# BLINDSIDED

## How Wall Street Stole the Economic Recovery

F.B. Wiseman



Abcor Publishers
New York

DISCLAIMER: While I have taken every effort to verify the accuracy of the information presented in these pages, I cannot accept any responsibility or liability resulting from any misinformation presented or any of the information, opinions, or conclusions set out in this work. Further, this publication is sold with the understanding that the author and publisher is not providing accounting, legal, or any other professional services or advice. Please speak with a trusted, competent attorney or other qualified professional before making any decisions involving personal or business financial and investment decisions.



ISBN # 978-0-9859556-0-1

Library of Congress Control Number: 2012946113

First published in the United States by Abcor Publishers, 2012

# Dedication

To Rachel, who had to close her mom-and-pop store because the bank raised the interest rate on her line of credit even though her bank was still borrowing at close to zero percent from the US government (tax payers). This book is for you.

To Dave, who has been frustrated that many people are unaware of current events and would like to find more information about why the economy is still not back to pre-recession levels. This book is for you.

For Mrs. Blackman, who was given the runaround by her bank while she was trying to refinance, even though she was using her house as collateral, had a high-paying job for income support, and has been a loyal mortgage payer for decades. This book is for you.

To Lee Ann, who was laid off from her job as a full-time teacher only to be rehired as a contractor with less pay and with fewer benefits. This book is for you.

To Michelle, who took out loans in an effort to earn a college degree and increase her standard of living, but currently has to defer that dream as she moves back home and joins the high number of unemployed Americans whose financial future is now burdened by the high cost of a college education that has continued to outpace both inflation and cost of living adjustments in both good and bad job markets. This book is for you.

To all those who would like to find out more about where this country has been, where we are, and where we are heading. This book is for you.

To the younger generations that rely on us to make responsible and unselfish decisions so that they will have a prosperous and sustainable future. This book is for you.

To all those who have contributed to the completion of this book by researching, writing, editing, illustrating, encouraging, or supporting in any other way. This book is also for you.

# Acknowledgements

The completion of this book is due in part to many individuals who have provided their help by researching, writing, editing, and illustrating in order to make this material a higher quality than it otherwise might have been. I especially want to thank my editor, Stefanie, who spent countless hours enhancing this manuscript. I also want to thank Elizabeth for her design work and bringing this book to life. I also owe a great deal of gratitude to my family, friends and all those who have supported this endeavor. For all the help and support I am truly grateful.

Thank you.

# Table of Contents

# SECTION I

## Economic Crisis

*"Those that do not know or acknowledge the lessons from history are condemned to repeat them."*

-George Santayana,
*Reason in Common Sense* (1905)

CHAPTER 1

# Reaction to the Financial Crisis

The United States has seen its fair share of financial hardships before, and we have always overcome them. In the past, we have managed to work our way out of our failures mostly by finding and holding the source accountable for the disaster, correcting the cause of the problems, and finally working our way out of our mess by utilizing great minds to find a sustainable solution to set us back on course. The idea of borrowing your way out of debt without changes to the root of the problem is not only foreign to American ideals, the very idea has also proven to be disastrous in practice. The direction our government has taken in an attempt to overcome the crisis we face today could arguably be worse than the results of taking no action at all. However, looking at the recent government reactions to the economic collapse and comparing them to similar solutions from the past is a telling exercise and a reason for concern.

## A Short History of the Crisis from 2007 to Today

The current financial crisis began to rear its head early in 2007, when the Federal Home Loan Mortgage Corporation (Freddie Mac) announced in a press release that they would no longer buy the most risky subprime mortgages and mortgage-backed securities. Less than two months later, a leading subprime lender, New Century Financial Corporation, filed for Chapter 11. By the summer, Standard and Poor's and Moody's had downgraded over one hundred bonds backed by second-lien, subprime mortgages.

Through the summer, the problems began to pick up steam as Standard and Poor's put over six hundred securities that were backed by subprime residential mortgages on credit watch, Countrywide Financial, the nation's largest subprime lender, warned of "difficult conditions," and Bear Stearns liquidated two hedge funds that invested in the risky securities. A second major mortgage investment corporation filed for Chapter 11 shortly thereafter, and by the end of the following January, the Federal Reserve, in an effort to keep the financial system liquid, had reduced its target for the federal funds rate five times—to nearly zero.

The following month, President Bush signed into law the Economic Stimulus Act of 2008. During this time, Countrywide had been severely downgraded, and Bank of America announced that they would purchase the company in an all-stock deal—a deal that was approved by the Federal Reserve in June of 2008.

Back in March of 2008, the New York Federal Reserve announced that it would finance the purchase of Bear Stearns by J.P. Morgan Chase & Co. The deal was secured through $30 billion of Bear Stearns assets controlled by an LLC newly formed for this purpose and would be known as Maiden Lane. Through this transaction, J.P. Morgan would be responsible only for the first billion dollars of liabilities, while the Fed would shoulder the remainder, using the near-worthless paper as collateral. In September of 2008, the director of the Federal Housing Finance Agency (FHFA), under the leadership of then Treasury Secretary Henry Paulson, announced his decision to place Freddie Mac and the Federal National Mortgage Association, commonly known as Fannie Mae, under conservatorship of the FHFA, whereas before this, they were only government-sponsored enterprises (GSEs). While the government maintains that this acquisition is temporary and is not indicative of a trend of nationalization, the trails of breadcrumbs that began with the bank bailouts and continued through bailouts of other areas of industry is reflective of nationalist, or as some have argued even fascist tendencies.

At the time, General Motors and AIG were two of the largest corporations deemed "too big to fail," and with the case of AIG in particular, the public grew to have a demonstrative disdain for that and other bailouts. The bailouts are widely viewed as bits of "crony capitalism" as allegations arose of the government giving financial support to the failing businesses rather than bailing the public out of its mess. The decision was made to pump money into the banking system, which was seen at the time as the best course of action, instead of finding an original solution to the current dilemma.

Many have faulted Timothy Geithner and Ben Bernanke for the failures of the course of action that the Obama administration took. This duo argued before the president and his advisors that if the banking system was flooded with nearly free money, then the banks were going to do the right thing and lend out the funds to businesses and the public. Their idea was relying on the theory of the multiplier effect of lending in which every dollar lent out by the bank to businesses and the general public would increase ten-fold as the money is spend in the economy.

If the banks lend out the free money, then such a solution has shown to work in the past. However, their gamble proved incorrect as the banking industry chose instead to restrict lending to potential job creators and potential consumers who could jump-start the economy. These recipients of the taxpayers' money chose instead to make loans to other financial institutions, to use the money for their own trading and investments, and to increase their other lines of businesses that were failing at the time. More astonishing to the public was the fact that there were few strings attached to this free money given to the banking industry. As the process unfolded, it would be clear that the banking industry was not going to be the panacea to revive the economy or help businesses or the general public to get back on financial course.

The program for helping those institutions that were "too big to fail" was known as the Troubled Asset Relief Plan, or TARP. As mentioned, it has been widely referred to as a bailout of the banking and financial sectors. Many have criticized it as a failure, and of the $700 billion allocated for the program, only $432 billion is now expected to be spent, according to the Congressional Budget Office. The banks and lenders received their money—even some like Wells-Fargo, which initially declined the hand out was eventually "encouraged" by the Treasury to take it. Unfortunately, for the taxpayers and the economy, the funds have not trickled down to the consumer or businesses, as loans and mortgages remain at historically low levels.

This leads many to believe that these funds were nothing more than favors to businesses and that much of the money ended up in the pockets of those who had been compliant with the government's low-income lending schemes. Others have also said that they believe the government is playing favorites in the distribution of the bailout funds by deciding which companies should survive. Others have also alleged that the money is being funneled to smaller players in certain districts in return for political support, but hard evidence of such occurrences is unfound. The reason that many are critical of the administration's effort to revive the economy is due to the actions of Geithner and Bernanke. Many have alleged that it was under Geithner's watch as head of the Federal Reserve Bank of New York that many of these financial problems occurred. Many have argued that President Obama's trust in these individuals resulted in an economy that would barely stay afloat years after the initial bailouts were distributed. Paul Volcker was thought to be the one that the president was going to rely on to reform the banking industry and chop down the too-big-to-fail institutions into manageable businesses. However, the opposition and political lobbying against his appointment was too great.

It seems that Wall Street's powerful financiers, including Geithner and Bernanke, pulled one over on President Obama's administration. The president also could not fire these people midpoint because it would look bad politically. However, many argue that if he would have gotten rid of them and hired brilliant people who could attack the root of the problem, hold wrongdoers accountable, and find a real sustainable solution, we could have been further along economically than we are now. Wall Street was bailed out, but Main street businesses and citizens are bankrupt, still financially underwater, or have succumbed to their financial situation.

Even economist and Nobel Prize winner Paul Krugman, who usually supports the current administration policies, has been very critical of the program, indicating in his *New York Times* column that these loans, which have no recourse for non-payment, seem to lead to hidden subsidies that can end up in the accounts of corporate managers, their shareholders, and their creditors. The expected trickle-down effect for the trillions of dollars put into the system has been a disappointment, as the money remained bottlenecked in financial institutions that are seeing record profits and billions in bonuses from taxpayers' dollars and are still very reluctant to lend out those funds to the real job creators. It is a sad day for America.

By the end of 2008, the assets of the Fed had risen nearly 300 percent, from $900 billion (with $790 billion being US treasuries) to about $2.28 trillion, with assets ranging across the board. While these proceedings began under the Bush administration and Henry Paulson, the Obama administration, with Timothy Geithner as Treasury Secretary, has willingly taken up the reigns of these actions and has spurred them on to new and greater heights, ultimately tripling the national debt in the process. There would be various names for the different strategies taken to revive the economy, but the plot was always the same: give the banks more money and see if they will hand it out. The plot is actually a tragedy, because the same thing would be tried in different ways, expecting to yield a different outcome. I think it was Albert Einstein that said insanity is doing the same thing over and over again and expecting a different result. Let us look at some of these strategies to see if maybe there was some careful pondering to come up with a unique solution to one of the greatest economic collapses the country has ever seen.

## Quantitative Easing

Quantitative Easing, or QE, is a strategy that was put into place by the Bank of Japan in the early 2000s to combat deflation. Although the measure was unsuccessful in Japan, Federal Reserve Chairman Ben Bernanke hinted as early as 2002 that the United States could fight the possibility of deflation through this tactic. However, he made the distinction that the effort would be more focused on purchasing government and financial securities and debt rather than just flooding the market with newly printed currency. Started in late November, 2008, QE1 saw the Fed purchasing billions of dollars' worth of risky financial products, such as mortgage-backed securities from troubled financial institutions and agency debt. This effectively tripled the Fed's assets by the end of the year. The stated intention was to reduce short-term rates and provide liquidity to the markets. Rates certainly dropped, but there was no uptick in borrowing or lending, so the results of the process are questionable. Many argue that QE1 did, in fact, prevent a second Great Depression, but this will remain no more than fortune-telling, as it is impossible to know what would have happened had the markets been left to work themselves out. What is clear is that as a result of QE1, the Fed went beyond its traditional role as a supervisor of the markets and instead became a major player in the markets by increasing its balance sheet and assets. There is now much speculation as to when and how the Fed can remove itself from this position without having a large negative impact on the market and the economy in general.

QE2 was a different animal altogether, wherein the Fed purchased US treasuries and supplied cash reserves to banks, although the reserves have largely sat in vaults and have been unproductive, since both borrowing and lending demands have remained stagnant. QE2 was much more like Japan's efforts and ended with similar results. The Fed has boosted the value of its assets—artificially, many claim—but the general economy has actually cooled during the time frame of QE2.

QE3 could be coming, as central banks are globally trying to come to the rescue of worldwide stock markets. While a third "easing" may encourage market investors' short term, the economic landscape has changed considerably since QE2 was instituted, and deflation no longer seems to loom. Instead, inflation may be the new dragon to slay. The Fed was keeping a close eye on this situation going into the end of 2011while downplaying the dangers in public statements. Consumer price index numbers rose throughout 2011 and early 2012, although the core inflation percentage, to which the Fed pays more attention, has gone up at a much slower pace. The Fed has even suggested that a slightly higher target of 3-percent inflation may help the economy get back on track. The idea of a QE3 does not promote widespread hope for helping the economy or consumers; however, it may bolster the stock market to an extent.

Detractors from all sides, including some regional Fed chairs, have roundly accused the QE measures of being nothing more than monetizing the nation's debt, more commonly called printing money.

Debt monetization by a government has historically been the beginning of the end, economically speaking, for the country in question. Perhaps the most famous example of debt monetization was in the Wiemar Republic of Germany. This tragic debacle resulted in hyperinflation that eventually destroyed the currency and increased unemployment to a staggering level, dropping the standard of living there dramatically and driving companies out of business at unprecedented rates. This is certainly something we do not want to see repeated in the United States.

## Operation Twist

Operation Twist is a highly controversial move by the Fed to lower interest rates on short-term loans and increase borrowing and lending for things like mortgages and business loans. By selling $400 billion in short-term treasuries in exchange for the same amount of longer term bonds, the Fed is essentially just shuffling money around, and this has been tried before.

This move dates back to the Kennedy administration in 1961, when the Fed attempted to address two economic problems at once: the balance-of-payment deficit with foreign governments and the domestic recession. The strategy was to purchase long-term bonds while at the same time selling short-term bills. This, it was thought, would raise short-term interest rates to stimulate the domestic economy while lowering the long-term rates to attract foreign investors, creating an influx of dollars. On the surface, it appeared somewhat successful at flattening the yield curve. However, other forces, such as raising the interest rate ceiling on deposit accounts and introducing negotiable-time certificates of deposit, actually contributed much more by providing banks with a wider availability of deposits. This allowed them to take advantage of arbitrage opportunities in the unstable and ineffective market. It also allowed for the yield curve to naturally flatten as the economy recovered through 1969.

Unlike the 1961 attempt, today's do-over no longer has the advantage of the interest rate ceilings on deposit accounts, so the rates cannot be artificially held at any particular level. In addition, the idea of lowering rates on things like mortgages to stimulate borrowing and lending is almost ludicrous at this point. In a September 22, 2011, story on the CNN Money website, Frank Sorrentino, CEO of North Jersey Community Bank, quipped: "This is not a situation where people are saying, 'Gee, I really want to buy that house, but interest rates are too high.' Rates are already at historic lows, and over the last six to nine months, we have not seen loan demand go up."

While the solution to the ailing economy in the United States and abroad is not clear, it is painfully obvious to those who can see fairly clearly through the filter of history that we are not taking actions that will get us to where we need to be. Austerity is necessary to some degree, accountability with real reforms and personal responsibility is what is needed and to a much greater degree than we have now. Regardless of future reforms, the one thing that is certain is that the printing presses of the Federal Reserve need to be shut down; in the absence of real solutions, the insanity of throwing money and hoping it will be distributed must stop

CHAPTER 2

# Government Bailouts

## How do Government Bailouts of Businesses Affect the Taxpayer?

The obvious answer to this question is that the money for the bailouts comes from the taxpayer. The question leads us to whether the taxpayer sees that money again and whether the bailouts actually benefit them. If there is no significant benefit to the supplier of the funds (taxpayers), then the simple business idea of receiving a return on an investment should point to the bailout as a bad idea. It remains to be seen what the return on investments for the current round of bailouts will be to the taxpayer, but the information is becoming clearer with time; and looking at the history of government bailouts in this country should provide some hint at the possibilities.

## A Short History of Bailouts

Over the last century, there have been more than a few bailouts by the government, so this is not a new idea. The trend has increased in the last forty years, however, as have the scope and size of this strategy. Below is a list of some of the largest bailouts since the turn of the last century, with some figures and results included so that we can get a better feel for where we are today.

**1907: Bank Panic** During the National Banking era of 1863 to1914, the bank panic of 1907 was the most severe financial crisis in the country and was focused in New York City trusts companies. Although the bailout in this case was spearheaded and funded primarily by banking magnates like J.P. Morgan, the Treasury did supply help to the tune of $73 million (approximately $1.6 billion today). Within a month, however, the working capital of the Treasury had shrunk to $5 million, leaving it unable to supply any more funding to the trusts. This scare led in great part to the creation of the Federal Reserve to help stave off such bank runs in the future.

**1933: HOLC** Four years after the stock market crash, FDR and Congress set up the Home Owners' Loan Corporation, a government agency that would reduce the number of foreclosures occurring in the country. Over $3 billion was issued to home owners as the government bought mortgages and refinanced them at lower rates for fifteen-year terms. The agency closed in 1951 with over 80 percent of the loans repaid and a small profit earned. The Federal Deposit Insurance Corporation (FDIC) was also set up in 1933 in response to Great Depression–era banking problems.

**1970: Penn Central Railroad** In 1970, Penn Central Railroad appealed to the Federal Reserve for a bailout based on the idea that they supplied essential national security services, and while the Fed and President Nixon agreed to the proposition, Congress refused, leading the railroad to file for bankruptcy that same year. The next year, the Fed supplied $676.3 million in loan guarantees to them, but by 1976, the government had consolidated the still-struggling railroad company with five others that were in similar financial conditions into Conrail and developed Amtrak. While the government sold the enterprise for $3.1 billion in 1987 and received $579 million in dividends for the Treasury, the cost of the initial consolidation and the funding to get it to a profitable position in the meantime was over $19 billion.

**1971: Lockheed** The Lockheed Corporation, an aircraft manufacturing firm, was the first recipient of the Emergency Loan Guarantee Act of 1971. This legislation was meant to provide needed financial assistance to major business enterprises in times of crisis. The emergency loan of about $1.4 billion was desperately needed by the Lockheed Corporation to pay down its burgeoning debts and avoid insolvency. These debts had materialized from a series of canceled contracts by major clients such as the government, production delays, non-recoupable cost overruns, and missteps by the management team. Despite its many problems, Lockheed was able to pay its loans off by 1977, and the government earned over $112 million in loan fees.

**1974: Franklin National Bankruptcy** The Franklin National Bank lost over $63 million in the first half of 1974, and the FDIC stepped in to bail it out. Eventually, corruption was discovered, leading to convictions. The FDIC sold the assets, but was ultimately left with a deficit of over $185 million in interest payments.

**1980: Chrysler** The Chrysler Loan Guarantee Act provided $1.5 billion to save the automaker from going under, and those funds were matched by US and foreign banks. Chrysler repaid the loans by 1983, seven years ahead of schedule, and the government came away from the deal with a net profit of more than $660 million.

**1984: Continental Illinois National Bank** The eighth largest bank in the country at the time, the Continental Illinois National Bank experienced severe losses after purchasing approximately $1 billion in energy loans from a failed bank. The Federal Reserve and the FDIC purchased 80 percent of the company and restructured it, replacing the top executives at the bank. By 1991, it had been returned to the private sector, but the FDIC lost $1.8 billion in the bailout effort.

**1989: Savings and Loan Industry** The debacle with failing savings and loans led to a bailout of roughly $220 billion. The American taxpayer was responsible for over $178 billion of this bailout.

**2001: Airline Industry** After the attack on the twin towers of the World Trade Center in 2001, the airlines suffered a blow to their already-ailing industry. The Air Transportation Safety and System Stabilization Act to stabilize the airlines cost the taxpayers $18.6 billion, though the money was recovered due to stock warrants allowed in the bill, similar to the Chrysler deal in 1980s. The reports on the net profit earned varied greatly, from $14 million to $327 million.

**2008-2011: Global Recession Bailouts from the Fed** Compared to past bailouts, these amounts handed out during recent years are startlingly higher:

- Bear Stearns: $30 billion in loans plus another $29.5 billion in purchased assets to help the firm be acquired by J.P. Morgan.
- Morgan Stanley: $107 billion
- Citigroup: Nearly $100 billion
- Fannie Mae/Freddie Mac: $400 billion
- AIG: $180 billion
- TARP: $700 billion Bank of America: $142 billion

**Auto Industry** Former auto czar Steven Rattner stated on December 15, 2011, that the estimated loss to taxpayers on the $82 billion bailout of Chrysler and General Motors would be $14 billion. He also admitted that "we the government didn't extract a big enough price from the banks for what was spent to rescue them. They got a lot of capital at really cheap prices, and almost no one lost their job at the senior level."(1) The picture gets even worse, however, according to *Washington Post* editorial writer Charles Lane, who suggests that GM should buy back the roughly one-quarter stock holdings of the American taxpayer via the Treasury. According to Lane, GM currently has triple the amount of cash reserves necessary for the repurchase. He also reports that in November, 2011, the Treasury estimated the loss to taxpayers as being $23.6 billion, significantly higher than Mr. Rattner's estimate.(2)

You can see from this list that prior to the 2008–2011 period, the total cost of the other listed major bailouts of the last century paled in comparison to the current round and totaled less than half of the TARP funding alone. If the TARP numbers are excluded from the total, since some of that money is included in the individual figures, the remaining total is still in excess of $900 billion, even by the most conservative estimates.

The most responsible businesses that have received this type of help have paid back the money they borrowed in full and on time, if not before. The 1980 Chrysler bailout is a prime example of this. It is not yet clear if the banks that have been given money in recent years have the same level of urgency to return the money they have borrowed, but a recent report by the organization The New Bottom Line seems to indicate that they do not. According to their report, seven of the largest banks in the United States, all of which received taxpayer-funded bailout money, are projected to have an overall 3.7-percent increase in compensation packages for their employees and executives in 2011, totaling $156 billion. This follows a record-breaking year in 2010 in terms of compensation for them.(3)

### Bailouts Benefits to Taxpayers

The stated intended purpose of the many government bailouts of these businesses was to protect the economy from free fall and to subsequently ensure that the American taxpayers would avoid high unemployment. This has so far not been the actual result, as unemployment has remained above 9 percent, and the lack of significant business lending has left the private sector in states of stagnation or decline. While the long-term effects of these actions remain to be seen through the lens of hindsight, the evidence of short-term growth is nowhere to be seen by objective observation.

The costs to the people of the country are not only in dollars, however, as moral questions have been continuously raised about whether these actions send the right message to both the public and the business community.

### Moral Hazards

When a company mishandles its business and verges on collapse, should it be bailed out or allowed to fold? The question has received varied responses from every stripe of elected official, pundit, and journalist alike. The government's position in these cases has been that the companies in question were "too big to fail," meaning that their failure would affect the economy, and therefore the public, in a way that would be catastrophic and possibly irreversible. If corporate leaders in other sectors perceive that they can also manage carelessly without fear of consequences and that they will also be forgiven via public funds, this could lead to corporate irresponsibility on a much larger scale.

In addition to businesses, individuals could also come to the conclusion that welfare is part of life and that their actions will not be held against them. Some argue that the moral compass of the country has been tilted or even destroyed by the government's handling of the banks, with families left to wonder why they need to follow a budget themselves if there are no consequences.(4) The point could be a valid one, as public events tend to shape the views and behaviors of those who observe them.

The failure of these companies to take care of their own financial houses has essentially become the responsibility of the taxpayer. When the government provides the legs for them to stand on after they have reached the edge of the financial cliff, they are handing the burden of the losses and failures on to those who did not create the problem and excusing those who did. This may set dangerous precedents for future scenes on the stage of our economy.

## Possible Causes and Solutions

One thing that may have helped along the worldwide banking crises was the consolidation of the investment and lending arms of these institutions. The Glass-Steagall Act of 1933 officially separated these different branches in the belief that the interests of each could conflict and cause the kinds of problems that we have seen. President Clinton and the Republican Congress effectively repealed the last part of this act in 1999 with the Gramm-Leach-Bliley Act, paving the way for the mega-banks that we see today. The creation of Citigroup in the late 1990s was one of the first moves toward this current trend, combining investment and commercial banking ventures under one roof. After the Gramm-Leach-Bliley Act, corporations such as Bank of America followed suit, and smaller investment firms like Goldman Sachs and Morgan Stanley were compelled to participate in the expansionist trend in order to stay competitive.(5)

There are movements currently underway in opinion and policy to return to smaller, more manageable banking structures, following the Glass-Steagall Model. In the United Kingdom, the government has endorsed John Vickers's report on banking, which calls for just such a move.(6) The same opinions have been voiced by more than one journalist or public figure in the United States in recent months, although the proposed solutions vary in relation to their bolstering of, departure from, or repeal of the Dodd-Frank financial oversight rules put into place in 2010.(7)

The Federal Reserve, for its part, is in the process of applying the Basel III rules set out by the Basel Committee on Banking Supervision(8), an international group of central bankers established in 1975 for the purpose of introducing regulatory guidelines for banking. The rules raise the minimum liquidity percentage for banks with more than $50 billion in assets, although the Fed has said that it will tailor the rules to smaller institutions and other industries, as well. There is opposition to these implementations from the major banking institutions, who argue that the regulations being considered will actually hinder lending rather than help it. The Fed will decide which other institutions the rules may apply to, such as hedge funds and insurance companies they deem important to the functioning of the markets and the economy.(9)

### To Whom are Banks Accountable?

The future of the financial sector seems uncertain at best, and with each passing month, there are new revelations of the past and new suggestions for the future. The taxpayer will not be able to sustain the bailouts at the rate we have seen in the past few years forever, and most believe they should not be expected to. However, most of the bigger institutions are bigger than before the bailouts and in some cases are still engaging in business practices that can potentially cause major disruption to our financial system given the right market winds.

The questions of whether these bailouts should have occurred will be answered over time and through the actions of those institutions that received funding. Most outside of the financial sector agree that the banking institutions in particular should have less power and influence, but that is not likely to happen. With the courts' declaration that corporations should be given similar rights to those of regular people, the power of corporations can only grow. It is often said that with great power come great responsibility, but if flesh-and-blood persons can fail to live up to those words, what hope is there that a corporation, whose action or inaction is attributed to the failings of sometimes nameless individuals in the firm, can live up to such responsibility. The dangers of the powers of these institutions were foreseen and addressed by President Andrew Jackson in 1832, when he said:

It is maintained by some that the bank is a means of executing the constitutional power "to coin money and regulate the value thereof." Congress have established a mint to coin money and passed laws to regulate the value thereof. The money so coined, with its value so regulated, and such foreign coins as Congress may adopt are the only currency known to the Constitution. But if they have other power to regulate the currency, it was conferred to be exercised by themselves, and not to be transferred to a corporation. If the bank be established for that purpose, with a charter unalterable without its consent, Congress have parted with their power for a term of years, during which the Constitution is a dead letter. It is neither necessary nor proper to transfer its legislative power to such a bank, and therefore unconstitutional. (10)

CHAPTER 3

# Wall Street Fines and Settlements

Every corporation has a management group that is responsible for establishing and managing financial and operational policies and procedures with dual goals. The first goal is to operate the business in a way that promotes growth and appropriately records all financial information so that it assists decision making and that the business adheres to accounting principles and governmental regulations and laws. The second purpose is to institute loss protection through antifraud and anticorruption controls. This is a necessary precaution, because not all managers and staff are honest, and history shows that fraud and corruption have existed as long as business has existed. Fortunately, as societies have become more civilized, government has increasingly assumed some of the responsibility for overseeing the protection of investors and the marketplace from these dangers perpetrated by corporations and other businesses.

There are many governmental agencies that are responsible for overseeing financial compliance and investigating corruption. In fact, you can find agencies at both the state and federal levels with state fraud investigators who usually report to the state attorney general. However, most corporate regulation and enforcement is the responsibility of federal agencies, with the states and local agencies playing a more supportive role. This may seem a bit odd if you remember that corporations are formed by state laws, but many corporations operate nationally or internationally, or both. These businesses' extensive scope and reach makes the federal government better-equipped than states to deal with cases of financial fraud and other wrongdoings that may arise.

The federal corporate fraud and corruption monitoring agencies are decentralized. The approach that has developed over time involves agencies like the Securities and Exchange Commission (SEC) or the Department of Justice (DOJ) regulating businesses through capital markets. There many other federal agencies that also regulate specific types of fraud or corruption. They include the Federal Trade Commission (FTC), which oversees consumer fraud perpetrated by corporations; the US Postal Service, which investigates mail fraud; the Federal Communications Commission (FCC), which regulates communications fraud; and the Food and Drug Administration (FDA), which verifies the validity of food and drug claims.(1)

The SEC certainly received the most attention recently because of the massive fraud that was uncovered and is still being uncovered after the collapse of the financial markets that started in 2007. The SEC can work alone, but fraud and corruption investigations are often joint efforts between several US federal agencies. The FTC may work with the SEC, or sometimes the DOJ may coordinate an investigation with the FTC. These agencies are some of the main players, but they are not the only ones that investigate corporate fraud and corruption.

## Internal Revenue Service

The Internal Revenue Service (IRS) audits public and private corporate financial records and may uncover cases of fraud in doing so. Sometimes, the IRS is notified by a whistleblower that a corporation is committing fraud and will initiate an investigation if the notification appears valid. The magnitude of a corporate violation of the Internal Revenue Code or other legal statutes is measured by the economic consequences on financial markets, investors doing good-faith business with the corporation, lenders, and employees.

The Internal Revenue Service maintains a staff of special agents in its Criminal Investigation Division (CID). These agents are actually law enforcement personnel who do corporate financial investigations and are also trained in the audit of sophisticated computerized financial systems. The CID can recommend criminal prosecution to the DOJ and/or impose civil penalties.

The IRS can also call on other federal agencies for assistance or to ensure a thorough investigation. For example, if the IRS is unable to prove tax fraud, then the SEC may be able to prove securities fraud.

## Federal Bureau of Investigation (FBI)

The Federal Bureau of Investigation (FBI) investigates a range of cases that includes everything from kidnapping to financial crimes. Because the agency's mission includes defending and protecting the United States against terrorism and intelligence threats and upholding the US criminal laws, it has a large variety of cases. The two parts of the mission are not necessarily independent of each other, either. Corporate fraud has been committed in order to fund terrorism groups, and this has become more common as federal agencies cut off sources of funding from legitimate business activities. Terrorists use various types of criminal activities that include fraud and organized crime that is covered up under the guise of a legitimate corporation.(2)

The FBI investigates terrorism, public corruption, white-collar crime, domestic and international terrorism, organized crime, and much more. The agency frequently works with other state and federal agencies during investigations. The FBI also has special agents who investigate computer-related crimes that impact computerized financial and banking systems. The FBI is a law enforcement agency and, therefore, can make arrests and charge people with crimes. Since, by law, business management personnel can now be held responsible for corporate fraud, the FBI also has the power to enforce laws against fraud and corruption relating to these types of criminal offenses.

### United States Secret Service

The United States Secret Service is well known for protecting the President and other important government officials. It is also responsible for criminal investigations and has a goal of protecting the "integrity of the nation's financial infrastructure and payment systems."(3) These cases include investigations into electronic crimes, computer-related fraud, currency counterfeiting, identity fraud, bank fraud, electronic funds transfer fraud, Federal Deposit Insurance Corporation investigations, fraudulent foreign securities, and fraudulent commercial instruments. Obviously, the investigations by the US Secret Service will probably be coordinated with the other federal agencies that are more accustomed to dealing with corporate fraud and corruption investigations.

### Securities and Exchange Commission (SEC)

The mission of the Securities and Exchange Commission (SEC) is to protect market investors, to maintain efficient and orderly markets that are fair, and to promote the formation of capital. The SEC regulates businesses and exchanges that sell bonds, stocks, and other securities. Therefore, with the intent of verifying that transactions are fair, market-related information is disclosed according to law, and fraud is prevented, the SEC oversees securities dealers, brokers, exchanges, mutual funds, and investment advisors.

Some types of fraudulent activities that the SEC might investigate include deceptive accounting practices, insider trading, and deceptive and noncompliant investment disclosures. The SEC can bring civil or administration actions against any individual who has violated securities law. However, the SEC works closely with all of the agencies mentioned plus the Federal Reserve, Treasury Department, states, and several commissions and task forces dealing with the financial markets.

The agency does not have law enforcement power but works closely with criminal law enforcement agencies to bring about prosecution of corporations and individuals when warranted. The SEC can also take a case to federal court to request a remedy or sanction, or it can recommend bringing an administrative action heard by an administrative (regulatory) law judge.(4)

## Sarbanes-Oxley Act of 2002

A number of laws govern the securities industry, including the Securities Act of 1933, which requires financial disclosure; the Securities Act of 1934, which created the SEC and regulates market conduct; the Investment Company Act of 1940, which regulates companies organized to invest in securities; and the Investment Advisers Act of 1940, which regulates investment advisors. One of the most important and far-reaching legislative acts impacting securities trading is the recent Sarbanes-Oxley Act (SOX) of 2002, and it deserves special mention. SOX was borne out of the prevalent deceptive accounting practices and corporate scandals in the early 2000s that were perpetrated by the now-infamous firms Adelphia, Enron, Tyco, and WorldCom, to name a few; the resulting investigation drew public outcry for transparency and stronger regulation. Designed to combat fraud and corruption, SOX expanded financial disclosure requirements and established the Public Company Accounting Oversight Board.

The Sarbanes-Oxley Act is an important piece of legislation for any corporation registering with the SEC. The Sarbanes-Oxley Act has various sections that specify where management or the auditor can be held accountable. The main SOX sections include:

| PUBLIC LAW 107–204 ("Sarbanes-Oxley Act of 2002") |
|---|
| Title I — Public Company Accounting Oversight Board<br>Sections 101-109 |
| Title II — Auditor Independence<br>Sections 201-209 |
| Title III — Corporate Responsibility<br>Sections 301-308 |
| Title IV — Enhanced Financial Disclosures<br>Sections 401-409 |
| Title V — Analyst Conflicts of Interest<br>Sections 501 |
| Title VI — Commission Resources and Authority<br>Sections 601-604 |
| Title VII — Studies and Reports<br>Sections 701-705 |
| Title VIII — Corporate and Criminal Fraud Accountability<br>Sections 801-807 |
| Title IX — White-Collar Crime Penalty Enhancements<br>Sections 901-906 |
| Title X — Corporate Tax Returns<br>Sections 1001 |
| Title XI — Corporate Fraud and Accountability<br>Sections 1101-1107 |

The Sarbanes-Oxley Act applies to all US companies and international enterprises that are registered with the SEC to sell debt or equity securities. For the first time, a law clearly held top management responsible for accurate financial and other important disclosures. The law also includes requirements for the accounting firms that audit companies registered with the SEC and hold CPA firms more accountable for ensuring that management and auditors are reporting correct, thorough, and accurate financial transactions.

The Sarbanes-Oxley Act is a very comprehensive document, and discussing all the sections and its details is beyond the scope of this book.

However, it is important to discuss some of the key and often contentious sections of SOX, notably sections 302 and 404.

Section 302 of the Sarbanes-Oxley Act requires senior management to actually certify that they are responsible for the internal reporting procedures and controls of their companies as well as certifying the accuracy of their company's financial statements. This is important, because many in senior management previously claimed they were not aware of many of the wrongdoings that their corporations and businesses were accused of.

Section 404 mandates that the management team and the external auditor assess whether the internal reporting system meets acceptable standards. This section, in effect, requires that auditors and managers work together to establish internal controls and accurate reporting methods. Section 404, along with section 302 greatly expands management's responsibility for limiting the possibility of fraud by establishing appropriate controls designed to prevent, identify, and detect fraud.(5)

SOX also established new penalties for when wrongdoing is uncovered. The ultimate goal of SOX is to protect investors by raising the bar for corporate accountability. This piece of legislation effectively puts management and auditors on notice in case there were thoughts of returning to the accounting schemes and shenanigans that brought down previous corporations that the public had trusted and invested in.

## Types of Civil and Criminal Penalties

There are many ways that corporations and their management can be punished if wrongdoing is found.

**Civil Action** Civil actions include being prohibited from carrying out business in a certain way in the future, monetary penalties, disgorgement or return of illegal gains, suspension or barring of an individual from a corporation's management or board of directors, and barring an individual from the brokerage industry.

**Administrative Action** Administrative actions include revocation or suspension of broker or investment advisor licenses, disbarment of a person from a public accounting firm, disgorgement, barring a person from working in the securities industry as well as censures, cease and desist orders, and civil monetary penalties.

**Criminal Penalties** Criminal penalties include house arrest, probation, prison terms, restitution, and fines. The public views the criminal penalties from the last financial collapse as almost nonexistent—a crime in and of itself.

## When Corporations Break the Law

White-collar crime, a term credited to professor Edwin Hardin Sutherland back in 1939, has been a concern to law enforcement agencies for decades, but the discussion has taken a new direction in the last few years as a result of the current recession. Whereas corporate fraud and corruption was mostly of interest to government officials in the past, the recession has created a level of public resentment based on the fact that managers of companies losing billions of dollars on bad investments continue to collect millions of dollars in salaries and bonuses. To add to the absurdity, corporations judged to be financially sound right before they collapsed have made people more aware of the importance of government regulatory agencies, corporate transparency or lack of transparency, and their accrued legal and ethical track records.

Until the recent financial crisis, there was a fair amount of indifference toward punishing corporations, especially their managers, for fraudulent activities. The investing public is said to have a very short-term memory when it comes to the potential of financial frauds and scandals, especially when the markets are doing well and the majority of investors are seeing their portfolios increase. However, like the philosopher George Santayana wrote in *Reason in Common Sense* in 1905, "those that don't know or acknowledge the lessons from history are condemned to repeat them."(6)

Laws and regulations are written for a reason. From the earliest written accounts, it has been shown that man needs laws and rules and their legal enforcement or threat of punishment in order to be compelled to live civilly among his fellow human beings. In the financial world alone, there are numerous laws and regulations that were created (always after the fact, it seems) to curb illegal and unethical behavior. But do not take my word as fact; I encourage you to take a look at the current financial laws that have been enacted over the years and the reason for their existence.

Technology has aided the financial crimes but has also exposed more of those once-closely guarded financial criminalities to the public. It is a fact that computers have made fraud easier to commit through elaborate and complex electronic maneuvers. The sheer complexity has thrown up roadblocks to uncovering fraud and corruption in its early stages, and unfortunately, it is only after the damaging effects have started to materialize en masse that action is taken, albeit usually too late.

The Racketeer Influenced and Corrupt Organization Act, enacted in 1961, punished organized criminal activity operated through business activities. The law, often referred to as RICO, led to fines, prison terms, and property forfeiture for those convicted. RICO laws also allowed civil suits to be brought by injured parties. Though business fraud and corruption has been in existence since before RICO, the modern-day public first became painfully aware of the continued existence of illegal activity in some corporations during the late 1990s.

By 2001, large companies like WorldCom, Enron, and Arthur Anderson became household names due to financial scandals, out of which grew Congressional response through the passage of the Sarbanes-Oxley Act. The Enron scandal should have been a wake-up call in 2001 that prevented the events leading to the 2008 Lehman Brothers collapse, but it obviously was not. The Enron financial story ending in the company's collapse involves a series of complex transactions that hid debt by failing to report the debt in the financial statement. The *Wall Street Journal* did a story on Enron that raised questions about the company's financial status. Making a very long story short, the SEC eventually opened an investigation and discovered that there were significant accounting errors and that the CPA firm Arthur Anderson had ordered the destruction of financial records to cover up possible illegal acts.

It took over five years, but fifteen Enron executives were sentenced to prison or probation, and several were assessed millions of dollars in restitution for helping to commit or hide fraud. Enron went bankrupt and emerged only to sue financial institutions that were determined to have helped cover up the fraud. Some monies were eventually collected through litigation and were later distributed to creditors. The Arthur Anderson CPA firm still exists but on a much smaller scale after being found guilty of fraudulent accounting practices by the SEC, leading to criminal convictions.

WorldCom, another company guilty of scandalous financial wrongdoing, had $3.3 billion of accounting "errors." This long distance telephone company handled the communication services for tens of thousands of domestic and international companies and managed much of the Internet traffic back in the late 1990s and early 2000s. The company grew by assuming sixty-five acquisitions that required sophisticated accounting practices in six years. Such major acquisitions, as it turned out, also gave the company the opportunity to manipulate earnings and expense amounts, including goodwill amounts for brand acquisitions, to make it appear as if the company profits were increasing over time.

In 2002, the US government refused to allow WorldCom to acquire Sprint, and the truth came out. WorldCom declared bankruptcy in 2002, and the web of deception began to unravel. The SEC investigated and found that the financial records of WorldCom included sweetheart loans to top management and a variety of accounting irregularities with the sole intent of deceiving investors. Arthur Anderson was once again involved in helping the company falsify accounting records, including a $2 billion capital expenditure accounting entry, overstatement of some of the acquisitions, pretax profits that didn't exist, and unrecorded expenses.(7)

As a result of the SEC investigation, top executives were once again convicted of criminal activity and sent to prison. The charges included conspiracy to commit securities fraud, commission of securities fraud, and filing false statements with the SEC.

Often, the people who cooperate with government officials receive a lighter prison sentence than those who do not. Even though it is a controversial practice, the government still utilizes this method in order to overcome perceived roadblocks in their investigations. This practice was generally used and accepted in 2005, when the WorldCom scandal was still being settled; however, many question the continued usage of this tactic.

### The Accused

So what is the general process when allegations of wrongdoing are lodged with the various regulatory government agencies? When a government agency accuses an investment firm of fraud or corruption, auditors begin combing through records, interviewing management and staff, and tracking transactions through computerized accounting systems. This laborious process can literally take years to complete. As discussed earlier, the steps the agency takes once the investigation is completed depends on its authority, but there will usually be fines and penalties assessed against the organization, restitution at the corporate and individual level ordered, and possible prison time determined for management or other personnel committing the fraud.

Over the years, the government has held those who commit financial crimes accountable, especially when the investing public has suffered immense losses; however, many critics have said the government is still too lenient on corporate criminals and wrongdoers. In reviewing the major corporate fraud and corruption cases over the years, it is clear that the punishment and fines have changed over time, but the process is far from being perfect and being impervious to undue influence.

### History Repeats Itself—Again

Business scandals are certainly nothing new. As far back as 1795, thirty-five million acres of land in the Yazoo area of Georgia were sold by the state to four businesses for the bargain price of a penny and a half per acre. The politicians had accepted bribes in return for the favorable contract sale terms. Additional scandals in the 1800s included Civil War profiteering agreements and the Credit Mobilier Scandal in the 1860s involving a dummy construction company formed by the Union Pacific Railroad. Also, in September, 1869, a financial panic resulted from wealthy speculators like the infamous Jay Gould and James Fisk, who attempted to control gold prices with the cooperation of President Grant's administration. Gould and Fisk failed in their attempt, which resulted in the government dumping gold on the market.

In a case of déjà vu, an 1873 economic collapse occurred after a number of risky loans made to railroad businesses went bad. The economy fell into a long depression that lasted until 1878.

In 1922, the Teapot Dome scandal was uncovered. This scandal involved Interior Secretary Albert Fall, who had secretly leased valuable US naval petroleum reserves located in Wyoming to an oil company without going through a competitive bidding process. Fall went to prison for corruption, but the precedent that this case would set was just as important. Fall's trial contributed to the 1927 Supreme Court decision in McGrain v. Daugherty: a decision that established the right of Congress to require witnesses to testify before Congressional members.(8)

In 1924, Calvin Coolidge, a man who was known to favor big business, became president of the United States. Coolidge's sentiments on big business were not news considering the period he was living in. The 1920s, or the Roaring 20s, as they are often called, are remembered as a time of great US wealth and big business. This period saw the stock market rise on speculative trades to unsustainable levels and extreme volatility. This all came to a head on the now-infamous day in the middle of the fall season. On Black Thursday, October 24, 1929, the stock prices began a precipitous decline, which led to panic selling that dragged the market down even further. The stock market decline continued until mid-November, briefly showed signs of a possible recovery, and then resumed its downward trajectory. This, of course, ushered in the Great Depression, a period recalled for being one of the longest and most pronounced economic declines in US history, a period in which well over 9,000 banks failed and from which a full recovery would not be seen until 1954, over three decades later.

One of the scandals to emerge out of the stock market collapse in 1929 was the fact that so many people had been allowed to buy stocks on margin when they could not afford to cover losses. Franklin Roosevelt was elected in 1932, and he decided to restore public confidence in both government and big business. He ordered the prosecution of Wall Street bankers. One of the first institutions to be targeted was National City Banks, which is known today as none other than Citicorp. The president of Nation City Banks (NCB) was well known for selling bonds on insider information, but there was also evidence that NCB was pushing brokers to sell Peruvian bonds that were about to default. Some of these activities were certainly perceived as deceptive, unethical, and unjust and were a failure in terms of the accountability and responsibility to the nation's financial system even though they were not legally seen as crimes at that time. However, these events did lead to the creation of the Securities and Exchange Commission and a slew of other regulations. But by far the most important regulation that came out of that period was the separation between the banking industry and Wall Street investment firms, a marriage that would not be reconciled until the 1990s, over fifty years later.

Thanks to government regulations and the socioeconomic state of the period following the Great Depression, corporate scandals remained relatively muted or well hidden until the 1970s. The 1970s saw the emergence of new corruption headlines. This included the Gulf Oil Corporation allegedly bribing Korean and Bolivian government officials and hiding the payments in their financial records. This was shocking not because of the bribery (bribing foreign governments was legal at that time—as long as the payments were reported to shareholders), but because Gulf Oil was now spreading the use of bribery not just internationally, but nationally, as well. In 1975, it was made public that over $300 million in illegal payoffs had been made nationally. At the time, the 1971 Federal Election Campaign Act (FECA) made it illegal for corporations to make donations to political candidates, a practice that is the norm today. The result of the scandal was amendments to FECA and the creation of political action committees, which were formed to accept corporate donations for political candidates.

The 1970s also saw a flurry of mergers and acquisitions that led to massive fraud and manipulation, foreshadowing the Enron scandal that would occur in the late 1990s. Financial scandals involving General Services Administration, uncovered by the SEC, and Equity Funding Corporation of America, uncovered by a whistleblower, revealed fraudulent contracts, fake documents, inflated profits, and so on. These scandals would pale in comparison to what was about to happen in the decade ahead.

In the 1980s, insider trading was the scandal du jour, and while there were many characters, none was as representative of that period as Ivan Boesky. He was a Wall Street speculator who made over $50 million on insider information supplied by investment banker Dennis Levine. Levine was the first to be ensnared by the SEC, and after some plea bargaining, he led investigators to Boesky. Levine admitted to insider trading deals and went to prison. Boesky was found guilty of insider trading and was ordered to pay $50 million in fines in addition to $50 million in disgorged profits. It was time for Boesky to engage in his own plea bargaining to lighten his sentence.

Boesky testified against other people he knew and worked with on Wall Street. Among the other infamous swindlers that Boesky testified against were financiers Michael Milken and Victor Posner. Milken, who worked at the prominent firm Drexel Burnham Lambert, Inc., pleaded no contest to six felony charges of stock parking and stock manipulation. He was fined $650 million. Posner was a wheeler dealer who developed the leveraged buyout and drained Sharon Steel through payouts to himself and his son. Eventually, he pleaded no contest to fraud for inflating donated land values and to tax evasion. In 1988, he was also charged with working with Drexel Burnham Lambert to conceal a large stock purchase. In 1993, he was barred by the SEC from being a director or officer of any public company.

After helping the Federal investigators, Boesky agreed to plead guilty to initially lying to federal regulators and was sentenced to three years in prison. He only served about two years, but his participation in the securities industry was restricted for the rest of his life. These scandals so dominated the public imagination that the character Gordon Gekko in the popular 1987 movie *Wall Street* is alleged to be based on Ivan Boesky.

In a domino effect, US attorney Rudy Giuliani prosecuted Boesky and Robert Freeman of Goldman Sachs, who each pleaded guilty to one felony. Other indictments were made but had to be dropped because the government did not have time to properly prepare for trial.

The time factor involved in successful indictments still has relevance today. This is the reason that so much time is spent on investigating before making an indictment, because the prosecutors want to reduce this risk due to lack of preparation. Investigators from the SEC or other government agencies hope to ensure that their case is solid before making a public accusation. Even then, the actual criminal indictment or conviction or civil or administrative action may take years.

## Savings and Loan Crisis

Now let us take a look at the institutional scandals of the 1980s, which were perpetuated en masse across the country. By far the biggest national financial failures of the 1980s were what are now called the Savings and Loan (S&L or "thrifts") scandal.

Savings and loans financial institutions were different from banks in that they received savings deposits from their customers and, in turn, made consumer loans and mortgages. They were traditionally known for providing attractive rates for savers and financing individuals and homeowners throughout the nation.

A key driver for the S&L growth was the amount of funds that savers would deposit in these institutions. Whether these depositors were going to choose an S&L depended largely on its advertised interest rate and market alternatives. S&L interest rates at that time had limits that were set by the government. All things being equal, however, if market rates were high, then potential savings depositors had the option of going to traditional banks or other financial intuitions, where rates were as competitive, and vice versa. So S&Ls tended to do better in a low-interest environment than a higher-interest environment. Unfortunately for these thrifts, the 1970s experienced slow economic growth, increased inflation, and high interest rates that were due to the extremely high oil prices. This economic environment proved very challenging for S&L growth and success, and in fact, saw many S&L institutions fall into bankruptcy. These S&Ls needed assistance or risked industry-wide failure.

The answer finally came in a series of new laws aimed at deregulating the industry and giving them alternative means to generate income. Congress passed the Depository Institutions Deregulation and Monetary Control Act of 1980. The importance of this act was to allow thrifts to offer checkable deposits and to allow most financial intuitions, including thrifts, to decide their own interest rates.

Much to the delight of the thrifts, this was followed up with more deregulations. This time, Congress passed the Garn-St. Germain Depository Institutions Act of 1982, which allowed banks to offer adjustable-rate mortgages. These deregulations, although meant to aid the banking industry, created a situation that allowed the S&Ls to act like regular banks, but without all the regulations and other restrictions that traditional banks had to follow.

Investment firms and other financial firms took little time to exploit the loopholes and opportunities that were now presented to them by these deregulations. The rest of the decade would see a period marred with over-lending to unqualified individuals and businesses that defaulted on these obligations, improper internal controls, poor analysis of financial ventures, and increased competition, which exacerbated some of the already-loose banking policies. Tie all this in with inadequate regulation and understaffed regulators, and the stage was indeed set for a financial crisis.

One of the first notable savings and loan scandal participants of this period was Penn Square Bank back in 1982. Penn Square Bank was alleged to have made fraudulent energy loans. Making matters worse, the accounting firm of Coopers & Lybrand had conspired with the bank to promote fraudulent drilling ventures, as well. The result of this financial failure was the closing of Penn Square Bank. However, this was just the tip of the iceberg of fraudulent practices that was quickly becoming the norm in the savings and loan industry.

By far one of the biggest names to emerge out of the group has to be Charles H. Keating Jr., who looted his own Lincoln Savings & Loan Company for $2.5 billion, but Keating cannot alone be held accountable. This is yet another case in which individuals in the government were seen as playing a key role in detrimentally affecting the events that would follow. In all, five US Senators, infamously known as the Keating Five, were accused of corruption and specifically of helping Keating avoid charges of fraud in exchange for campaign contributions. Ernst & Young, the auditing firm that was supposed to alert the company and the investing public of any potential misstatements or material losses, did not perform its duty. In fact, Ernst & Young admitted that it, too, had failed to catch the fraud in its audits and would later settled out of court for $400 million for its role in the scandal. However, no accountants at the savings and loan were prosecuted.

The scandals and frauds from the S&L fiasco resulted in the failure of over 700 savings and loan institutions; that is over 20 percent of the 3,200 S&Ls that existed at that time. This represented a direct cost to taxpayers of well over $120 billion dollars. The indirect cost and ensuing financial downturn from the crises' fallout would last for years. This period so scarred the S&L industry that, by 1995, there were a little over 1,645 S&Ls in the United States; that was a decrease of over 50 percent from its peak of 3,234 in 1986.(9)

One of the positive changes that came out of the S&L financial scandals was a campaign reform bill that was not passed until 1991 and a crime bill that increased prison terms for crimes committed at the federal level. This was also a time when financial deregulation received increased scrutiny which, not surprisingly, is the same discussion going on today, years after the fallout from the mortgage fiasco.

The stock market crashed in 1987 as the bull market ended, but it rallied quickly and was fully recovered within two years, unlike the stock market crash of 1929, which took twelve years to recover from. The cause of the 1987 crash is assigned to derivative securities, trade deficits, budget deficits, and computer trading by large institutional investors. This was yet another foreshadowing of the 2008 market collapse. After the crash, as is customary nowadays, the FBI and SEC began investigating whether stock manipulation existed.

The 1990s, as discussed, saw the Enron, WorldCom, and Arthur Anderson financial scandals. However, they were not the only ones. Tyco, Ltd., a company that was incorporated in Bermuda but operated its headquarters in the United States, was also part of this scandalous circle. In the end, the Chairman and CEO, Dennis Kozlowski, and the CFO, Mark H. Swartz, were convicted of twenty-nine counts of theft from their company in the amount of $600 million, and both were sentenced to eight and a third to twenty-five years in prison.

In the 1990s, hedge funds got attention because of the risk that can be built into them and also because they were not regulated like other investment funds, such as traditional mutual funds. One of the infamous was Long Term Capital Management (LTCM), an absolute-strategy-type fund, which was founded in 1994 by John Meriwether, the former head of Salomon Brothers's bond trading desk. Meriwether had resigned years earlier in light of financial scandals that occurred on his watch. Despite the previous scandal, investors still supported his hedge fund venture. One of the reasons that he garnered investors' support was probably the fact that Meriwether had hired some very intelligent individuals to work the complex mathematical models and strategies that the fund was going to use. Two notables were Robert Merton and Myron Scholes, both future Nobel Prize winners. The LTCM hedge fund was known for using highly speculative strategies that impressed its investors by generating 40-percent annualized returns in its first year. However, as with investment vehicles that have the potential for high returns, so, too, is the potential downside for losses and, in some cases, bankruptcy.

LTCM was the poster child for capital risk in that period. The fund was leveraged about twenty-five times over at some point, with about $125 billion against less than $5 billion in equity. The fund's off-balance-sheet holdings were even more shocking, with over $1.25 trillion in derivatives securities. LTCM, however, would not be immune to the market risks and managed to lose $4.6 billion in four months in 1998. It has been said that the fallout from the 1997 Asian Financial Crisis compounded with the 1998 Russian Financial Crisis caused the fund's eventual demise. It was during this period that LTCM unfortunately had to liquidate many of its positions at prices and terms that were detrimental to the fund, and losses continued to increase. This forced liquidation is built into the market, however, to protect the other market participants' interest in these transactions. This scenario would also be played out in the 2007 derivatives debacle, with similar losses flowing through the financial system as market participants demanded payment from other participants who had to sell at whatever prices the market would pay—which oftentimes amounted to a fire sale on the securities.

Meriwether would receive a bailout under the supervision of the Federal Reserve from other financial firms on Wall Street—firms that were linked intricately in the LTCM's highly leveraged network. This bailout would not prevent the catastrophic losses that ricocheted throughout the financial system, possibly because of LTCM derivatives holdings and the fact that it was so highly leveraged. The bailout would only stem the losses enough to keep it afloat temporarily, but this just postponed the inevitable. The fund would finally fold in 2000.

Also important to mention is Barings Bank. Though it was a London-based financial institution and, at the time, the oldest merchant bank in the venerable city, it shook the financial markets with an amazing discovery. One of its employees had lost $1.4 billion on futures contract speculation and then manipulated the records to hide the losses. When the enormous losses were discovered in 1995, the Singapore-based employee was tracked down, convicted, and ordered to spend six and a half years in prison. Barings Bank no longer exists, but this scandal led to increased scrutiny and oversight by government regulators. Management was also put on alert for rogue traders and was told that they had to be more accountable for the actions of the company's employees.

In the decade of the 2000s, the fraud, deception, and corruption continued beyond Enron and WorldCom. Adelphia Communications Corporation, a cable company, amassed a $2.3 billion debt by 2002 and was accused of internal corruption. The company founders were charged with securities violations. Two officers who were family members were sentenced to prison for taking $100 million from the company and giving it to businesses owned by their family.

The recent corporate financial scandals uncovered after the collapse of Lehman Brothers in 2008 pale in comparison, however. For example, Bernard Madoff ran the largest Ponzi scheme in the history of the US through Bernard L. Madoff Investment Securities. The firm was founded in 1960 and generated steady and, in most cases, predictable returns that were unique, it seems, to each investor's expectations for over forty years until its reasons for stable returns came to light. It was not until 2008 that the Ponzi scheme was finally reported by Madoff's sons. The FBI then arrested Madoff, which led to the unraveling of a scheme that was essentially carried out in plain sight for decades. This scheme involved $50 billion and defrauded thousands of investors, many from prominent firms and families, of their life savings. Madoff was sentenced to 150 years in prison and is not expected to ever get out.

One aspect of this fraud is embarrassing for government regulators. The Madoff company had been investigated by the SEC well over eight times, but the investigations did not uncover fraud. In fact, investors and analysts were quick to point out they did not understand how Madoff could be getting such large returns, but that did not seem to encourage anyone to dig deeper. The fact that the SEC did not uncover the fraud for more than ten years led investors to question their ability to trust government regulators to protect the public from fraudsters like Madoff. In addition, Madoff had managed to fool big banks, including Bank of America, UBS, and Citi.

Another Ponzi scheme that was run by a Sir Robert Allen Stanford through the Stanford Financial Group also unfolded in 2009. However, the alleged amount of $7 billion, which, compared against history, was a fairly large sum, unfortunately paled in comparison to the Madoff scheme. This speaks volumes about not only the direction that these frauds and schemes are headed in but also what is being done to curb these unscrupulous individuals and firms who exploit our financial system to the point of crippling our economic system as we know it.

The collapse of the housing market that began in 2007, and is still ongoing in many ways, is also an end result of a series of fraudulent transactions. The difficulty for regulators has been being able to pinpoint blame. A series of activities led up to the housing market decline; this included giving loans to people who should not have qualified or who could not provide adequate documentation, approving loans to people with bad credit, and creating mortgages with adjustable interest rates that eventually made payments unaffordable. On the financial institution side, these subprime mortgages known to have a high risk of default were bundled as securities and were resold to other financial institutions. In other words, the original mortgagor was selling bad loans before they went bad.

Where is the fraud in all of this? The people obtaining many of these mortgages knew they were not telling the truth about their financial condition or ability to pay a mortgage payment. The financial institutions were selling securities with mortgages as collateral, knowing the mortgages were close to worthless, but did not disclose that information. In addition, bond ratings agencies were approving these securities bundles while knowing, if they did any research at all, that they were extremely high-risk investments.

In 2010, the SEC charged Goldman Sachs with fraud. According to the press release, "The SEC alleges that Goldman Sachs structured and marketed a synthetic collateralized debt obligation (CDO) that hinged on the performance of subprime residential mortgage-backed securities (RMBS). Goldman Sachs failed to disclose to investors vital information about the CDO, in particular the role that a major hedge fund played in the portfolio selection process and the fact that the hedge fund had taken a short position against the CDO."(10) In other words, an investment firm was letting a client who believed the mortgage market would collapse influence the packaging of the mortgages into securities bundles while telling investors that an independent party had made the selection. Goldman Sachs never admitted guilt. However, the firm agreed to make some business practice changes. The SEC fined the company $550 million.

As mentioned earlier, due to changes resulting from early corporate fraud cases, Congress can call people to testify before its members. Senators formed a commission and called former Chairman and CEO of MF Global, Jon Corzine, and other executives of the same company to Washington to answer some questions. MF Global, a financial derivatives broker, went bankrupt on October 31, 2011, and now the firm is unable to locate $1.2 billion of money invested with the firm by 36,000 clients. Interestingly, Corzine was once head of Goldman Sachs. This case is ongoing as of 2012. Certainly, it does seem that history repeats itself.

## Do Big Wall Street Corporations Care?

One of the most interesting questions being debated is: Do Wall Street companies care about the threat of fines and prison for committing fraud? If you consider the examples given and realize this is a small sample, then the answer is probably that they do not really care. In fact, the risky behavior that led financial institutions to sell derivatives with faulty underlying assets and led to a major global crisis has not stopped. History seems to indicate that where there are high profits to be made, fraud and corruption cannot be far behind.

In the last ten years, there has been a trend toward giving corporate executives prison time for committing fraud. However, in the case of Goldman Sachs, no one went to prison for committing fraud. In fact, the $550 million fine really had little significance to a financial giant like Goldman Sachs. The company's first quarter 2010 profits were $3.3 billion. In other words, the fine equated to approximately two weeks of profit. No prison time and a small fine for the fraud committed—was this just added as a small fee of doing business in this new financial reality?

Interestingly, the government itself seems to be at odds over whether these fraud perpetrators should be punished. The SEC allows companies to settle cases without admitting fault. Recently, Judge Jed S. Rakoff of the United States District Court in Manhattan rejected an agreement between Citigroup and the SEC. The judge was not saying that Citigroup was guilty, but rather that allowing a settlement without proving a claim of fraud made it impossible to know if the settlement is fair and in the public interest.(11) The SEC plans to appeal the rejection of the settlement.

Citigroup was accused of the same thing most of the large banks have been accused of: failing to inform investors buying into a mortgage fund that the securities would probably fail. Like Goldman Sachs investors, Citigroup's investors were led to believe that an independent party was selecting the securities for the fund. The SEC recommended a settlement amount of $285 million.

If you want a historical reference to determine if the SEC has made any progress in convincing investment firms to avoid conflict of interest and follow government regulations and ethical rules of behavior, then consider a 2003 press release. The SEC announced that "Ten of Nation's Top Investment Firms Settle Enforcement Actions Involving Conflicts of Interest between Research and Investment Banking."(12) The whole point of the 2003 agreement was that investment banks would stop influencing brokerage firm research efforts. On the list of ten firms is Goldman Sachs, in addition to other big names like Citigroup, Bear Stearns, UBS, and J.P. Morgan. Now consider this fact: Citigroup paid $300 million in 2003 to settle with the SEC and is being asked to pay $285 million in 2011 for a larger repeat offense.

It is clear that no government agency is deterring big financial firms or their executives from committing fraud and corruption. This is not a judgment call but rather an assessment based on historical facts. To the large Wall Street firms and particularly global investment firms, the SEC fines and even the risk of prison are simply costs of doing business.

For investors, their best protection is to diversify their holdings and do even more due diligence on where their money is invested. The people who invested their entire life savings with Madoff learned that criminal activity can lead to total loss. If they had spread their investments among several brokers, they would not have lost everything. Finally, one golden rule of investment is this: if it is too good to be true, then it is probably fraud, a scam, or a bubble that is going to collapse.

CHAPTER 4

# Flash Crashes: High Frequency Trading

In the modern financial world of discount brokers, online trading, and foreign exchange (forex or FX) trading signal indicators, the world of market investing and trading is very different than it was only two decades ago. Individuals are much more involved, and the different types of securities that can be traded keeps on increasing, seemingly on a weekly basis. With the many changes that have taken place in this new market environment, many controversial practices have arisen in the markets, and perhaps none are as controversial as high frequency trading, or HFT.

The origins of high frequency trading date back to the 1980s, when electronic trading first came into vogue. It may be surprising to those outside the industry, but the stock market crash of 1987 was widely blamed on computerized trading.(1) After these and other implications, the US Securities and Exchange Commission (SEC) authorized new rules on electronic exchanges in 1998. It was around this time that a new wave of electronic trading began, mostly behind the scenes and out of the view of both the public and regulators. With the perfect combination of algorithmic science and electronic acumen, HFT is reminiscent of the scheme hatched by Richard Pryor's character in the movie *Superman III* (or the revision of the plan from the cult classic *Office Space*) to steal fractions of pennies from millions of transactions, a method known by the slang term "salami slicing." The difference is that HFT is legal, at least for now, and skilled securities firms are making millions of dollars using these computerized trading programs to sometimes earn as little as fractions of a penny on transacted trades.

## "Traditional" Trading Techniques

Trading has undergone so many changes in the past that listing a technique as "traditional" is perhaps not an accurate term, but the idea here refers to trading done with a human component, versus computerized HFT, which is almost completely automated. However, even with advanced signals, stock forecasting tools, and other helpful computerized and electronic trading, there is generally a human decision maker involved before trading actually commences. Before we get into HFT strategies, let us briefly look at some of the more traditional trading techniques that have been employed in the past.

**Contrarian Trading/Investing** is a method in which traders go against the grain of popular market opinion. These strategists are usually buying into stocks or similar securities that have been falling out of favor, usually indicated by price declines, or are selling or shorting stocks whose prices are still rising when they feel the market is overvaluing these securities. Warren Buffet is one of the more famous Contrarian investors who has built an investment empire buy purchasing undervalued securities and business that were often neglected in the marketplace. This method can use electronic analysis, but typically a lot of fundamental analysis is employed to look at the core value of the businesses and securities being observed.

**Price Action Trading** is trading based on the current price of the stock and the action, or movement, of the stock. This strategy is typically seen in volatile markets where prices and thus the action can vary quite frequently. Many see this strategy not just as technical analysis but also as a blend of behavioral analysis since these traders are trying to anticipate the trending price direction that the market will eventually move in for the securities under observation. Different variations of this method are extremely popular today with computerize advancements seen online with streaming charts.

**Range Trading** is also based on charts but does not take into account the immediate price of the stock during the trading day. Rather, the "range" of the stock price is charted with highs and lows touching parallel trend lines drawn on the chart. Traders sell when the price touches the top of the channel and buy when the price touches the bottom of the channel. These trending prices are usually based on the closing price at the end of a trading day or even week, rather than intra-day pricing. These technical strategists also use advanced computer charting programs to plot vast amounts of data to determine the high and low resistance points or trending ranges.

**Rebate Trading** is a much closer relative to HFT, in that it often involves trades that can open and close in seconds or minutes. Buying stock in high volumes through an electronic communications network (ECN) has been a practice among firms since its inception in 1969. The ECNs provide an alternate market outside the stock exchanges where stocks and currencies can be traded among the vast networks of traders. ECN will tend to charge traders a premium or commission for priority trades that must be filled immediately. However, ECNs also pay a rebate to traders who add liquidity to the market by making limit-order trades in marketable securities. These limit-order trades are non-priority trades that are filled when certain price, time, and other specified requirements are met. However, depending on market conditions, some of these trades can take days or weeks, if they are ever filled at all. Therefore, most profitable rebate traders exploit strategies that generate high volumes at a low price or cost to them. These traders will thus attempt to purchase stocks that trade with high volume so as not to affect the price with the purchase, and then sell after a very small gain, which can be pennies. However, these trades are done often to get the more valuable rebates per share than the pennies in trade profits that can be realized from these transactions.

**Scalping** is the method used by market makers and some traders who buy at the bid price and sell at the ask price very quickly to "make the spread." They are generally just trading to exploit the difference between the buy and sell prices. These types of trades are done often in fractions of a second, depending on how advanced the trading system being utilized is, and the goal is to profit on these price-spread differences. These types of trades generally make the market more efficient, because they narrow the differences between the buying and selling prices on securities. Market makers typically use this method to keep liquidity in the markets. This is probably the closest relative of HFT in terms of technique.

**Trend Following** is the technique of watching for a trend in price movement to be established and then taking a position to take advantage of the momentum. This is essentially a jumping-on-the-bandwagon style of investing, where the trader sees the current trend as continuing for a while and, therefore, tries to profit from continued price increases or tries to short sell and profit from price decreases. Trend investors use many and varied criteria for determining whether a trend is established, but they all generally forgo the profits at the upturn or downturn of the price to wait for momentum to build.

## Trading at the Speed of Light

High frequency trading, in contrast, is a completely automated and computerized system of trading, with the only human elements being the initial development of the algorithm used and turning the machine or computer program on or off. HFT machines initially were able to complete their transactions in a matter of seconds, but as technology has advanced and more advanced algorithms, or "algos" as they are often referred to in HFT lingo, have been developed, machines that now take seconds to complete a trade are seen as obsolete. Today, HFT is now measured in microseconds and nanoseconds, with speeds measuring in picoseconds (one trillionth of a second—yes, that is fast) close at hand. The race to zero in terms of time frame is high, with the speed of light actually being a goal for many HFT users. To understand the speeds that are being utilized and are in development, think about this: a fast trader can submit perhaps five trades within a one-minute time frame, while HFT systems will soon be able to execute more than sixty million trades in the same sixty seconds. This is based on the assumption that the HFT system can process trades at about 740 nanoseconds or a trade in 0.00000074 second, a feat that boggles the mind.(2) Clearly, the prospects for technologically challenged traders continue to remain bleak for obvious reasons.

These speeds do not come cheap. At the slower end of the spectrum, startup costs for the necessary equipment can far outstrip the $10 million mark, and this does not include other costs of doing business. Traders must also ensure their equipment does not malfunction or disrupt the functioning of the network, as there are penalties for such actions. Recently, the Chicago Mercantile Exchange (CME) fined a firm about $850 thousand for recurring HFT programming errors that were noticeable in the marketplace.

Then there is the location cost, and in this fast paced business, location does matter. In HFT, the proximity to the traditional exchanges data center often determines the time a trade can take to complete in addition to having quicker access to market data from the exchanges. In fact, many are arguing that these new data centers are becoming the new exchanges. Securities firms therefore often spend between $50 thousand to upward of millions of dollars annually in what is known as location or co-location fees in order to have specialized equipment placed within or near securities exchanges in order to gain an edge over their competitors by shaving seconds off trade times.

A new industry of exchanges data centers co-locations (CoLo) sites has been developed to meet the needs of securities firms that are looking to get closer to the securities exchanges. In some cases, these data centers are developed by the securities exchanges themselves, but there are also many other locations that provide alternate CoLo data centers access if traders do not have the capital to invest in direct contracts with the exchanges. Also, as exchanges move their data centers to new locations, the industry of data center providers also moves their locations in order to gain that proximity advantage.

However, while the costs of the equipment, necessary software, location fees, compliance penalties, and other charges to run these operations can be high, these costs become minuscule in comparison when the possibility exists to make the kind of profits that were made in 2009 and 2010, which were about $12.9 billion. And as long as the market has volatility and inefficiencies, there will be HFT programs there to generate revenues around the clock. And HFT is not limited to the typical big-name investment firms. HFT operations are run by both known and relatively unknown global companies, including high-profile names like Goldman-Sachs and Chicago hedge fund Citadel Investment Group, LLC. However, there are international financial powerhouses that also play in the US markets.

## HFT Strategies

There are several different strategies employed by HFT traders, all of which take advantage of speed. Market making, traditionally done by specialists, is now handled more often by HFT outfits. This is the simultaneous buying and selling of a security at the bid and ask prices in order to supply orders to traders. Market makers make their profits from the spread, the difference between the bid and ask price.

**Ticker tape trading** is another strategy employed by HFT outfits. Ticker tape trading is the practice of using HFT machines to analyze the information embedded in market data before it crosses the news screens, which is legal since all quote and volume information is public. The HFT machines can simply get the information quicker.

**Event arbitrage** is another practice used by many traders that involves trading based on recurring events that cause normally predictable short-term movements, such as earnings releases or end-of-quarter sales. Again, the machines can simply do this faster.

**Statistical arbitrage** uses information from many different market sources to predict deviations from stable statistical relationships between securities, such as forex interest rate changes. The machines can almost instantaneously analyze prices on a number of different aspects of a situation and predict short-term changes within a security.

**Low latency trading** is simply using the fastest speeds possible to accumulate minuscule profits on trades as quickly as possible. Latency refers to the delay of signals sent; the lower the latency, the faster the information travels. This form of trading relies on ultra-low-latency networks, which bring vital market data, such as the pool of bid and ask prices, often seconds before the rest of the market sees the information.

By having this data before the rest of the slower market participants and the right data-mining algorithms to take advantage and transact on the data, millions can be added to the bottom line over time.

**Layering trading** is often seen as a form of spoofing in which a trader usually knowingly places and cancels trade orders in an attempt to manipulate market prices. These types of strategies are almost an illegal scheme if intent can be proven. These traders might place multiple or frequent orders to buy a particular security, thereby driving up the price of that stock. Once a predetermined target price is reached, the traders would then unload or sell that particular stock from their own inventories and cancel the orders that they placed to buy the stock. This is indeed a form of price manipulation since the traders had no intention of buying the stock, but were only trying to drive up the price to get a higher return in the marketplace. Price manipulation intent can sometimes be difficult to legally prove, but firms like Swift Trade, who had to pay millions in fines, show that the practice of price manipulation does occur.

### Trading Algorithms Crimes and Penalties

In addition to being penalized for malfunctioning equipment and code, there are also fines for those who attempt to manipulate the financial system by using HFT technologies. There have been numerous fines in the last few years for HFT strategies that illegally profited due to various market manipulating schemes. In most cases, HFT misconduct is just part of the list of allegations against these securities firms, but there are other times where the focus seems to be on HFT. Let us take a look at a recent securities firm and an individual case to see some of the issues that are plaguing the HFT industry and our greater financial markets, as well.

In 2010, the Financial Industry Regulatory Authority (FINRA) fined Trillium, a New York securities firm, about $2.3 million for its role in market manipulations schemes utilized under its HFT system. There was no jail time; instead, the firm simply paid the fine without admitting to any wrongdoing. Like other firms that engage in similar market manipulations and are penalized, these firms will more than likely see this as a cost of doing business in today's increasingly competitive environment. However, the cost is far greater than that. While some firms see relatively insignificant financial penalties as a cost of doing business, the cost to the overall financial system is very significant. With each "insignificant penalty," the foundation of the market system gets weaker, because those that rely on it for fairness and transparency see that might not be the case.

Individuals or employees on the low end of the Wall Street totem pole do not fare as well when implicated in scandals on the street. In 2010 for example, the US Federal Courts affirmed that Sergey Aleyniko, an HFT algorithm programmer, had been found guilty of stealing computer code from Goldman Sachs before resigning from the company. He received an eight-year jail sentence and over $12 thousand in fines. Aleyniko was one of Goldman Sachs's top programmers, making upward of $400 thousand a year to write HFT code that earned the company hundreds of millions annually. His sentence sent a clear message to employees everywhere—do not steal from your employer or else you will be fined and jailed.

Although, in this case, it appears that the motive was selfish profiteering versus self-preservation as an employee. There still have been numerous cases of individuals who, once justifiably found guilty of wrongdoing at corporations, were ordered to pay steep fines and even do jail time. Here is a list of some rogue traders and the penalties for their actions dating back to 1995:

| Name | Date(s) | Loss | Institution | Market Activity | Sentence |
|---|---|---|---|---|---|
| Nick Leeson | 1995 | £827 million | Barings Bank | Nikkei index futures | 6.5 years prison |
| Toshihide Iguchi | 1995 | $1.1 billion | Resona Holdings | U.S. Treasury bonds | 4 years prison |
| Yasuo Hamanaka | 1996 | $2.6 billion | Sumitomo Corporation | Copper | 8 years prison |
| John Rusnak | 2002 | $691 million | Allied Irish Banks | Foreign exchange | 7.5 years prison |
| Gianni Gray, David Bullen, Vince Ficarra, Luke Duffy | 2003 - 2004 | AU$360 million | National Australia Bank | Foreign exchange options | 16 mths prison, 3 years and 8 mths prison, 2 years and 4 mths prison, 2 years 5 mths prison |
| Chen Jiulin | 2005 | $550 million | China Aviation Oil | Jet fuel futures | 4 years and 3 mths prison |
| Jérôme Kerviel | 2006–2008 | €4.9 billion | Société Générale | European stock index futures | 5 years prison (2 years are suspended) |
| Boris Picano-Nacci | 2008 | €751 million | Groupe Caisse d'Epargne | Equity Derivatives | Investigation in progress |
| Kweku Adoboli | 2011 | $2.3 billion | UBS | S&P 500, DAX, and EuroStoxx index | Investigation in progress |

**Source: Wikipedia (Largest Rogue Trader Losses)**

Imagine if that same system of justice applied to those at the top of these organizations—where much of this culture is sometimes fostered and trickled down to the underlings who carry out the various policies. A fair system should require that those who are directly responsible or who contributed directly to these actions should be held accountable, not just the individual who pushed the button.

## Shining a Light into the Shadows

While many HFT groups operated for years out of the limelight and in the shadows of the financial system, in recent years, they have been given much attention, partly due to the so-called "flash-crash" of May 2010, when the markets plunged some seven hundred points in a matter of minutes and eliminated almost a trillion dollars in securities market values before recovering a percentage of the losses. There are various theories as to what caused the crash, including assertions that it was an individual typing a *b* for billion instead of an *m* for million or even that someone shut off one of the HFT machines. What is clear is that after the trigger was pulled, the HFT and other automated machines that were programmed to react to events in the marketplace began cannibalizing each other in what appeared to be an endless feeding frenzy, collapsing the markets. If the exchanges and other human participants had not pulled the plug, this activity would have more than likely continued till either the entire market collapsed or the program itself crashed.

## 2010: Flash Crash of 2:45

The Thursday, May 6, 2010, Flash Crash (aka the Crash of 2:45) significantly affected the Dow Jones Industrial Average (DJIA), the index reflecting relative prices of selected stocks traded on the New York Stock Exchange (NYSE), and changed the way people viewed computerized trading and exchange traded funds (ETFs) in the financial markets. Let us take a quick look at what happened on that day.

| Dow Jones Industrial Average (DJI) Prices | | | | | |
|---|---|---|---|---|---|
| Date | Open | High | Low | Close | Volume |
| 5-May-10 | 10,918.40 | 10,984.05 | 10,754.30 | 10,868.12 | 6,795,940,000 |
| 6-May-10 | 10,862.22 | 10,925.86 | 9,787.17 | 10,520.32 | 10,617,809,600 |
| 7-May-10 | 10,519.42 | 10,622.27 | 10,221.50 | 10,380.43 | 9,472,910,400 |

May 6, 2010, had started out pretty rough for the markets due to the uncertainty caused by the looming Greek and European debt crisis being scrutinized by the media from Europe to New York. Traders were making and adjusting their trades in a tireless effort to stay a step ahead of the news that was coming out of Europe. All this uncertainty in trading created a volatile trading environment for securities, especially stocks. In fact, the morning trading session showed that the DJIA price was already trending downward amid the growing negative sentiment of traders and investors. This meant that the markets were already anticipating a sell off for stocks.

Around midafternoon, at 2:42 p.m. EST, the DJIA was trading down almost three hundred points from its opening price, and traders were getting a little nervous. However, no one—and I mean no one—was prepared for what was about to happen next. As some traders looked on in horror, the DJIA began to drop, plunging more than seven hundred points in a matter of minutes and eliminating almost a trillion dollars in securities market values before it stopped and then reversed direction, with prices climbing back to its level before the crash began. So what happened?

Shortly after the crash, speculation about what actually took place was rampant. Many blamed the high-frequency computerized trading systems, some blamed ETFs, some blamed rogue traders, while others blamed the whole trading system for being so fragile and susceptible to large erroneous trades. Unfortunately, most of the rumors about what occurred proved correct as the SEC validated some of the claims about five months later, after its investigation and report.

In its reports that were made public on September 30, 2010, the SEC suggested that the crash was caused by volatility and the placement of a large erroneous order through a computerized trading program into the financial markets. However, that is an oversimplification of what actually happened. Let us go back to that day in May, 2010, and see what the SEC found during its investigation.

According to the SEC report, the fiasco started around 2:32 p.m. and continued as follows:

A trader at a financial firm programmed a computerized trading system to sell seventy-five thousand E-Mini S&P 500 contracts valued at approximately $4.1 billion in the financial markets. The trader initialized the system to automatically process the trades if the volume of the markets could support the trades without regard to price or how long it took to process the trades. SEC investigations would later note that the sheer size of the trade and its loose terms of processing would be the critical driver in the ensuing chaos. Portions of the seventy-five thousand E-Mini S&P 500 trades began to be executed in the futures market. High-frequency trading automatic systems took notice and began responding to the trades. HFT began buying and selling thousands of trades in blinks of an eye.

Selling pressures pushed the price of the E-Minis down further. SPY, an exchange-traded fund which represents the S&P 500 index, began a steep drop. With no large buyers to support the fall, HFTs began a vicious cycle of buying and selling to each other, relying on their algorithmic programs' instructions, in an effort to stabilize their positions. HFTs with positions in the general stock markets began pulling down those stock prices. This led other HFTs in the stock markets to respond, which made a bad situation worse.

Trading volume spiked within this period as buy-and-sell trades climbed into the millions then further into the billions. The DJIA was down almost one thousand points from its opening at about a 9-percent decline. In a matter of minutes, over a trillion dollars in securities market values evaporated. Some HFT systems and others were also canceling orders when they realized that the market was dysfunctional.

Smart human traders, realizing that something was wrong, essentially shut down their trading systems and exited the market to find out what was really going on in the markets. Some sophisticated HFT programs with automatic "kill" switches also disengaged from the market when the volume spiked abnormally. Procter & Gamble, which was one of the "victim" securities that had sell contracts issued on it, witnessed an unprecedented drop from its opening price of $62.12 per share to $39.37 per share (about a 37-percent decline) during the fiasco.

**Source: CNNMoney**

At 2:45:28 p.m., the Chicago Mercantile Exchange (CME) Stop Logic Functionality safety mechanism kicked in and halted trading. At 2:45:33 p.m., trading was allowed to resume, and buyers began coming into the markets again, leading to a more stable trading environment and a start to recovery. Trading in the E-Mini also recovered from the previous blitz selling craze.

By 3:00 p.m., the worst was over, and the market had resumed regular trading again. The flash crash was over. By closing bell, the markets had stabilized; however, the DJIA was still down over three hundred points from its opening price.

In the aftermath of this chaotic trading day, over twenty-one thousand trades (mostly ETFs) were eventually canceled or reversed by regulators. Most of the trades were reversed due to automatic systems selecting any available price that was seen in the trading market. Trades with extreme prices, typically as low as a penny or as high as $100 thousand, were reversed. Those types of trades were meant to serve as placeholders in portfolios rather than actual available trading prices.

In the hours and days after, many market participants were still in shock that something like this could take place. They were sure that HFT systems had built-in safety mechanisms. However, the live scenario in the markets had made it clear that after that erroneous trade was programmed into the system, the HFT and other automated machines that were programmed to react to events in the marketplace began to cannibalize each other in what can be summed up as an endless feeding frenzy that led to the collapse of the markets. Only the exchanges and human participants who pulled the plug avoided a market collapse and the crash of the computer programs.

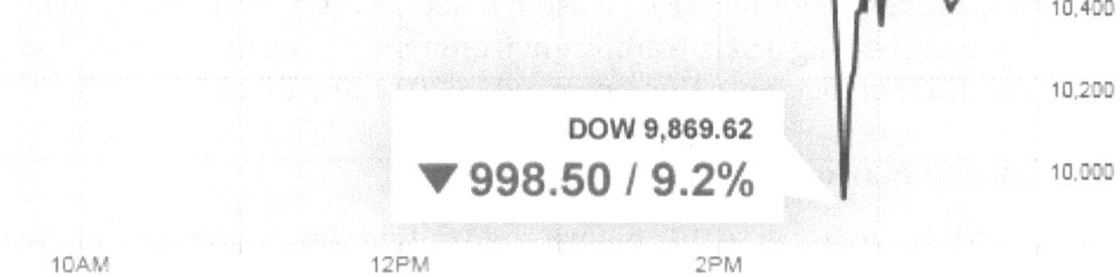


**Source: CNNMoney**

The SEC has also launched an investigation into the practices of HFT traders and debated the potential regulations that should be imposed on them. Many HFT organizations have also subsequently come forth and attempted to polish their images in order to gain favor in the regulators' sights.

In recent months, regulators have actually requested HFT traders to hand over their trading strategies, and in some cases, even their written code for their algos. These HFT trading systems are also required to have circuit breakers in place to prevent a similar event from happening in the future. In September, 2010, the SEC also expanded its Stock-by-Stock Circuit Breaker system, which temporarily stops trading activity for a stock if its price swings more than 10 percent in a five-minute period between the hours of 9:45 a.m. EST and 3:35 p.m. EST.

On May 31, 2012, the SEC approved proposals to replace the single stock circuit breaker system with the Limit Up-Limit Down plan as well as a plan for a market-wide circuit breaker system. The Limit Up-Limit Down plan arose due to complaints about the existing single-stock circuit breaker system, the need to maintain elements of the single stock circuit breaker system, and the need to create a practical system that does not erroneously get triggered by certain market events. The new plan, which trading firms have to adhere to once implemented, was formulated through negotiations between the various securities exchanges, the Financial Industry Regulatory Authority (FINRA), and the SEC. Both of these measures will go into effect on February 4, 2013, on a one-year pilot basis and will be reviewed at the end of that period.

Some have heralded these events and the aftermath of regulations as the beginning of the end of HFT, and to many critics, this is a good thing.(3) Unfortunately for the industry, the exposure of some additional incidents has shed a bright light on the secretive world of some of these trading firms and their systems. While there are new global safety nets in place to hopefully prevent another HFT disaster, it seems there is still some work to be done in creating a safe trading environment. Let us take a quick look at two additional incidents that occurred in 2011 and 2012.

## 2011: Broad Market Flash Crash Averted

On Thursday, August 4, 2011, before the trading day began on the East Coast of the United States, the market was already jittery with global economic news and more bad news coming out of the European markets. It seemed that the Asian and European financial markets were in the middle of responding to the negative news coming out financial markets. As a matter of fact, governments around the world had already given the go ahead for their central banks to take measures to stabilize the markets.

US traders with access to other markets began selling off some of their holdings, putting additional negative pressures on securities and stock futures. As the clock slowly ticked away the last few seconds to the opening bell for trading in New York, the stage was already set, with tensions and anticipation being held back like cattle before the running of the bulls. The bell rang and the sell-off began. Out of the gates, all signs indicated that there would be a blood-red day led by massive stock sell-offs.

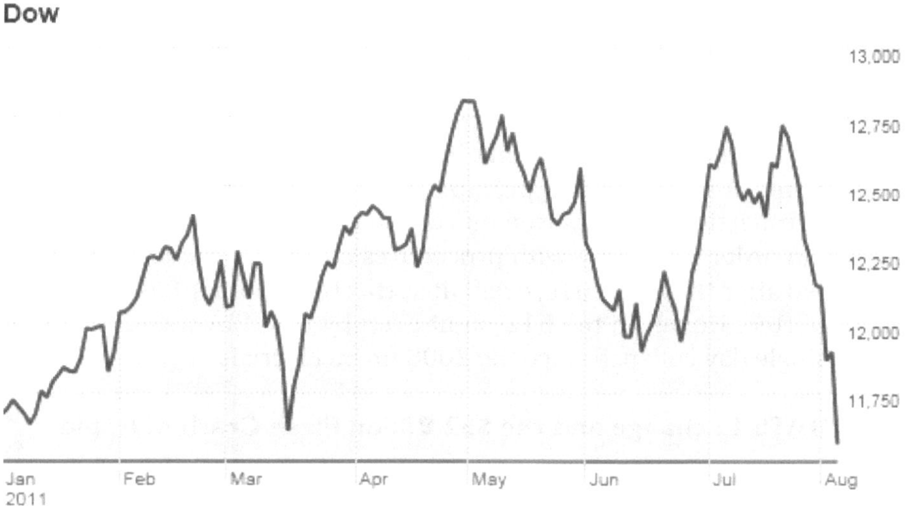


**Source: CNNMoney**

HFT systems, which were accounting for over 60 percent of the volume of trades, traded at lightning speeds, following their preprogrammed algorithms in order to trade their positions. As more bad news regarding the economic recovery rocked the market, those that were hesitant about selling before now joined the already-frenzied mob in the stampede to the exits.

Over thirteen billion shares would be traded (a normal day sees about two billion shares trading) over the day. It is estimated that the May, 2010, Flash Crash generated a trading volume of over 19 billion shares changing hands. However, some of that related volume was later adjusted due to regulators stepping in to investigate the "real" trades from the "fake" trades. There were also technical problems with trading systems, such as

NYSE Euronext (trades derivatives), which did little to boost confidence in some of the panic-stricken investors.

Fortunately, market circuit breakers (exchange and private trading systems) kicked in whenever security prices dropped below a certain level or fluctuated too widely in order to prevent a global free fall in the markets. For example, Vodafone had opened at $27.14 per share and was trading in a tight range between $26 and $28 when the market price suddenly jumped to $57.50. It eventually settled back to around $27.57 per share. The NYSE Amex would eventually cancel the bulk of the trades above $28.89.

Trading information also slowed to a crawl on certain electronic systems as the system tried to deal with the increased volume and adjustments that were being made globally. Trades were rerouted to various exchanges whenever an exchange got overheated with activity. The final half hour of trading saw increased trading in certain financial instruments and securities, prompting additional triggers to engage. Certain restrictions were placed on certain types of trades, such as short selling, in order to comply with procedures and best practices that were instituted after the May, 2010, event. It seems that another flash crash had been averted. However, the 512 point drop by the DJIA was dubbed the worst single day collapse since the 2008 financial crisis.

## 2012: BATS Exchange and the $52 Billion Flash Crash of Apple

On Friday, March 23, 2012, the BATS Global Markets Exchange (ticker: BATS) based in Kansas, United States, began its first day of public trading after its $100 million IPO was cleared the night before. This was its first corporate IPO on the BATS Exchange.

At 10:45 a.m., the BATS Exchange noticed that one of its trading system's matching engine programs was malfunctioning, apparently because of some sort of software bug. At 10:48 a.m., the BATS Exchange sent out an alert to the markets letting them know that it was experiencing technical difficulties with the trading system and was apparently having issues with secures with symbols from *A* to *BF*. At 10:57 a.m., the BATS Exchange sent an Apple stock (ticker: AAPL) trade to the market for $542.80 per share. The previous market price was for $598.26. This sent the price of Apple's stock falling.

The single-stock circuit breaker rule kicked in after a 9-percent rapid decline in Apple's stock price triggered it, and trading stopped for about five minutes. Trading was cleared to resume shortly thereafter, and regular trading began again with prices at about $598.20 per share.

The BATS IPO price fell from a high of more than $15 to less than four pennies during the market debacle. The NASDAQ Stock Exchange, the second-largest stock exchange globally, was able to summarily cancel the BATS trades, which allowed it to cancel its IPO.

Between 11:49 a.m. and 12:35 p.m. EST, the erroneous trades in Apple stock were able to be cancelled. The BATS Exchange, whose IPO trading was also stopped, would eventually withdraw the IPO from the markets on March 28, 2012. Since no monies had been exchanged with the new buyers of the stock, its withdrawal did not pose a problem. Clearly, it would have been a disaster to let the IPO trade in the public markets after that incident.

The acronym BATS supposedly means Better Alternative Trading System. And in an open letter, the CEO admitted to the failures of that fateful trading day and vowed that he and his team would "do better." The CEO states that prior to this incident, the company had a performance record of being "up" more than 99.9 percent of the time. He also remarked that the markets' single-stock circuit breakers did their job. The company will work to regain its investors and market confidence and uphold its mission of "making markets better." Advocates say that BATS's goal of creating a better trading market should be applauded. Critics, however, are skeptical.

It should also be noted that the BATS Global Markets Exchange was founded by a computer programmer whose expertise was in the development of securities exchange software—software that is probably still being used by some of the prominent exchanges. The SEC continues its investigation in the BATS Global Markets Exchange and its HFT systems.

### Is HFT Good or Bad for the Financial Markets?

This is a matter of opinion, and opinions vary, as they always do. Those in favor of the practice argue that HFT provides much-needed liquidity to the markets, lowering the spread on bid and ask prices and the commissions on trades and speeding up execution times, all of which are benefits to the average trader. Others argue that these benefits are not necessarily the result of the HFTs, but simply benefits of rules enacted and reformed by the SEC, which helped the HFTs and would be benefits even if the HFTs disappeared.

The detractors of high-frequency trading argue that the high volume creates artificial liquidity due to the extremely short duration of the positions. In addition, concerns about future flash crashes have been expressed not only by regulators but also by many economists and individual traders alike. The argument that the practice hurts the individual investor or trader has both merits and unwarranted concerns. By most assessments, in normal, uninterrupted trading, the volume does not affect individual traders very much, if at all, in a negative way. The largest fear comes from the flash crash event and the potential of algorithm- or HFT-induced malfunctions where such a large volume of trading and liquidity is left to automation. These are quite valid concerns, considering that HFT accounts for over half of the volume on the market today, and it only takes one "trigger" event that is common to the HFT algorithms to usher in a market collapse.

# SECTION 2
## Business as Usual

*"It is to be regretted that the rich and powerful too often bend the acts of government to their selfish purposes. Distinctions in society will always exist under every just government. Equality of talents, of education, or of wealth cannot be produced by human institutions. In the full enjoyment of the gifts of Heaven and the fruits of superior industry, economy, and virtue, every man is equally entitled to protection by law; but when the laws undertake to add to these natural and just advantages artificial distinctions, to grant titles, gratuities, and exclusive privileges, to make the rich richer and the potent more powerful, the humble members of society--the farmers, mechanics, and laborers--who have neither the time nor the means of securing like favors to themselves, have a right to complain of the injustice of their Government. There are no necessary evils in government. Its evils exist only in its abuses. If it would confine itself to equal protection, and, as Heaven does its rains, shower its favors alike on the high and the low, the rich and the poor, it would be an unqualified blessing. In the act before me there seems to be a wide and unnecessary departure from these just principles."*

-President Andrew Jackson in vetoing the privatization of the United States National Bank bill (1832)

CHAPTER 5

# Gramm-Leach-Bliley Act

At one time, financial institutions could sell personal information without your knowledge. The personal information included account numbers, bank balances, and credit information. Though it may seem like a complete invasion of privacy today, the selling of personal information was common practice before the Gramm-Leach-Bliley Act (GLBA) passed in 1999. This act is also called the Financial Services Modernization Act of 1999 and was designed to limit the right of companies to sell your private financial account information and to limit pretexting. It also infamously allowed banks to sell securities for profit, thus reversing the Glass-Steagall Act of 1933.

Like most laws, the GLBA had unintended consequences. However, to understand those consequences, you must also understand why the law was passed and what it was intended to correct. The GLBA actually has its historical justification in the Glass-Steagall Act passed by Congress in 1933 after the Great Depression. The GLBA is typical of laws in that one law is passed to correct problems, and the new law creates new problems.

In 1933, the Glass-Steagall Act was passed, prohibiting affiliations of national and state banks with security companies. This was followed by the Bank Holding Company Act in 1956, which barred banks from controlling non-bank companies. In 1982, that same act was amended to prevent banks from underwriting general insurance businesses. The Gramm-Leach-Bliley Act repealed many of the limitations of prior acts and restored the rights of the banks to engage in certain business activities.

To understand why the GLBA exists, it is important to understand the history of the legal relationship between brokerage investment companies and banks. This relationship has changed over the decades as a result of three intertwining factors: market risk, fraud and corruption, and laws and regulations.

## History of the Gramm-Leach-Bliley Act

| The Gramm-Leach-Bliley Act Time Line | |
|---|---|
| **Year** | **Banking Legislation Changes** |
| 1933 | Glass-Steagall Act separates commercial banking (CB) from investment banking (IB) |
| 1956 | Bank Holding Company Act limits banks venture into non-banking activities |
| 1982 | Bank Holding Act is amended to curtail banks' insurance underwritings |
| 1999 | The Gramm-Leach-Bliley Act removes separation between CB and IB |

The history of the Gramm-Leach-Bliley Act actually begins during the Great Depression, because events of that time laid the foundation for the changes to the law. The purpose of the Glass-Steagall Act was to prohibit state and national banks from affiliating with securities companies. In 1956, additional limitations were placed on banks with the passage of the Bank Holding Company Act. The 1956 law disallowed banks from having control of a non-bank business. Then, adding yet another degree of separation, the Bank Holding Company Act was amended in 1982. The 1982 amendment forbade banks from certain activities, like general insurance underwriting.

In 1999, the Gramm-Leach-Bliley Act was passed. In a reversal of a decades-long trend that had widened the gap between banks and non-banking activities, the GLBA allowed banks to sell financial services once again. The reversal of many of the provisions of pre-GLBA laws opened the way for banks to do international business by modernizing financial services. Modernization recognized the globalization of financial activities. Before the passage of the GLBA, banks, insurance companies, and brokerage firms were not allowed to merge. This kept banks smaller, reduced risky behavior, and also lowered the risk of private information being shared between companies.

The GLBA was prompted by several events. The Charter Pacific Bank in Agoura Hills, California, sold millions of consumer credit card numbers in 1997. The bank sold the credit card numbers and information to an adult website company. The adult website company then proceeded to bill customers for services never requested, including pornographic site access. Knowing it was breaking the law, the adult website company created a number of business accounts with different names so that they were difficult to track. Over 700,000 customers had been fraudulently billed for more than $40 million. The Federal Trade Commission (FTC), an independent consumer protection government agency, eventually won a $37.5 million judgment against the company in 2000, with the bank maintaining it did nothing wrong.(1)

In 1998, yet another bank shared information from customer accounts in violation of securities law. NationsBank, which was merged with Bank of America, shared the account information with NationsSecurities, an affiliate broker-dealer subsidiary. NationsSecurities then sold high-risk investments to customers like senior citizens who traditionally purchased low-risk securities. The Securities and Exchange Commission (SEC) and the National Association of Securities Dealers (NASD) brought enforcement action against both firms, claiming violation of the antifraud securities laws provisions. The charges included not clearly differentiating the bank and the broker, thus misleading customers into buying investment products, distributing misleading information to customers, distributing false information to customers, failing to advise customers of investment risks, and making unsuitable sales to investors.(2)

NationsBank and NationsSecurities were ordered to cease and desist by the SEC, which also fined these companies $4 million in civil penalties. The NASD also imposed a fine of $2 million to be paid by NationsSecurities. The NASD charged NationsBank and then censured, suspended, and fined several of NationsBank's officers and managers.

In 1999, U.S. Bancorp was sued by the Minnesota Attorney General for sharing customer information with third-party marketer Memberworks. The bank violated its own internal policies and shared private information without informing or seeking permission from customers. The telemarketer Memberworks then proceeded to charge customers for services they never authorized. Eventually, thirty-nine other states also sued U.S. Bancorp for fraud, deceptive advertising, and violation of the Fair Credit Reporting Act. This was the first time a large bank was charged with sharing private customer information with telemarketers, which had become a common practice in the banking industry.(3) Lawsuits were also filed naming Memberworks as the defendant. The bank and Memberworks eventually settled the lawsuits; however, it was discovered that other big financial institutions like Citibank and Chase Manhattan were also selling information to telemarketers.

In addition to these events, US businesses were rapidly going global. The European Union passed the Data Protection Directive in 1995. This directive required that any international data exchanges that involved the personal information of European Union citizens must meet the requirements of the directive. The US self-regulatory practices in the financial industry were looser than the directive requirements, meaning changes were needed. The stage was set for the passage of the Gramm-Leach-Bliley Act on November 11, 1999.

## Dismantling and Rebuilding

The Gramm-Leach-Bliley Act (GLBA) applies only to financial institutions, which includes businesses that sell stocks and bonds, give financial advice, provide banking services, do investing, and insure. The law has specific provisions concerning information sharing that include the following:

**Privacy of Consumer Financial Information Rule** This rule requires applicable financial institutions to notify customers via delivery of Privacy Notices about any customer-information-sharing policies and procedures. The business must also give customers the right to not have their personal or account information shared with non-affiliated businesses. Also, any business that does obtain customer financial information is restricted as to how the information can be reused or disclosed.

**Safeguards Rule** The Safeguards Rule requires any business within FTC jurisdiction to develop and implement measures to maintain the security of customer information. The financial institutions must also establish measures that ensure affiliates also safeguard customer information.

**Pretexting** Businesses are barred from using deception or false pretenses to obtain customer information from financial institutions.

However, consumers cannot stop information from being shared with affiliates of financial institutions. Also, financial institutions can report nonpublic personal information to credit reporting agencies and financial regulatory agencies. Additionally, under no circumstances, even if there is no opt-out, can a financial institution disclose or sell access codes or account numbers except to credit reporting agencies.

In addition to the consumer protections put into place by the GLBA, important provisions concerning the relationships between banks and investment companies were also included in the Glass-Steagall Act. The Glass-Steagall Act, which was passed in 1933 and is also called the Banking Act of 1933, applied to Federal Reserve member banks. It also restricted commercial banks from underwriting, holding, and trading corporate securities and prohibited commercial banks from being affiliated with securities firms and having interlocking directorships or close employee or officer relationships with underwriting firms, strengthened the Federal Reserve powers, and established the Federal Deposit Insurance Corporation (FDIC).

These regulations were put into place as a result of the 1929 stock market crash and the ensuing bank failures of the Great Depression. However, the law only applied to member banks, thus savings and loans and non-member banks were free to form affiliations with securities or investment firms.

The Gramm-Leach-Bliley Act dismantled two important provisions of the Glass-Steagall Act. First, it allowed banks and securities firms to form affiliations as they were allowed to do before 1933. (Yes, history was about to repeat itself.) In addition, the interlocking prohibition was also reversed. This meant that banks and investment firms could now pretty much do whatever they wanted to do in terms of merging or partnering and even sharing officers.

Another important provision of the GLBA allowed financial institutions to group mortgages and other securities into packages to be sold to investors. The stage was set for another financial disaster.

## A Financial Crisis in the Making

Clearly, some of the roots of the 2007 financial crisis were germinated with the passage of the Gramm-Leach-Bliley Act. The GLBA is recognized as important deregulation legislation that ended almost sixty-six years of regulation of the financial services industry put into place after the Great Depression. The intent of the GLBA was to give the banking and investment industries more flexibility and to remove obstacles to growth in the constantly changing economic environment.

Today, the GLBA is often quoted as setting the stage for the financial crisis that began in 2007 by removing firewalls within the financial services industry. It was the removal of the affiliate limitations that had contributed to the development of huge financial institutions that were said to be "too big to fail." These loosely regulated, bloated, and uncontrollable behemoths of institutions' sheer size in terms of assets and influence on the global economy makes failure or bankruptcy a disaster that reverberates throughout every financial market. Regular-sized financial institutions experienced accelerated growth in gaining the right to bundle securities and sell them as investments en masse, a practice which tied together financial institutions around the world in a tight, intricate network. It also promoted risky behavior as banks used customer deposits to invest in risky securities for self-profit. The separation that was in place before with the Glass-Steagall Act was eradicated, and speculative bankers and other unscrupulous financial operatives were chomping at the bit to get at the new opportunities this deregulation provided.

It is ironic that the GLBA swept away the very reforms instituted in 1933 to correct financial industry speculative behavior believed to have caused the Great Depression. The irony lies in the fact that the GLBA restored the ability of banks and investment firms to resume speculative behavior, and in less than ten years, another market crash ensued.

Though the 2008 recession cannot be blamed solely on the passage of the GLBA, it is clear that the capital market crisis is at least partly due to the deregulation of the financial industry, the formation of megamergers, and the willingness of banks and their affiliates to sell high-risk products to make greater profits. In other words, megabanks making risky loans and selling risky derivatives created a situation in which failure meant taxpayers would have no choice but to bail them out or witness a global financial industry collapse. The GLBA allowed two types of inherently risky businesses, banks and brokers, to form affiliations with very little oversight or regulation. They became "too big to fail" and then failed, forcing the government to bail them out.(4)

### Dismantling the GLBA

The question now is whether the Gramm-Leach-Bliley Act should be repealed. If dismantling the Glass-Steagall Act led to a new financial crisis, then it would seem to make sense to rebuild it by dismantling the Gramm-Leach-Bliley Act. Re-establishing the separation of banks, investment firms, and insurance companies by barring affiliations would stop the development of the megabanks and firms that are too big to fail. It would also reduce conflict of interest within financial holding companies.

Realistically, it would be difficult to prohibit bundled securities that were allowed with the passage of GLBA. In fact, the same banks bailed out by the government to prevent failure are now selling bundled derivatives again. Instead of limiting bundled securities, the GLBA could be strengthened by adding stricter disclosure requirements, which could limit unintentionally risky investments. For example, being fully informed of the risks of subprime-mortgage-backed securities would have discouraged many investors. It is a fact that consumer investors, global banks, and investment firms buying the mortgage-backed securities were not always informed of the high risk of probable failure of the mortgages.

Perhaps the most important provision in revised legislation would require banks to divest their investment and insurance operations, thus forcing them to scale down. Banks should also be barred from using customer deposits to make risky investments.

A revised financial reform law should also include severe penalties, including criminal charges brought against executives should the laws be violated. It is clear that SEC penalties currently assessed are not discouraging risky behavior within the financial industry. The penal amounts paid are seen as part of the cost of pursuing risky transactions and hence are incorporated into the fee schedule. These callous sentiments clearly need to change.

Some people believe that the current financial crisis would not have occurred if the Gramm-Leach-Bliley Act had not allowed banks and investment and security firms to merge operations and then sell bundled securities. That is an oversimplification of the set of circumstances that led to the 2008 recession, and strengthened oversight is needed to prevent another similar financial crisis. However, there are some individuals who knowingly assumed too much risk while chasing profits and greed-laden dreams of opulence. There is no law that can prevent that type of behavior.

CHAPTER 6

# New Lending Policies: Why Some Banks Will Not Lend

*"It is not by augmenting the capital of the country, but by rendering a greater part of that capital active and productive than would otherwise be so, that the most judicious operations of banking can increase the industry of the country."*

- Adam Smith

The famous economist Adam Smith seems to be speaking to our current financial crisis. Although his quote is from over two hundred years ago, it is prescient and appears as almost a prophecy of how the current banking situation has materialized.

Interest rates are at an all-time low. The government is flooding the banks with very cheap money. Why then are banks reluctant to lend to businesses and consumers? The answers to this question are debated by politicians and economists alike, but an objective look at a few key points can offer a relatively good understanding of what is going on with the economy today and why it is not growing at the rate it should be.

## Banks Operate by the Rules of the Fed

The Fed decided in October, 2008, to start paying interest on cash reserves; at the same time, the financial crisis came to the forefront of people's attention as a serious problem. The FEd started paying on not only the required reserves but also on the excess reserves, which quickly jumped. Whereas banks would traditionally use customer deposits as reserves for their liquidity needs such as backing loans and clearing checks, today, they borrow their liquidity from other banks, the money market, or the commercial paper market. By paying interest on the cash reserves the banks are holding, the Fed is essentially competing with these private sector markets for short-term funds, which inhibits lending between banks and causes a squeeze on liquidity. The upshot is that the banks are not lending because it is less profitable to do so. Businesses have to resort to credit cards with rates that average 16 percent—more than double the rates they usually get on bank loans. The obvious result of this increase in rates is less borrowing, which means less expansion, growth, and investment.

A look back at the events in the fall of 2008 provides a clearer picture than we had at the time and demonstrates that the action taken by the Fed in deciding to pay interest on these cash reserves was not only unwarranted but also helped to greatly accelerate the decline in lending. Even after Lehman Brothers filed for bankruptcy on September 15, 2008, the daily amount of inter-bank lending transactions remained relatively steady near the $200 billion mark. However, within weeks of the Fed deciding to pay interest on the cash reserves in banks, the daily transactions dropped to less than half of where they were. As a result, by the end of June, 2011, the Fed reported almost $1.6 trillion in excess reserves—twenty times the amount needed for banks to meet their reserve requirements. The graph below from the St. Louis Fed's research shows the dramatic increase in these reserves after being at zero since the 1960s. Banks are simply sitting on their reserves because the Fed has made it profitable to do so, and with zero risk.

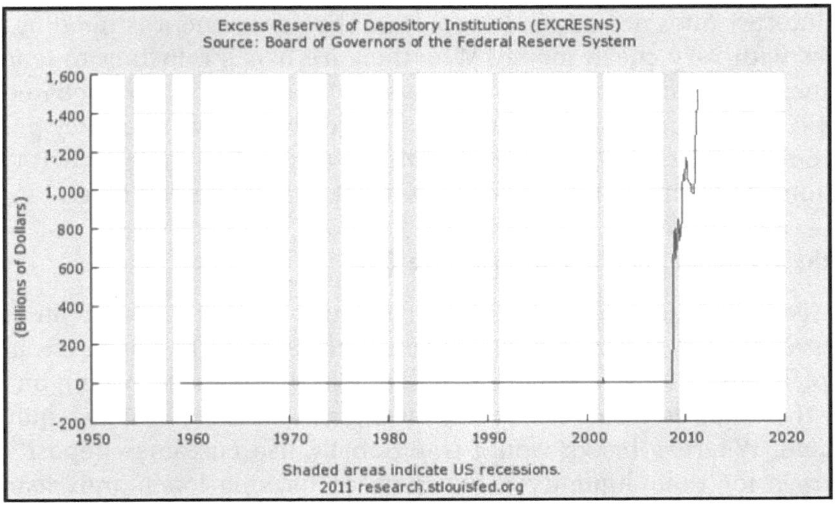

Any lender must take into account two important considerations when making loans: it has to be able to price the risk accurately, or it has to limit its risks with fewer loans, smaller loans that reduce the risk profiles of the recipients. The current administration and Congress have been on a regulation spree for the past few years, massively increasing the costs and, therefore, the risk factors of small business loans. In the face of such increased risk, these lenders are essentially being forced by the government to limit their lending. All the while, the same government publicly pleads for increased lending. Critics of both the banking institutions and government policies claim that cronyism is a major issue at play in this, with policy makers creating problems and then providing solutions that benefit those in power and those they favor, while presenting the solutions to the public as the solution that will help "the people." An example of this is the Credit Card Accountability, Responsibility, and Disclosure Act of 2009, or the "Credit CARD Act." On the surface, this seemed like legislation that would help individuals, and some provisions of it are mildly beneficial. The bigger picture, however, is that most provisions of this law hurt the general public by interfering with accurate risk-based pricing by the lenders, like limiting the ability to raise interest rates or declare a default when the risk of the borrowers increases.

## Who is Holding all the Money?

While the belief exists that banks no longer have the need for inter-bank borrowing due to the excess of cash reserves, the fact is that these reserves are concentrated in the larger banks. Over half of the aggregate reserves are held by the twenty-five largest banks in the United States, and 21 percent of the reserves are held by only three banks.(1) These large banks holding the reserves are finding ways to use them that are much more lucrative than loaning to small businesses and consumers who are awash in government regulations, which highly increase the risk factor of lending to them.

It is worth noting that while local and regional banks have been closed by the Fed around the country in the hundreds, larger banks have become much more powerful by holding more cash reserves than ever before in history. In addition, many of the policy makers in government and in the Fed system have increasingly been recruited from these larger banking institutions.

## Effects on Small Businesses and the Overall Economy

The concentration of cash reserves in the larger banks and the reluctance of these institutions to engage in lending to small businesses in any great measure over the last few years has been a driving force in the stagnation of the economy as a whole. According to a 2009 report by the Small Business Administration, an independent government agency, over 60 percent of new jobs added over the past fifteen years has been created by businesses with five hundred or fewer employees.(2) Almost one-third of American workers are employed by small businesses with less than fifty employees, and these businesses have been hit the hardest in the economic downturn, accounting for around 45 percent of the job losses the country has experienced.(3) This does not bode well for the country's financial stability as a whole. With history showing that the majority of jobs are created by smaller businesses, nearly half of current job losses being within that same business demographic, and small business lending lagging, the prospects of an economic recovery seem bleak without a reverse in the lending trend.

## States Looking to Alternative Solutions

One option to end some of the problems that big banking has caused is the one taken by North Dakota, which set up the Bank of North Dakota in 1919. After a long and difficult fight with opponents of the state-owned institution, the bank finally began to fulfill its original mission in 1991. The core mission for the Bank of North Dakota was simple: to meet the needs of its citizens by promoting businesses such as agriculture, commerce, and industry. To that end, their business lending grew 35 percent from 2007 to 2009, during the worst time for bank business lending nationwide, and their story has been a successful one. As of mid-2012, fourteen other states have either introduced legislation or have formed committees to discuss the same possibility.(4) In light of the fact that the financial crises we have been experiencing have been in part caused or exacerbated by both governmental policies and larger banking institutions, a local or regional answer could be more viable than a federal solution.

CHAPTER 7

# A Golden Parachute

One of the first "golden parachutes" on record was created in 1979, when Reliance Electric was in takeover negotiations with Exxon. Because Reliance executives had agreements that offered them generous termination benefits in the case of a takeover or merger, otherwise known as golden parachutes, as part of their exit strategies, they were able to do what they needed to do, according to those who were close to the deal. However, as it turned out, that meant accepting Exxon's bid, thus losing their own jobs while supposedly benefitting the shareholders by making the deal.

A more high-profile golden parachute scenario happened in 1982 when William Agee, head of Bendix Corporation, instituted a takeover bid for Martin Marietta. Marietta, in turn, made a hostile bid for Bendix, which, in turn, was acquired by Allied Corp. Agee bailed out and took his $4 million parachute with him—the largest known at that time. However, this is a mere pittance in comparison to some of today's grandiose corporate exits. We will get into this a little more later, but, first, let us take a look at some key factors relating to the proliferation of the golden parachute phenomenon.

## Executive Compensation and Layoff Packages

Originally, the golden parachute concept was developed to put the interests of management and shareholders on the same page. The board of directors and management knew that if a hostile bidder came and offered a takeover premium that was higher than the firm's market value, it was possible that the shareholders would want to accept that premium offer, often to the detriment of the firm's employees. However, management would traditionally resist such hostile actions, because such an agreement would surely mean that they would lose their jobs. However, if they already had an exit strategy in place, then the decision-making process would be different. An exit strategy, or parachute, would enable them to make a strategic decision without being distracted by where their next paycheck would come from.

But, like mushrooms left alone in the dark, the parachute has grown and evolved significantly from its humble inception. The range of situations where parachutes are applied has expanded significantly, especially when those benefitting from its establishment are involved in the agreement process. In the beginning, only a hostile takeover would trigger the provision. Now, most top executives say that whether the deal is hostile or friendly should not matter. In some cases, the exiting executive not only benefits from the parachute agreement but also gets hired by the newly merged company—much to the dismay of some shareholders.

Today, a golden parachute has simply become a standard piece of the compensation agreement reached between top executives and the company that hires them. Even if the executive is fired or resigns under pressure, he gets what is known as a "soft landing," courtesy of his golden parachute.

## Corporate Governance and Shareholder Involvement

What causes one firm to offer the golden parachute while another does not? One possible factor is the composition of the board of directors, since this board ultimately approves executive compensation. Some observers say that directors who are insiders are likely to be less independent of senior management than are directors who are outsiders. So it follows that a board that tilts heavily toward insiders will be more likely to include the golden parachute in a compensation package.

Another influencing factor is the amount of stock that members of boards of directors own. Directors who own substantial amounts of stock will be more inclined to put the interests of stockholders above those of management. To the extent that golden parachutes are gratuitous diversions of stockholder money, they will more often be seen in firms whose boards own relatively little company stock.

## Legal and Ethical Issues

In the beginning, it was thought that golden parachutes would insure effective corporate management and preserve the firm's value for all its stakeholders. Companies and their boards would offer parachute agreements to protect human capital during periods of financial uncertainty or threats of takeover. Seen from that viewpoint, golden parachutes are certainly both a legal and an ethical choice that is valuable to stakeholders, because they encourage management to choose merger or acquisition in lieu of bankruptcy.

Whenever we question whether a golden parachute is ethical or unethical, we must first look to see if the compensation is given to a CEO who is responsible for a firm's poor performance and that the subsequent takeover also proves to be harmful to other stakeholders as a group. If the CEO is not responsible for a firm's financial woes and few stakeholders are harmed, the golden parachute would probably be considered ethical. On the other hand, recent highly publicized departures of top CEOs with cash in-hand while the company burns may provide evidence to the contrary in some cases.

### The Famous and the Notorious

Several infamous individuals have exited with severance packages that were significant for the time. Up first is Leo Apotheker who became HP's CEO in 2010, and lasted less than a year. He was fired and walked away with $13.2 million in cash and stock while the company's performance was in a downward spiral. His predecessor, Mark Hurd who started at HP in 2005, left in 2010 with $12 million after being terminated amidst a sexual harassment inquiry and scandal involving expense-account irregularities. Hurd's predecessor Carly Fiorina who started as CEO in 1999, left HP in 2005 with $21 million while her performance as CEO was widely criticized in the financial press.

But Hewlett Packard is far from unusual. Robert Kelly, fired from the Bank of New York-Mellon, left with $17.2 million. Carol Bartz left Yahoo with $10 million in a similar scenario. Ian McCarthy departed Beazer Homes USA with $6.3 million and Beazer Homes USA paid his legal bills when the company was sued by the SEC for filing false statements.

Perhaps one of the most notorious and widely discussed parachutes is that of Franklin Raines, who presided over the disastrous decline of Fannie Mae. As a result of accounting "mistakes," Raines was allowed to retire and will enjoy a pension that pays $1 million annually in addition to millions in stock and options worth over $148 million.

Although mismanagement or malfeasance is not always involved, some of the executive payouts triggered by corporate mergers and takeovers have likewise triggered outspoken commentary on the part of politicians, pundits, and ordinary citizens.

A notable example is Nabors Industries's former CEO, Gene Isenberg, who got $126 million when he exited as chairman. He could have received five times as much. A corporate spokesperson commented, "It used to be a hell of a lot bigger until the board reduced it."(1) Meanwhile, IBM CEO Sam Palmisano pocketed $170 million. And Google's Eric Schmidt received $100 million in stock after leaving as CEO. While none of these payouts is illegal, or even unethical, they do raise eyebrows in an environment of layoffs, bailouts, and declining profits. In his *USA Today* article "CEOs' exit packages blow past $100 million," Gary Strauss justifiably comments that "the golden parachute is evolving into the platinum kiss."(2)

Below is a list of some CEOs' golden payouts data by Governance Metrics International (GMI). They also have more detail breakouts in their report that includes areas such as salary, bonuses, perks, severance, equity profits, pension, and other relevant information.

**Table 1: 21 CEOs over $100 million (Source: GMI)**

| Company | CEO | Tenure | Total Payout |
|---|---|---|---|
| General Electric | John F. Welch Jr. | 1981-2001 | $417,361,902 |
| Exxon Mobil Corp. | Lee R. Raymond | 1993-2005 | $320,599,861 |
| UnitedHealth Group Inc. | William D. McGuire | 1991-2006 | $285,996,009 |
| AT&T | Edward E. Whitacre Jr. | 1990-2007 | $230,048,463 |
| Home Depot Inc. | Robert L. Nardelli | 2000-2007 | $223,290,123 |
| North Fork Bank | John A. Kanas | 1977-2006 | $214,300,000 |
| Merck & Co., Inc./Schering-Plough | Fred Hassan | 2003-2009 | $189,352,324 |
| International Business Machines | Louis V. Gerstner Jr. | 1993-2002 | $189,005,929 |
| Pfizer Inc. | Hank A. McKinnell Jr. | 2001-2006 | $188,329,553 |
| CVS Caremark Corporation | Thomas M. Ryan | 1998-2011 | $185,415,435 |
| Gillette Co. | James M. Kilts | 2001-2005 | $164,532,192 |
| Target Corporation | Robert J. Ulrich | 1994-2008 | $164,162,612 |
| Merrill Lynch & Co. Inc. | E. Stanley O'Neal | 2002-2007 | $161,500,000 |
| U.S. Bancorp | Jerry A. Grundhofer | 2001-2006 | $159,064,090 |
| Omnicare, Inc. | Joel F. Gemunder | 2001-2010 | $146,001,476 |
| Wachovia/South Trust | Wallace D. Malone Jr. | 1981-2004 | $125,292,818 |
| United Technologies Corporation | George A. L. David | 1994-2008 | $122,631,309 |
| eBay Inc. | Margaret C. Whitman | 1998-2008 | $120,427,360 |
| WellPoint Health Networks | Leonard Schaeffer | 1992-2004 | $119,041,000 |
| XTO Energy Inc. | Bob R. Simpson | 1986-2008 | $103,485,972 |
| Viacom | Thomas E. Freston | 2006 | $100,839,772 |

## The Future of the Parachute

In January, 2011, the Securities and Exchange Commission adopted the Wall Street Reform and Consumer Protection Act, otherwise known as

"Dodd-Frank." This bill provides rules for implementation of the say on pay, say on pay frequency, and say on golden parachutes. These are rules and terms that have become part of corporate law. The bill details the shareholder advisory votes required to implement any policy relative to executive compensation. When it comes to golden parachutes, Dodd-Frank lists strict disclosure requirements for all pieces of the compensation package. This includes advanced disclosure of offers made and elimination of some of the more egregious practices of compensating executives in the face of poor performance or outright fraud.

So the future of the golden parachute may not be as golden as some executives have forecasted. At the very least, corporate boards now know they are being watched, not only by the SEC and their shareholders but also by the public at large. In the end, the real culprits may have been the boards of directors who paid CEOs outrageous sums for failure. And they have been aided and abetted by the institutional shareholders who repeatedly voted for the same old board members while paying lip service to corporate transparency and ethical standards.

CHAPTER 8

# Corporate Handouts and Welfare

Calling anything "welfare" gives you the sense that something is being given away due to circumstances. However, is it fair to call government financial incentives or tax breaks given to big corporations "corporate welfare," implying a handout of sorts? Some think yes, and some think no. Corporate welfare is defined as benefits, preferential treatment, or advantages given by governments to specific industries or businesses. Use of the term "welfare" in conjunction with "corporate" implies financial aid that is unjust.(1) However, this is financial aid with the ultimate goal of providing societal benefits that may take the form of tax breaks, subsidies, grants, loans, or other special financial or competitive benefits that include marketing or commercial support, visas for foreign workers who are willing to work for less in the United States, foreign trade barriers to protect domestic business from competition, and regulations that favor particular companies.

Subsidies can be direct or indirect. An example of a direct subsidy is a farm loan. An indirect subsidy would be a protectionist regulation that gives a domestic firm a competitive advantage over an international firm. Yet you do not have to go overseas to find corporate welfare, because sometimes the preferential government treatment is used solely to promote domestic business activity.

In the following sections, I will discuss corporate welfare and how it compares to social welfare. This is a topic with no definitive answer, but it's also a topic of importance. The review can start on common ground, too, because in both cases, you are talking about the best use of taxpayer dollars.

## Corporate Welfare in Action

One of the simplest ways to understand corporate welfare is to first consider some of the many forms it has taken over the years. It is certainly not a new concept, and it goes back to the forming of the nation as the first Congress imposed tariffs that subsidized manufacturers. Another early program of corporate welfare is the Mining Act of 1872. This act was intended to promote the development of land and settlement of the Wild West by allowing private companies that discovered gold to buy the acreage over the gold reserves for as little as $5 per acre. Remarkably, this law is still valid today.

Since 1872, there have been a number of corporate welfare programs that supported development of railroads, waterways, aviation technology, and much more. The government has been giving private companies preferential treatment in some manner as a way to:

- Promote the development of natural resources
- Encourage research and development in new technologies and science
- Encourage businesses to expand into particular locations
- Promote domestic-international partnerships
- Bailout large companies in financial difficulty
- Reward political supporters

Though the laws allowing the government to give preferential treatment to businesses do not include rewarding political supporters as a motive, history has shown that is certainly one of the ways it has been used. Though guised under lofty goals of promoting business expansion or job creation, corporate welfare has long been criticized as a method of legal cronyism that interferes with free market operation. It is important to understand this view in order to understand the criticisms corporate welfare garners.

Corporate welfare has not been limited to just the federal government. State and local governments have also been shown to participate in corporate welfare. Corporate welfare is handed out in a variety of oftentimes creative ways. In some cases, a law is passed that specifically names a corporation or industry. However, billions of dollars are also spent through organizations like the Import-Export Bank of the United States, created to finance American exports. The Import-Export Bank, which was established by an executive order from Franklin D. Roosevelt in 1934 and issues loan guarantees to large corporations selling American products in foreign markets.

Another popular program is called the National Institute of Standards and Technology (NIST) Advanced Technology Program. This program, which was originally established under President Bill Clinton in 1995, is meant to encourage early stage development of innovative technologies, especially when no other funding seems to be available. The NIST programs assist corporations with researching and developing cutting-edge technology. Other successive technology development programs such as the NIST Technology Innovation Program were created under the America COMPETES Act (H.R. 2272) in 2007. The America Creating Opportunities to Meaningfully Promote Excellence in Technology, Education, and Science Act of 2007 (America COMPETES Act) was enacted with the goals of supporting research and development (R&D) in the important and competitive technology industry.

Of course, one of the earliest industries to get corporate welfare was the farming industry. The American public has a love-hate relationship with farm subsidies in that they romanticize the funding of smaller farm operations while, in reality, subsidies go to large corporate farming businesses. The Agriculture Department's Market Access Program, the Defense Department's Technology Reinvestment Project, the Small Business Administration, and many other government programs also offer subsidized loans or insurance.

Following are some examples of corporate welfare through the years, designed to display the many forms government support can take.

- **1971: Penn Central Railroad** is given $673 million in federal loan guarantees.
- **1971: Lockheed Aircraft** gets $250 million in federal guaranteed loans, and the loans were fully repaid by 1977.
- **1980: Chrysler Corporation** receives $1.2 billion in federal loan guarantees.
- **1989: Savings and Loans** defaults prevented when the government injected $293.3 billion into the financial institutions.
- **1991: National Cancer Institute** licenses Bristol-Meyers Squibb to sell the government-developed drug Taxol and gives up control of pricing, leading to wholesale prices that were at least twenty times greater than the manufacturing costs.
- **1994: Alabama** offers a package of incentives to build a plant that includes $300 million in tax breaks, and also agrees to buy the plant site for $30 million and lease it back to Mercedes-Benz for $100.

- **1997: Federal Communications Commission** donates up to $70 billion in broadcast licenses in support of digital television licenses.
- **2003: Washington State** gives Boeing $3.2 billion in tax breaks to build 7E7 Dreamliner jets.
- **2005: Farm Subsidies** in the amount of $24.3 billion are authorized by federal government.
- **2005: Florida** promises J.P. Morgan Chase & Co $21 million in benefits and $74.5 million in tax breaks and includes worker training, road improvements, and state tax refunds in its concessions to the company.
- **2006: New York State** gives a $665 million cash grant plus other incentives for a total of $1.4 billion to GlobalFoundries for a computer chip factory.
- **2008: The Emergency Economic Stabilization Act of 2008 (EESA)** authorizes $700 billion of Treasury investments to stabilize economy; the Troubled Assets Relief Program (TARP) created by EESA invests $205 billion in banks and $20 billion each in Citigroup Inc. and Bank of America Corp.(2)
- **2008: Automakers** General Motors and Chrysler receive $14 billion short-term federal guarantee loans made to prevent bankruptcy.
- **2010: Alternative Energy** Solar panel company Solyndra, LLC receives $535 million federal in loan guarantees to develop new alternative energy technology, but later company filed for bankruptcy in 2011.
- **2010: Farm Subsidies** totaling $3.5 billion were paid to US corn farmers.(3)
- **2011: North Carolina** gives Chiquita Brands International $20 million in state incentives and $2 million in local incentives to move global headquarters from Cincinnati, Ohio to Charlotte, North Carolina.(4)

The examples given of actual government tax incentives, cash grants, and subsidies hint at the variety of ways in which they are used. However, it is not just the actual incentives that develop supporters and critics alike—it is the politics, too. In some cases, it appears that government favoritism in the way of corporate welfare is intended to reward political supporters, campaign donors, and so on.

On the other hand, corporate welfare is found in almost every industry, and it represents big business. The Cato Institute, a nonprofit public policy research organization, attempts to estimate the amount of grants and subsidies given to businesses by the federal government each year. In 2006, the total of federal subsidies was estimated to be $92 billion, but that number grew considerably as a result of the 2008 recession, the collapse of the financial and housing markets, and the passage of the Emergency Economic Stabilization Act of 2008 (EESA).(5) This number does not include state and local incentives, either.

Based on a US Treasury list of 2011 tax subsidies given to businesses and investors, the Citizens for Tax Justice estimated the 2011 total economic cost of these subsidies to be $365 billion.(6) Professor Kenneth Thomas at the University of Missouri estimates that state and local government subsidies are over $70 billion each year.(7)

The growth of corporate welfare is spread across various industries, as well. The energy industry is one of the main recipients of federal energy subsidies. Following are the totals for the years 1950 to 2010(8):

- Oil: $369 billion
- Natural Gas - $121 billion
- Coal: $104 billion
- Hydro: $90 billion
- Solar and Wind: $74 billion
- Nuclear: $73 billion
- Geothermal: $7 billion

Other industries or businesses participating in tax breaks, grants, and subsidies beside the ones mentioned in the examples (banks, financial institutions, automotive, railroads, aviation, pharmaceutical companies, agriculture, and high tech companies) include:

- Manufacturing (variety of products)
- Maritime (ship building and waterway development)
- Defense Technology (weaponry development and construction)
- Forest Service (road and trail construction)
- Travel and Entertainment (hotels and casinos)

Unfortunately, it is impossible to state a definitive amount of corporate welfare the United States has given to businesses. The various numbers put forth by organizations depend on how they define corporate welfare and what is included in the total. For example, some include Medicare and Social Security while many do not. It is safe to say that the total of all federal, state, and local welfare exceeds $1 trillion each year if you include subsidies, tax breaks, loans, and grants.

## Social Welfare as a Moral Imperative

Corporate welfare refers to government benefits that give corporations a competitive advantage of some kind. Social welfare is different in that it refers to government cash services and benefits given to individuals with certain essential needs. The social welfare programs funded by government usually represent financial assistance programs that in theory serve one or more of the following purposes:

- Assist people who fall on hard financial times and need temporary assistance (bridge funding) such as unemployment and housing assistance
- Provide assistance to people who are unable to support themselves, such as children and the disabled, with food and nutrition programs such as Women, Infants, and Children (WIC) and Supplemental Nutrition Assistance Program (SNAP), Temporary Assistance for Needy Families (TANF), and Social Security Disability Insurance
- Supplement retirement programs, including Social Security and Medicare, which are partially funded by payroll tax deductions
- Provide access to healthcare through Medicaid and the National Health Care Act, which is in the process of implementation
- Assist low-income individuals with obtaining an education through student grants and aid
- Provide veterans' benefits to assist veterans

However, this is not a comprehensive list of the social welfare programs. In addition, some analysts do not include Social Security and Medicare as social welfare programs, because they classify them as entitlement programs. They are called entitlement programs, because most people contribute to the funds and are thus entitled. However, the expansion of Social Security benefits to include payments to people who never work, like some spouses and disabled, would make it seem more like social welfare. The same is true for Medicare, because everyone is eventually insured through the federal program after a certain age.

To qualify for social welfare, you must meet certain requirements as defined by the law. Those requirements consider annual family income, age, and employment status. The social insurance programs like Social Security pay benefits based on lifetime contributions. The means-tested programs provide benefits based on need, using income figures.

The social welfare programs now account for over half of the federal budget and are approximately 4 percent of GDP. In 2010, the following amounts were spent by the federal government:(9)

- Social Security:$707 billion
- Medicare, Medicaid and Children's Health Insurance Program: $732 billion
- Anti-Poverty Programs: $496 billion

In addition, in 2010, states funded Medicaid and children's health insurance programs with $135 billion and assistance for the poor with $12 billion.(10) This puts the estimated total of social welfare costs at over $2 trillion per year.

## Welfare by Any Name

There is an ongoing discussion among policymakers, members of think tanks, religious groups, citizens groups for just government, and analysts concerning corporate welfare versus social welfare. Whether someone supports or opposes corporate or social welfare depends on his or her view of the role of government. Is it to promote business and thus economic prosperity? Or is it to regulate the population and to ensure that all basic needs are met? If its primary role is to ensure that all basic needs are met, how do you define those needs and acceptable well-being levels? Is higher education a basic need, and does it justify the billions spent on financial aid?

The issues are complex any way you look at them. Both types of welfare have stigmas attached to them, offer benefits to the recipients, and have costs that are frequently in the trillions of dollars. And as the economy continues to falter, these discussions have gotten even more heated. There are arguments for and against both types of welfare.

The proponents of corporate welfare cite a number of reasons why these government handouts and tax breaks are important and justified. They stimulate the economy and promote innovative research and development. Incentives to businesses create and save jobs while encouraging private sector activity that supports public policies such as green technologies and alternative energy sources. It also promotes domestic and local development by corporations in designated areas while protecting businesses from unfair foreign competition.

The opponents of corporate welfare believe that it is government interference in the free market and that it gives designated businesses an unfair competitive edge and unfair access to and influence on policymakers.

They argue that companies will look to the government for success instead of relying on their ability to be competitive when unlimited funding without restrictions is available. Unlike shareholders, taxpayers have no recourse against the companies should they waste the government incentives that often promote growth only in large corporations that can afford to be inefficient. These programs also divert funds from social programs, which are based on need, unlike the corporate welfare. Opponents also argue that these programs encourage corporate influence and lobbying at the government level, which tends to promote wealth accumulation within the more influential corporations. And the expected results may not materialize.

Proponents of social welfare believe that providing this is a primary function of government and that government has a moral responsibility to do so. The arguments for social welfare include that it ensures children and those who cannot take care of themselves have access to basic needs and assists those who have temporary setbacks. It promotes employment and job training, which benefits society as a whole and defends human rights by promoting increased productivity by giving people a chance to participate in society on a higher level through access to housing, food, and healthcare.

Those who argue against social welfare believe that government programs promote dependence, discourage initiative, and weaken work ethic, creating a sense of entitlement. They reason that the government programs benefit individuals at the detriment of society, because increased funding requires increased taxation of the working class. Substantial increases in social welfare have not improved poverty rates and have actually harmed the social fabric by encouraging single-parent family units. And government bureaucratic distribution systems are inefficient and wasteful.

The discussion on corporate welfare can get very heated, while discussions on social welfare can be equally or sometimes more passionate. The problems that have emerged with increased corporate welfare include a series of what is viewed by many as abuses of tax dollars. For example, General Electric reported $14.2 billion in profits, of which $5.1 billion was made in the United States. Yet General Electric did not pay any taxes due to a mixture of tax breaks and offshore profiting.

There are also many examples of companies that received special government benefits only to go bankrupt, institute a workforce reduction, and pay large executive bonuses. For example, Solyndra received a US Department of Energy loan guarantee for $535 million in 2010 and went bankrupt in 2011, forcing the layoffs of 1,100 employees. Now there are questions about how much the government knew about the company's financial status when it granted the loan guarantee and how much Solyndra executives paid themselves in bonuses instead of repaying the loan. More significant is the fact that critics are asking whether Solyndra received preferential treatment in getting funding due to its political contributions or whether that funding was given solely on the merits of its business. The bankrupt Solyndra is still under federal investigation even as it tries to reorganize its business.

Corporate welfare does have success stories, and like most government programs, there are times when it has needed. For example, in 2006, there was one remaining US clothing hanger manufacturer, and it was facing closure. Chinese hanger imports had almost eliminated the US domestic hanger industry by undercutting its prices. In response, the US government imposed tariffs on Chinese hangers. As a result, the imports dropped significantly, and the US hanger industry thrived once again.

Supporters of corporate welfare see these stories as proof that the government's responsibility to society can be fulfilled through business support rather than through handouts to individuals. The people who worked at the hanger plant were able to keep their jobs, which meant they could fully contribute to the economy. Instead of becoming "handout takers," they could remain as taxpayers and consumer spenders.

Proponents of social welfare see it as an essential tool in ensuring that all of society's members have their basic needs met. The social welfare system becomes a wealth redistribution system in that working people are taxed, and that tax money is then used to fund the social programs. The redistribution of wealth is a strategy for fulfilling a moral imperative to satisfy the basic needs of those who are unable to meet those needs without assistance. In assisting the individuals, society as a whole benefits, because social welfare helps the sick, the hungry, the illiterate, and the poor.

The general arguments against social welfare are based on the fear that some people who are handed all their basic needs without working for them will then choose to not work or will fail to try to better their circumstances. They argue that it is too easy to live on the government handouts. However, it really comes down to one's view of human nature and, ultimately, of society.

Is corporate welfare more or less acceptable than social welfare? Most people will agree that some people need social welfare—children who are homeless or living in poverty, the mentally or physically disabled who have no family support system, the unemployed who have searched but were unable to find jobs, the elderly who cannot work, and so on. However, for both corporate welfare and social welfare, the real issue seems to be one of scale. Some corporate welfare is beneficial when it serves a broad societal purpose, is in the public interest, and does not interfere in healthy market functioning. Unsurprisingly, opponents of corporate welfare using these criteria argue that billions of corporate welfare monies should not have been spent given some of these corporations' actions, such as avoidance of taxes and massive layoffs after they received governmental financial support.

The same is true for social welfare. Fraud and waste are unfortunately commonplace in government programs. For example, the government reported that in 2011, it recovered $2.9 billion related to healthcare fraud. (11) However, such cases do not change the fact that a society based on principles of human rights cannot assist the neediest of its members. How "needy" is defined, however, is the real question of contention. While most people would agree that a starving child is needy, there could be a long debate about how much should be done for a capable person who is unemployed.

In general, social welfare is more acceptable than corporate welfare simply because it does fulfill basic human needs. Some want it scaled back, while others want it increased, but there are almost no calls for complete elimination of government assistance programs for the needy. In addition, corporate welfare has become a means by which corporations amass government benefits without regard for their responsibility to society in exchange for these benefits. For example, in 2008 Citigroup lost $27 billion and accepted $45 billion in TARP funds to prevent financial collapse. The company then decided to payout $5.33 billion in bonuses. It is stories like this that are the source of public ire and further boosts opponents' argument that corporate welfare funds should be reined in. Both corporate welfare and social welfare each have a purpose and can be effective if properly administered and scrutinized once funds are distributed. So perhaps the real question is whether the government is capable of managing either one efficiently.

CHAPTER 9

# Outsourcing and Other Offshore Business

Increasingly, a lot of businesses have chosen to take their businesses offshore. Some of these companies have moved only some of their operations offshore, while others have chosen to completely relocate their headquarters outside of the country where they were originally founded. As globalization transforms the marketplace, many businesses, and even governments, feel that they have no choice but to seek out the lowest cost of doing business. This might seem like a rational strategy in the short term, but these decisions can have devastating effects on long-term productivity and economic success of a nation that thoughtlessly embraces these ideals.

Business schools and the businesses community often cite many reasons for relocating businesses to foreign nations, but, unfortunately, these justifications rarely incorporate the necessary ten-year-plus analysis of the effect on the domestic economy. In this chapter, we will take a look at some of the common reasons for outsourcing and offshoring businesses, but first let us review one of the main reasons that companies preferred to go offshore in our not-so-distant past.

## Tax Havens

A tax haven is an independent legal jurisdiction, usually a small nation, that provides extraordinary tax benefits or incentives for businesses that have their headquarters or subsidiaries there. According to the Organization for Economic Cooperation and Development (OECD), there are four key traits that identify a tax haven from an ordinary jurisdiction:

- "The jurisdiction levies insignificant taxes."
- "A lack of transparency."

- "Laws or administrative practices that prevent the effective exchange of information for tax purposes with other governments on taxpayers benefitting from the no or nominal taxation."
- "An absence of a requirement that the activity be substantial."

Low taxes on capital and corporate income, particularly for non-residents, is an important benefit of tax havens. Multinational corporations can base their headquarters in a small room or apartment in a tax haven jurisdiction to gain the tax and legislative benefits without doing much—or any—business in that country. This allows them to avoid the higher taxes imposed by the countries in which they conduct business. Due to their small sizes, tax havens service foreign businesses almost exclusively, so they do not lose much money by taxing corporations at a very low rate.

Tax haven provinces and nations often have limited regulation on corporate management practices and structure compared to countries like the United States, which hold corporations to a higher degree of public accountability and transparency. Individuals and corporations using tax havens to shelter their income also benefit from bank secrecy legislation. These laws hinder other governments' attempts to investigate taxpayers' finances if they are suspected of tax evasion or avoidance. The secrecy policies of some tax haven jurisdictions are condemned by international organizations for encouraging tax evasion.

While tax havens currently provide significant financial and regulatory benefits, they may not be able to provide this security for long. For the last few decades, the United States and some European nations have been creating legislation to close loopholes that allow individuals and companies to abuse tax haven jurisdictions. Political and economic leaders of various developed countries agreed to deal with tax evasion problems during a G20 summit in November of 2011. The OECD administration plans to work with G20 leaders to combat the increasing amount of tax income that is lost to tax evasion and avoidance through tax havens.

## A Brief History of Tax Havens

Tax havens are a relatively recent development of the nineteenth and twentieth centuries. Tax havens originated from extraordinarily business-friendly jurisdictions, formed with the intention of attracting businesses from outside of their borders. The states of Delaware and New Jersey both passed laws in the late 1800s to draw founders of corporations and other businesses to their state in order to generate revenue through taxation. Technically speaking, these two states are not tax havens, but their policy designs did set the stage for true tax havens in the twentieth century.

During the 1920s and '30s, several smaller European nations, like Switzerland and Lichtenstein, began creating legislation to encourage outside business. These jurisdictions, which shared a common currency, created a unique type of business entity called an "Anstalt," which did not restrict the formation of new business entities based on the nationality or residency of the owners.

In the 1960s, several remote jurisdictions, like the Cayman Islands and Singapore, developed into true tax havens. Rising tax rates during this decade likely contributed to the advent of tax havens around the world. These modern tax havens adopted financial legislation designed to protect the identity and finances of those sheltering in the haven by restricting international access to pertinent documents.

## The Future of Tax Havens

In the first two decades of the twenty-first century, with the weakening of the US economy and turmoil in the Eurozone, tax havens have come under scrutiny and condemnation from the international community. A recent article in the *New York Times* titled "Tax Evaders Face Greater Scrutiny as National Debts Pile Up" noted the developing sentiment against tax evasion and havens. For the time being, tax havens do provide many large businesses and wealthy individuals with the means to hide a large portion of their income from government authorities. However, future legislation and policy changes may reduce the benefits or viability of tax haven jurisdictions.

Below are a few tables showing business tax rates in various countries. Some of the businesses in the developed world have for reasons that we will soon discuss decided to pursue business and tax strategies that lower their overall tax burden. Ireland, along with other countries, has proven a suitable place for businesses that choose to reduce their fair share of the tax burden. Some financial and other critics might push the envelope and suggest that these businesses are engaging in tax avoidance or tax evasion, straddling the line between legality and creative accounting schemes.

| Major Economies Countries Lowest biz tax Rates (2009) | |
|---|---|
| Country | Rate |
| Montenegro | 9% |
| Bulgaria, Cyprus, & Serbia | 10% |
| Ireland, Latvia | 12.50% |
| Nations of Hungary | 15% |
| Romania | 16% |
| Switzerland | 13-25% |

| Major Economies Countries Highest Biz Tax Rates (2009) | |
|---|---|
| Country | Rate |
| United States | 15-35% |
| United Kingdom | 21-28% |
| Canada | 11-16.5% |
| Japan | 40% |
| China | 25% |
| Germany | 30% |
| France | 34% |
| Australia | 30% |
| Brazil | 34% |
| Hong Kong | 16.50% |
| Mexico | 28% |
| Russia | 13-20% |

| Non- OECD Countries highest Biz Tax Rates (2005) | |
|---|---|
| Country | Rate |
| Congo Democratic Republic | 339.70% |
| Gambia | 292.30% |
| Sierra Leone | 235.60% |

Rates in non-OECD countries will be substantially higher. These countries are marked by social, economic, and political instability that sometimes lead to these higher rates.

### The Proposed Offshore Tax Holiday (Repatriation)

A businesses tax holiday is a temporary decrease in the tax rate or a complete elimination of said taxes for a temporary period in order to entice business investments or cash flow that is currently stashed away in foreign countries. Many corporations would like to bring those funds back to the mainland, but will only do so under certain conditions. We will take a brief look at the main points of this debate, but one point holds true if these tax holiday petitioners have their way. If the tax holiday is granted, the tax advantages gained will be substantial. Low estimates for tax savings are in the billions. The last federal tax holiday was granted in 2004 to allow American businesses to repatriate their foreign earnings back to the United States at a low tax rate. There are many positives and negatives in granting another tax holiday to these companies that have taken their businesses offshore.

## Tax Holiday Main Reasons and Criticisms

Offshore companies have well over a trillion dollars in cash stockpiled in offshore accounts. This stash of cash influx could stimulate the economy and generate over two million jobs.

A tax holiday was done unsuccessfully under the American Jobs Creation Act (AJCA) in 2004. The AJCA lowered the tax rate on foreign profits from 35 percent to 5.25 percent, as lobbyist wanted, and United States businesses repatriated or returned from offshore companies about $362 billion. The majority of these companies then used the monies to buy back their own stock from the stock market.

Other companies used the monies to increase dividend payouts to investors. However, most of these companies that got the tax break also went on to generate some of the largest job decreases, not increases.

The table below shows some of the recipients of the tax holiday and the resulting decrease in their workforce in the period after the tax holiday. Politicians in the US Senate did a study that showed that the companies promising to deliver millions of new jobs actually ended up reducing their workforce over time. Please bear in mind that this list, although far from comprehensive, is meant to give you, the reader, a general idea of some of the negative effects of granting another tax holiday.

| Sample of 2004 Tax Holiday Beneficiaries | | | |
|---|---|---|---|
| | | | |
| Firm | Amount Repatriated | Stock Buyback | 2005-2007 Proposed Layoffs or work - force Reductions |
| Pfizer | $35.49 Billion | | 11,700 workers |
| HP | $14.5 Billion | $4 Billion | 14,500 workers |
| Ford | $850 Million | | 30,000 workers |
| Merck | $15.9 Billion | | 7,000 workers |
| Honeywell Intl | $2.1 Billion | | 2,000 workers |

As you can see from the list above, there are a lot more reasons to deny these companies a tax holiday than to give them one. If the past behavior is indicative of future intentions, then these companies should, at the very least, give some written guarantees with monetary concessions attached before another tax holiday can be seriously discussed.

Many critics of the offshore-businesses tax holiday suggest that these companies are intentionally stockpiling record amounts of cash in lieu of receiving such a tax holiday—and not for the benefit of the American economy. Their suggested goals are to satisfy their own benefits and possibly greed. This, however, is not surprising, because as mentioned before, the rational entrepreneur or enterprise is in business to pursue its own self-interest. They are, therefore, looking to maximize shareholder value, even if it is shortsighted.

It is also not surprising that President Obama and most politicians in the Senate did not buy into the current tax holiday scheme. They were denied in March, 2011. Clearly, a new argument needs to be made. Maybe this time, it will include real and direct benefits to the American economy.

We are going to shift away from taxes for the time being and focus on the other reasons given for transferring business offshore.

### Advantages to Offshore Establishments

Most companies that moved operations to other countries did so to realize economic savings from labor costs. At first, it was only multinational corporations with business in other countries that were relocating, but this is no longer the norm. Today, domestic businesses and even state governments have found ways to relocate, in some cases, a majority of their operations offshore.

This trend is due in large part to businesses that have been created to facilitate the process of moving certain business offshore. It is no longer just call centers that are moving offshore; job functions that do not require a face-to-face interaction are also slowly making their way offshore, to places where labor costs are cheaper.

The cost savings realized by going offshore have arguably put some companies in a better competitive position on the global playing field. Some employers say that the initial productivity gains from workers in the countries where the businesses have relocated to are substantial. They argue that these gains arise because the workers in the new locations are more motivated by increased wages and a higher quality of life derived from this job transfer. Some offshore firms have also touted the fact that they are getting, on average, the same level of talent that these companies would have received in their home country, only at a lower cost.

The United States still has one of the highest corporate tax rates in the world. Due to this, many companies might feel pressured to relocate to other countries where the tax rate is substantially lower.

Generally, the workers in areas where companies relocate operations experience an increase in wages and standards of living. This increase in standard of living allows these individuals to purchase more goods and services they could not otherwise afford. This not only breathes life into those local economies but also gives the offshore company a foreign presence they might not otherwise have. This presence, with the aid of local workers who already know the customs and culture of these new areas, allows the offshore company to compete on par with the local business.

Another benefit of relocating part of operations to other countries can be the ability to have a twenty-four-hour workforce. Initially, companies use call centers in other countries to provide 24/7 service to customers, but the services offered have gone far beyond just customer service. Some financial companies are already utilizing international workers to create a truly twenty-four-hour workforce.

It used to be that if the work did not get completed at the end of the day, then the company would have to either require overtime hours or simply wait till the next day to complete the project or start new business. That is no longer the case. Companies can now have competent workers in other countries take over where workers in one country left off or start basic tasks that can be completed while the employees in the home country sleep. With the proper training, cost savings and productivity gains can be realized fairly quickly at some companies.

The table below demonstrates how other locations' time differences compare to US EST and how a twenty-four-hour workforce would function.

| Example of 24 -Hour Workforce | | | |
|---|---|---|---|
| NY, United States | Hong Kong, HK | Kolkata, India | Colombo, Sri Lanka |
| **Current Time** | **+ 12 hours** | **+ 9.5 hours** | **+ 9.5 hours** |
| 6 PM EST<br>END of workday | 6 AM<br>START workday | 330 AM<br>Off Work | 330 AM<br>Off Work |
| 9 PM EST<br>Off Work | 9 AM<br>Work Day | 630 AM<br>START workday | 630 AM<br>Off Work |
| 11 PM EST<br>Off Work | 11 AM<br>Work Day | 830 AM<br>Work Day | 830 AM<br>START workday |
| 12 AM EST<br>Off work | 12 PM<br>Work Day | 930 AM<br>Work Day | 930 AM<br>Work Day |
| 3 AM EST<br>Off work | 3 PM<br>END of workday | 1230 PM<br>Work Day | 1230 PM<br>Work Day |
| 6 AM EST<br>Off work | 6 PM<br>Off Work | 330 PM<br>END of workday | 330 PM<br>Work Day |
| 8 AM EST<br>START workday | 8 PM<br>Off Work | 530 PM<br>Off Work | 530 PM<br>END of workday |

We have already covered this reason before, but the topic bears repeating. As mentioned, some businesses might use a tax holiday to repatriate cash. And even though the chance of a tax holiday is a rare occurrence, some offshore-based companies would prefer to sit on their cash and wait for such an event rather than keep their headquarters or other business units in their higher-profit tax country. The savings that can be realized when such an event does occur is quite substantial for the companies and shareholders. The cost for those keeping their cash in other countries is worth it when they are finally able to bring those monies home.

In 2004, a tax holiday was given and offshore-based companies were able to transfer back (repatriate) $362 billion to the United States. Of that amount, only $312 billion was qualified for the lower tax rate. If it had been taxed at the 35-percent tax rate, these companies would have paid $109.2 billion. Instead, the monies were taxed at only 5.25 percent, amounting to about $16.38 billion overall. This was a savings of 29.75 percent or $92.82 billion in cash. That is one reason some companies would rather wait for such an event than pay the higher tax rates.

Overall, investors might be more attracted to companies that have some of their operations offshore because of the competitive advantage gained through cost savings and potential markets. This, however, is based on how efficiently the newly gained competitive advantage is managed or mismanaged.

Offshore business can offer several benefits to investors and the United States. The lower cost for goods and services increases the standard of living in our home country. It also offers the United States opportunities for better international relations, because countries that do business with us will eventually develop better relationships with us. Offshore business also encourages better trade agreements that benefit those other countries.

By doing away with labor-intensive jobs, Americans will turn to service and "intellectually challenging" jobs. This will lead to new innovations, and America will be more competitive in the global market. The United States also has better protections of patents and economic laws, so it makes sense to stay rooted in the United States.

### Disadvantages for Offshore Establishments

When jobs are relocated for any reason, unless those displaced workers are retrained or given other jobs within that business, those workers will be unemployed. That is simple fact. Now, suppose that it is not just one business moving offshore, but the overall trend in the economy is to offshore jobs. This will mean that those in that economy will have to be retrained and provided with new jobs or become entrepreneurs or unemployed. Some have argued that the period of this dislocation unemployment will amount to only a short period, but others have argued that in unfavorable conditions, such as a slumping economy, such unemployment can last for years.

Princeton economist Alan Blinder in his paper "How Many US Jobs Might Be Offshorable?" estimates that between 2006 and 2036, over 42 to 56 million jobs might be offshored. That is over 30 percent of the jobs currently in the United States.(1)

Unemployment is a disadvantage to the workers, but could excess cash surplus be a disadvantage to the business? Many would doubt that having excess cash could be bad for business, but that is exactly what appears to be happening with some of these companies that have moved their businesses offshore. Some of these companies have moved offshore to realize a much lower effective tax rate on their profits, but now they want to transfer these monies back to their home country. However, this transfer would be taxed at a much higher rate, currently about 35 percent, in the United States.

This puts these offshore companies in a difficult position, because they would like to use their cash profits. Although these offshore outfits realize that they are creating inefficiencies because they cannot put cash to use or invest in a more gainful way, some analysts have decided that it is better to sit on the cash and let it grow offshore rather than to transfer the surplus funds back to their home country to be taxed at a higher rate. So the United States loses tax revenue and revenue from real estate development and office space leases.

Employers fixated on cutting costs at all costs are creating a new economic and social model where wages will stagnate, benefits will be cut, local unemployment will remain high, and social programs will lose funding or be cut entirely. This could also spell the end of collective bargaining.

The initial cost of relocating a business is also expensive. The business will need to do studies to find the right location or country. The cost to deploy and hire workers is high, and the new workers will need to be trained and taught US culture and customs. This also includes keeping worker who are not necessarily familiar with common business practices in compliance with company policies. Businesses may experience difficulties in communicating with foreign mangers, and the cultural learning curve can be steep for both parties in various worksites. Poor customer service is common during training and transition phases.

### Conclusions

When jobs are relocated for whatever reasons, society should work together to meet the challenges of the displaced workers, loss of tax revenues, and cuts in social programs. The government, under its social contract with its society, should take measures and enact legislation where needed to ensure that offshore economic activity is not done to the detriment of long-term prosperity of the society it was created to protect. Offshore companies should also be given incentives to maintain and create economic opportunities in the local economy.

It is not enough to expect businesses to want to take morally correct actions. It has been proven for centuries that most enterprises and entrepreneurs are in the business to maximize their profits. These groups are by definition trying to produce as many goods and services within the limitations of their resources and the marketplace they have to compete in. What is becoming clearer, if it has not been obvious already, is that the economic environment is becoming more global. It is becoming increasing difficult for the non-global domestic companies to compete with multinational corporations just a block away.

These multinationals have global reach and have access to lower cost labor, materials, and other resources. In addition, some of these multinationals, because they are based offshore, do not have some of the tax burdens that a non-global domestic company might have.

Some may argue that in a capitalist society, the companies that know how to effectively use the system and its limited resources should win. However, the actual realities and spoils of the winners and losers appear to be blurred at best. Many wonder who the actual winners are in this new economic environment.

### Who is the real winner in the global economy?

Is it the individual who works for the large global company? Is it the state or local economy that sees tax revenues continue to decline? Is it the investor who pours funds into these companies?

The real winners and losers differ depending to whom these questions are posed. A society should be cautioned, however, if its long term goals of social stability and economic prosperity are not met by its social and economic policies. If an economy is not working toward the benefits of its society, then who is really benefitting? It is better to fix a malfunctioning system in the light than to try to create a new one in the darkness. It is, therefore, crucial that businesses and governments work together to ensure that the overall good of society is being rewarded as part of ongoing business operations.

CHAPTER 10

# Special Interests and Lobbyists

Lobbyist and special interest groups get a lot of attention from voters, politicians, and policymakers, because they represent groups of people and businesses that have particular social, economic, or political concerns. What sets special interest groups apart from other groups is the fact they represent a specific social base and concentrate on specific issues of interest to that social base. One of the most important characteristics of special interest groups is that they focus on these specific issues without regard for their impact on the wider constituency.

Special interest groups are created simply because, as the old saying goes, there is power in numbers. As the federal and state governments grow increasingly larger and complex, it becomes more difficult for individuals to present specific issues, opinions, beliefs, concerns, and proposals. That is why special interest groups form and hire lobbyists who are specifically directed to present the group's interests to legislators, policymakers, bureaucrats, legislative aides, agency heads, and other government officials.

A special interest group does not have to include lobbying as a function; however, that is commonly the main reason that they are established. Direct lobbying is an attempt to influence government legislators and policymakers to pass legislation or write government rules that specifically benefit the interests of the group. These special interest groups may have economic or non-economic goals.

Those with economic goals are seeking financial benefits for members in a variety of ways. For example, industry lobbyists may seek new tariffs on foreign imports, restrictive laws that create a market advantage, subsidies to control price fluctuations, or government agency rules that create an economic advantage.

The non-economic lobby groups usually have a cause they feel benefits everyone, not just the special interest group. As a note, it was mentioned earlier that special interest groups focus on their goals without regard for their impact on the general population. That often holds true even for non-economic groups, because everyone may not agree with a group's cause or goals. A good example is environmental groups that lobby for laws that restrict economic development to preserve wildlife areas. There is no economic benefit accrued by the environmental special interest group, but there are also those who might see these restrictions as being counterproductive to the general population's interests. The following are some examples of large special interest lobby groups.

### Economic Lobbying Groups

- **American Association of Retired Persons (AARP)** – focuses on needs of people over fifty years old
- **Planned Parenthood –** works to improve women's safety, health, and right to make choices
- **US Chamber of Commerce** – protects business interests
- **National Rifle Association (NRA)** – works to preserve gun rights and sales
- **National Federation of Independent Business (BFIB)** – promotes small business interests
- **National Association of Manufacturers (NAM)** – promotes manufacturing interests
- **American Federation of Labor and Congress of Industrial Organization (AFL-CIO)** – advances labor interests
- **National Association for the Advancement of Colored People (NAACP)** – focuses on civil rights, government policies, economic protection, and political action
- **Political Action Committee (PAC)** – influences federal legislation or promotes election of a candidate

### Non-Economic Lobbying Groups

- **Greenpeace USA** – promotes environmental protection
- **American Israel Public Affairs Committee (AIPAC)** – works to strengthen Israeli-US relations
- **American Civil Liberties Union (ACLU)** – protects human and legal rights
- **Christian Coalition** – works for the political preservation of religious rights

- **Common Cause** – promotes effective government
- **Mothers Against Drunk Driving (MADD)** – lobbies to create laws addressing drunk driving

It is estimated that there were over ten thousand lobbyists working in Washington, D.C. during the third quarter of 2011. In the first ten months of 2011, over $2.44 billion was spent on lobbyists. The top twenty industries spending the most on lobbying in 2011 were:(1)

- Pharmaceuticals and health products: $182 million
- Insurance: $117 million
- Oil and gas: $111 million
- Electric utilities: $106 million
- Tech industry: $93 million
- Television, movies and music: $92 million
- Manufacturing and Distributing: $89 million
- Securities and investment firms: $75 million
- Business Associations: $75 million
- Hospitals and Nursing Homes: $74 million
- Education: $71 million
- Civil Servants and Public Officials: $61 million
- Health Professionals: $59.5 million
- Air Transport: $58 million
- Health Services and HMOs: $54 million
- Real Estate: $49 million
- Commercial Banks: $47 million
- Defense Aerospace: $47 million
- Automotive: $46 million
- Telecommunications: $43 million

It would probably surprise many people to learn that commercial banks are seventeenth on the list. Financial institutions have been heavily criticized as being the constructors of the 2008 recession and then lobbying to prevent new regulations intended to limit their ability to cause similar problems in the future. However, the largest single organizational lobbying expenditures in 2011 was the US Chamber of Commerce at $46 million, followed by General Electric at $21 million, the National Association of Realtors at $16 million, the American Medical Association at $16 million, and Conoco Phillips at $16 million. Other large lobbying firms include AT&T, Blue Cross/Blue Shield, Comcast Corp, AARP, Verizon Communications, Boeing Co., and FedEx Corp.

## Brief History of Lobbying Industry

The goal of special interest groups is usually to influence politicians or policymakers in some manner. Lobbyists directly contact legislators, while some groups focus on raising money for specific political candidates they believe are supportive of the group's goals. As would be expected, the rise and fall of these groups has led to cycles that reflect political and economic conditions and a series of laws regulating lobbying activities.

The right of all people and businesses to lobby the government is protected by the First Amendment to the United States Constitution. It falls within the clause that prohibits making a law that bans the "petitioning for a government redress of grievances." The right to petition extends to Congress and the judiciary and the executive branches of the government.

The United States has struggled with interpreting this right since its inception, and at times, Congress has even limited the right to petition. Industrialization at the turn of the century saw the establishment of the first trade unions and agricultural groups in the 1920s, followed by professional associations in the ensuing decades. It was in the 1930s that President Franklin Roosevelt's New Deal was established to promote interest groups' participation and progressive policies intended to provide equal opportunity. The New Deal also solidified the institutionalization of special interests.(2) This would set the stage for later special interest groups to form with the goal of power equalization between the rich and the poor and the individual and businesses. Amazingly, these are the same themes that are still heard eighty years later.

Beginning in the post-industrial period of the 1960s, the numbers and types of special interest groups grew phenomenally. The way lobbyists interacted with Congressional members also changed. For a twenty-five-year period, until the late 1950s, the lobbyists used a combination of formal Congressional committee approaches and informal personal contact. Lobbyists knew who must be approached in Congress to promote particular issues, a practice that has become the hallmark of the institutionalized nature of lobbying.(3)

It was in the mid-1960s, however, that electoral politics began to change the nature of lobbying and the roles of special interest groups. The passage of the Voting Rights Act of 1965 and the Supreme Court decision concerning "one person, one vote" changed Congressional composition. Old-style institutionalized lobbying was no longer as effective, because new faces and new issues in Congress led to the disintegration of established committee connections. More power was pushed toward individual legislators and their corresponding parties.(4) This change is important to understand, because it laid the groundwork for political action committees and powerful special interest groups that are now often politicized.

The 1960s saw the rise of special interest groups, even those promoting civil rights for minorities and women. This period witnessed the formation of major environmental special interest groups, as well. The 1970s, by far, was the period during which public interest groups grew rapidly and began to encompass a multitude of social issues like domestic violence, low income housing, and rights for the disabled. It has been argued that these aforementioned lobbying issues brought about the passage of the equal protection laws in the 1960s and 1970s that led to a rapid decline in union membership participation in the periods that followed.

Government policy has been a key factor in influencing the rise of special interest groups. For example, when there are major wars, veteran's groups become more vocal. As the US population ages, senior citizen groups also expand. As the government increases the number of regulations and laws controlling businesses, corporations exert more lobbying efforts to minimize the impact of those laws.

As mentioned, the passage of more wage and benefits laws over the decades has led to declining labor union membership from about 33 percent of the labor force in 1960 to about 10 percent by the year 2000. For the most part, the members of the labor force felt comfortable with the rights and benefits that had been procured on their behalf, so their reliance on unions steadily dropped.

Broad economic developments had ushered in the emergence, expansion, and seemingly unwavering power of special interest and lobbying groups. For example, the 2008 collapse of the financial markets led to lobby groups representing the banking industry wielding enormous influence over financial reform legislation. Due to financial industry lobbying, banks were able to continue to sell derivatives—the same products that helped trigger the financial market collapse.

In 1995, the Lobbying Disclosure Act of 1995 was passed, followed by the Lobbying Disclosure Technical Amendments Act of 1998. These laws require accounting reports and disclosure of legislation influenced by lobbyists. The Legislative Transparency and Accountability Act of 2006 also imposed rules on gifts from lobbyists and expanded reporting requirements for this powerful and influential group.

Political Action Committees (PACs) are a type of special interest group that garners a lot of attention. These groups exert enormous influence over the political process. The first PAC, appearing in 1944, was formed by the CIO labor union to bypass the Smith-Connally Act, which had set limitations on direct labor union contributions to political candidates. Over the next twenty years, the union PACs grew in size and financial power. In response, businesses also began to form PACs in the 1960s and 1970s. In the 1980s, the leadership PACs formed by members of Congress to fund party members appeared. In other words, there are different types of PACs—business, labor, leadership, and ideological—and their purpose is to fund political candidate campaigns.

Legislatively, PACS were held in check by the passage of the Federal Election Campaign Act (FECA) of 1971, which was amended in 1974 to limit PAC donations and establish the Federal Election Commission to ensure finance law compliance concerning political campaigns. In addition, public financing of federal campaigns was allowed. With the 1974 amendment, strict limits were placed on contributions that PACs were allowed to make to federal political candidates or to political committees. Those limits, however, were eventually challenged as unconstitutional in the case of Senator Buckley and the Secretary of the Senate, Buckley v. Veleo. The Supreme Court ruled that candidates could contribute to their own campaigns and declared that laws prohibiting others from spending money outside of a political campaign violated free speech rights. However, the Supreme Court also reversed spending limits, ruling in favor of the candidate's campaign committees. In 1976, further amendments were made to FECA to align with the restrictions rulings on spending limits.(5)

The political contribution and election laws were amended a number of times over the years through 1984. However, the PAC contribution limits to political candidates were maintained. Only disbursement laws were loosened. Despite increased regulation and contribution limits, the number of PACs continued to grow until there were four thousand formed by 1988. In fact, large contributors to PACs continued to push the limits of the law.

The Bipartisan Campaign Reform Act (BCRA) of 2002 restricted individual contributions to federal political elections and restricted the raising of soft money (non-federal) by federal candidates and national parties. Labor unions and corporations were prevented from contributing to electioneering communications with money that comes from their general treasuries. In addition, any donor allowed to finance electioneering communications had to be identified if the amount was $1,000 or more. The goal was to regulate large campaign contributions, and for a time, this system worked.

Then in 2010, the rules for donors lobbying groups changed yet again. The Supreme Court ruling in January, 2010, Citizens United v. Federal Election Commission, eliminated limits on contributions to special interest groups, specifically PACs. By removing the limits, campaign finance laws were drastically changed. The court ruled five to four that corporations can fund candidate elections through PACs without limits and said that corporations have a right to political speech. It may seem unbelievable, but it is, in fact, true. Unbelievably, the courts ruled that corporations had rights, as do "natural persons," and therefore had protected rights under the Constitution.

Apparently, the Supreme Court has upheld that notion that corporations have the same rights as natural persons when it comes to entering into and enforcing contracts since Dartmouth College v. Woodward in 1819. Since 1819, the rights of the corporate personhood, as it is often referred to, have grown immensely, despite the many challenges from a host of outspoken critics, such as the Green Party and former Vice President Al Gore. All that the powerful lobbying industry did was take the corporate personhood argument a step further to confer additional rights upon corporations in order to get their contributions limit restrictions removed.

Fortunately, the Supreme Court did not bend to all of the lobbyist demands. The disclosure requirements on spending were upheld when the court wrote that the electorate has a right to the information. Just as importantly, the ban on corporations and unions making direct contributions to political candidates was also upheld.

With restrictions lifted, corporations, unions, and individuals could contribute as much as they want to PACs. Ending restrictions on donations to Political Action Committees has led to explosive growth in special interest group funding and the number of lobbyists. The Center for Responsive Politics estimates that as of the end of 2011, there were 12,242 lobbyists actively working in Washington, D.C.; that is a growth in the industry of over 300 percent in the last thirty years.(6)

### Job Title: Lobbyist

Special interest groups and lobbying groups are embedded in the US political system. The opponents of special interest groups accuse them of buying political influence, and they are able to do so by relying on large amounts of money coming from businesses and corporations. Ordinary citizens usually cannot compete, because they are unable to match the funding.

However, the laws allow anyone to start a special interest group that adheres to the law. Any special interest group can hire lobbyists or mount a publicity campaign intended to influence policymakers and/or the public. For example, special interest groups may send direct mailings to promote an issue or to raise funding, send e-mails, rent billboards, make telephone calls, create membership lists, build a website, or organize lawful assemblies.

Yet it is the lobbyist that has the direct contact with politicians, their aides, and political committees. They work for corporations, individuals, or the public. It should not be surprising that many lobbyists are ex-legislators or legislative aides who are familiar with how government works, have insider knowledge of the laws, and have established valuable contacts among lawmakers and policy makers. Indeed, lobbyists are among the most powerful and influential groups in the United States.

It is a fact that most current lobbyists have changed careers to become lobbyists. They have special experience and knowledge gained during their previous careers that makes them valuable intermediaries between the special interest groups and politicians. The majority of lobbyists have college degrees, but developed networking skills are invaluable. One of the interesting characteristics of a job as a lobbyist is that there is no hierarchy of lobbyists. Respected lobbyists who earn a high salary may have even started at that salary, but that entitlement is usually reserved for ex-legislators.

Lobbyists must register with the government at the federal or state level if they get paid for the work they do. Large lobby firms hire lobbyists and then contract with businesses or individuals, but some lobbyists work for themselves. The amount a lobbyist gets paid varies based on the type, size, and complexity of the project, and the amount is negotiable. Detailed salary information is not widely available, but surveys have indicated lobbyists make an average of $50,000 to $60,000 annually. A qualified, experienced lobbyist working in Washington, D.C. will earn as much as $300,000. A high-powered lobbyist with access to established key contacts can earn even more. A lobbyist working at the state or local level will usually make less.

The large lobbying firms earn millions of dollars each year. In 2011, Akin, Gump, Strauss, Hauer, & Feld, LLP earned $27.9 million; Patton Boggs, LLP earned $27.2 million; Podesta Group earned $20 million; and Van Scoyoc Associates earned $17.9 million—just to name a few.(7)

The power of lobbying and special interest groups cannot be overstated. Lobbying impacts government policies and regulations, laws, domestic commerce, and foreign trade. In addition to the examples given throughout this discussion, following are a few more lobbying successes:

- **Mothers Against Drunk Driving** - responsible for convincing states to pass legislation toughening the sentencing laws for driving while intoxicated
- **Oil company lobbying** - led to minimal government regulation, federal rules waivers, and limited accident liability(8)
- **Pharmaceutical industry lobbying** - prevented media restrictions being enacted concerning US drug advertisements
- **Corporate lobbying** - led to passage of the American Jobs Creation Act, which enabled corporations to pay a low tax rate on profits earned overseas

There are thousands of examples of how special interest groups have influenced legislation in every industry. The debate concerning whether lobbying is necessary and efficient or a perversion of democracy rages on. Despite frequently being derided by a number of derogatory terms including "influence peddlers," lobbyists have become an integral cog in the American business and political machine, and they are not planning on leaving any time soon. Special interest groups are also here to stay. Even those who find the influence of corporations and unions on policymaking to be distasteful can often take solace in that there are also ideological groups that promote causes they believe in and can improve the quality of life and the world in which we live.

# SECTION 3
## Brave New World

*"Money has no loyalty. It worships no gods, corrupts the best of society, respects no laws, observes no country's borders, and is accountable to no one. Therefore, it falls upon reasonable men to protect the wealth of society, from the inequity and tyranny of the evil men it corrupts."*

-F.B. Wiseman

CHAPTER 11

# Global Financial Crisis Update

As the world desperately tries to recover and move past the economic crises of the past few years, here is an update of how the different regions of the globe are faring today.

## Africa and the Middle East

The Middle East and North Africa economies, or MENA as they are commonly referred to, are as volatile as they come these days. While not a historically stable region, this was considered one of the areas to watch until last spring, and it still is by many. Africa has seen a surge of investors in recent years and is heralded by many as the investment spot of choice for emerging economies. Since the so-called Arab Spring revolts, however, the political climate has become extremely uncertain, giving pause to many would-be investors. Unemployment in this region stands at around 10 percent, while the unemployment rate among those under age twenty-five has climbed to 24 percent, an alarming statistic that will be closely monitored for its impact on the region in years to come.

In addition to the geopolitical issues at play in the region, the sharp drop in commodity prices and the lower demand for exports from Western nations have taken a toll on the MENA region. While the amount of exports is not as great as that of China, the impact has been felt more since the area has less to rely on in terms of diversity and growth. The price of oil is also being closely watched, as a recent drop has affected the region negatively, as well. The long-term prognosis for the MENA region at this point is as uncertain as it is anywhere, and unless some political stability comes to the area soon, this is unlikely to change. The World Bank is projecting that foreign investment deposits to the region will slow through 2012 and then pick up again in 2013, but this will largely depend on what happens in the various new governments there.

## Asia

Overall growth in Asia has remained at high levels as the global economic weather vane has shifted in its direction while the growth in traditionally stronger Western countries has slumped. Even with Japan's recent tragedies and political instability, its economy has not fallen as much as that of its Western partners, and the losses and pitfalls that it has experienced have been more than offset by the growth in China alone.

China has seen continued stellar growth in the past few years, to the point that the government there is attempting to slow it in fear of sector bubbles bursting. Recent reports show that China's growth rate in 2011 slowed a bit from the 10.3-percent rate in 2010 down to a still-amazing 9.5 percent. The Chinese government would like to see the growth rate even out at around 7 percent, for the sake of stability.

Concerns over China's economic growth center around the heated growth rate and exporting slumps. With the Western economies still slowing or remaining stagnant, the demand of imports from China has slowed, as well. However, many economists are more interested in China's capital expenditures than its exporting. While the traditional role of the country has been to provide cheap goods at low prices to the rest of the world, that focus is shifting in the wake of the global recession as China focuses on real estate and construction as major internal drivers. The manic currency policies in China also remain a concern, including the possibility of inflation, with the money supply having been increased over 50 percent in the last two years.

For now, Asia remains the focus of the global economic shift, with China predicted to become the world's largest economy in the next decade, followed by India. The region in general is expected to become the new economic hub as the world restructures following the worldwide economic crisis.

## Europe

The debt crisis in Europe is even more evident than in the United States when viewed through the public eye, due to the street rioting throughout the region in 2011 as many European countries introduce austerity measures to attempt to stave off the collapse of the European Union. With partners such as Greece, Spain, Portugal, and Ireland teetering on the edge of default, the instability within the Union has grown at an alarming rate.

With the European crisis rivaling that of the United States, the UK government recently embraced the John Vickers report on banking as new policy, saying that they would introduce the rules fully dividing investment and commercial branches of banking in the region to avoid a further debt crisis through the intermingling of these two enterprises. They expect this to bring stability to the banking industry by reducing the risk; however, major banks are opposed to the measure, which also limits their ability for riskier and often much more profitable ventures.

## North America

In Canada and the United States, the unemployment rate remains in the 9-percent range, despite the government bailouts and economic stimulus packages introduced by the government over the last three years. The primary reason for the high unemployment is a lack of growth in the private sector, particularly among small businesses, due to a lack of any significant lending and borrowing. Although cash reserves are at an all-time high, the liquidity is sitting and earning interest from the Federal Reserve rather than seeing movement on inter-banking loans and commercial loans. Like the UK government, the US government is considering new legislation and regulations that would divide the commercial and investment arms of major banks as well as plans to introduce the Basel III rules to not only banks but also other industries that are deemed necessary to stability in the financial sector and the economy.

## South America

South America is possibly in the best economic situation, next to China and India, to weather the economic storm of the past few years. Because of relatively solid banking systems that have emerged in the past decade as well as trade agreements for commodities with China, Israel, and Palestine, among others, the countries south of Panama have been essentially unscathed compared to most of the world, while Central American countries with closer ties the US economy have suffered.

Emerging economies in places like Brazil have been favorites for investors in recent years, and South American countries have been applying some protectionist measures as safeguards against cheap imports. In December 2011, the Mercosur trade bloc agreed to a 35-percent tariff on one hundred additional goods that are subject to Mercosur's common tariff on imports from outside the bloc. The IMF's managing director, Christine Lagarde, has reported that Brazil and Mexico have leaned toward offering funds to the IMF to bolster their lending war chest, should it be necessary in further bailouts to European countries.(1)

South America is expected to remain solid as China's growth increases demand on commodities from them, even as Europe's support through the same means has faltered in the wake of their debt crisis.

CHAPTER 12

# The Eurozone Experiment

By the end of the Second World War, Europe had seen years, even centuries, of intermittent and sometimes prolonged skirmishes, battles, and wars between its neighboring countries. This had culminated in two bloody and costly World Wars with their hub within the continent's borders. War weary and seeking a world stage from which greater influence could be exerted, its leading continental nations sought to bring harmony and economic, social, cultural, and political integration by forming a union of European countries.

In 1957, the European Economic Community, the forerunner of the European Union, was formed with just such aims. Its six founding members—Germany, France, Italy, and the Benelux countries of Belgium, Holland, and Luxembourg—continue to be the Union's strongest members today.

Continual evolution of the aims and breadth of powers within the European Union as well as its membership, which currently totals twenty-seven countries, finally led to a call for greater financial and economic integration. The idea of a single currency was born, and in 1979, the currencies of the European nations who wanted to participate in the European Monetary System (EMS) were bought under the control of the Exchange Rate Mechanism (ERM) as a forerunner to eventual monetary union. This pegged the currencies of participating countries within pre-defined bands against the value of a notional European Currency Unit (ECU), which was a weighted average of its members' currencies. Each currency within the ERM was allowed to fluctuate by no more than 2.25 percent to either side of the value of the ECU, except the Italian Lira, which had dispensation to fluctuate by up to 6 percent.

The UK joined the system in 1990, but was forced to withdraw in 1992 when speculation against the British pound drove the currency through its allowable fluctuation limits. The speculation against the currency had been prompted by two factors. Firstly, there was the poor economic climate in the United Kingdom, and secondly, Britain had gained an opt-out clause when signing the Maastricht Treaty in 1992.

The Maastricht Treaty obliged EU member states who had met pre-defined monetary and budgetary requirements to adopt the single currency once it had been introduced. The United Kingdom and Denmark gained exemption to this requirement. Sweden joined the EU in 1995, but refused the euro by referendum in 2003 and has since not met the necessary requirements to adopt it. All countries that now join the EU do so with the agreement that they will adopt the euro at the earliest possible opportunity.

By September, 1992, the UK government had spent over $6 billion to prop up the value of its currency and had endured nearly two years of recession after joining the ERM. After its exit from the ERM and subsequent currency devaluation, the United Kingdom enjoyed a period of rapid economic growth. With further attacks on the ERM and the French franc, in particular, the margin of allowable fluctuation was increased to 15 percent in 1993.

After more than five years of perceived ERM success, the Economic Monetary Union (EMU) partially developed with the introduction of the single European currency, the euro, as an electronically traded currency on January 1, 1999. On January 1, 2002, this currency came into physical being. The nations that adopt the EMU became part of what is called the Euro area, also known as the Eurozone. As of November, 2011, there were seventeen member nations in the Eurozone: Austria, Belgium, Cyprus, Estonia, Finland, France, Germany, Greece, Ireland, Italy, Luxembourg, Malta, the Netherlands, Portugal, Slovakia, Slovenia, and Spain.

## The Advantages and Disadvantages for Member Nations

From a collective point of view, one of the main advantages of adoption of the single currency is the continued move toward increasing economic and political integration. A nation's currency is seen as a keynote to national identity. Replacing the Lira with the euro, for example, is thought to promote a feeling of being European rather than Italian. Ideologically, such psychology is hoped to prevent war between neighboring states. It is also felt that, when trading with the rest of the world, a larger, more integrated economic block will have greater negotiating power than a group of separate sovereign nations.

Within the Eurozone's borders, the single currency brought with it a number of financial and bureaucratic advantages. The costs of conducting business between companies within the Eurozone would no longer be subject to the expense of currency conversion, and a true and fair comparison of the cost of goods and services could be made by corporate bodies and individuals. Investment capital should be more easily accessible from a wider supply in a wider single-currency trading zone where companies can achieve better forward planning. This should lead to more stability in finances and a healthier business environment, promoting greater economic growth in the region. Freer trade with fewer barriers to access, lower costs, and a clearer environment for forward planning should lead to greater economic growth and lower inflationary pressures.

However, there are also disadvantages associated with membership of the Eurozone. For certain countries, the fear of a loss of sovereignty and self-governance, which are already being eroded by laws introduced from a centralized European Parliament, was a step too far. Monetary and fiscal policy will naturally become more centralized. The European Central Bank is administered from Frankfurt, and it is this that sets interest rates for the Euro economies. Eurozone states whose economies are out of sync with others are unable to fully control their own fiscal and monetary policy to promote economic activity; individual companies' domestic markets might be reduced by competition from abroad and price wars could inhibit profit growth, which could, in turn, hold back investment and growth within individual countries.

## Current Eurozone Problems Identified

Current opinion is weighted toward the feeling that the Eurozone is floundering and has the potential to be an unsuccessful experiment. After a little more than a decade of the single currency, the disadvantages previously discussed, which formed the backbone of reason for opting out of the single currency for the United Kingdom and Denmark and Sweden's negative initial referendum result, seem to be outweighing the advantages.

Within the European Union and particularly within the Eurozone, the ease of currency transfer and the mobility of labor between the nations were once considered advantageous. However, this mobility has created a situation where the labor forces, when hit by recession in an industrial sector within a member country, move almost en masse to another. This is also the case when migrant workers, unable now to find work or to claim social security benefits in one country, return to their homeland, where they are paid social security benefits. Both scenarios cause problems to the homeland country—either as a depletion of the workforce or as a drain on that sovereign state's finances.

Labor and employment law as well as social and criminal law is increasingly also dictated from the European Parliament headquartered in Strasbourg, France. The implementation and administration of such laws puts extra expense on the sovereign governments and individual companies. Often, they are seen as unnecessary meddling, and animosity toward the European Parliament is increasing. This "anti-European" feeling within Europe itself is also increasing with the current economic problems brought on since the 2008 global financial crisis.

A recent survey in the Netherlands, one of the founding members of the European Union and home of the Maastricht Treaty that set the conditions for the single currency (the euro), found that 63 percent of the Dutch think their country should stop helping Greece through its well-documented financial troubles. Further than this, over half the people surveyed felt that the Greeks should be expelled from the EU altogether. These sentiments have been brewing, and its supporters are politically well organized. For instance, Netherlands's anti-European Party for Freedom (Partij voor de Vrijheid or PVV) was the third-largest political party in the Netherlands's parliament based on seats won in the 2010 elections. This is a great feat, considering that the PVV was formed in 2005 and was considered in 2006 to be the fifth-largest political party in the parliament based on the number of seats held.

Increasingly anti-European resentment has become a more pronounced political movement within the member states. One noticeable assemblage, called "populist" parties, that has been trading on the negative sentiments toward cheap migrant labor from the newer European Union member states of Eastern Europe is gaining traction in the popular vote across the continent. The right-wing parties of the Eurosceptic True Finns, the anti-immigration parties of Denmark's People's Party, Sweden's Democrats, Italy's anti-EU and anti-immigration Northern League, and Belgium's Vlaams Belang—campaigning for Flemish independence—are all gaining in political strength within their own countries. Austria's Freedom Party of Austria, led by ultra-right-wing Heinz-Christian Strache, has 27 percent of voter approval, and many feel they have a real chance of gaining power in the elections in 2013. These political problems are also mirrored by financial strife across the region.

The global financial crisis of 2008 was met by relaxed regulations within the Eurozone that enabled money to be pumped into the economy. In conjunction, the European Central Bank (ECB) cut Eurozone interest rates to their lowest levels for decades. The net result was that some euro nations' budget deficits exploded through previously agreed limits based on the perception that these deficits would soon be reversed by increased taxes created from rapidly increasing economic activity. These forecasts were unfortunately wrong, and a deepening financial crisis began.

Across Europe, the governments commenced with a crusade of financial bailouts with aims of keeping the banking system solvent. Previously profitable banks were pushed to the verge of ruin by decreasing property values and increasing debt defaults by both corporate bodies and private individuals. These financial institutions were thus privatized in efforts to prevent a total collapse of the financial framework of the European Union and the Eurozone. However, the weight of money pumped into the European economy has only masked the systemic problems of the region. The more industrially diversified nations have weathered the economic storm better than the highly indebted and narrower economies of the so-called PIIGS (Portugal, Ireland, Italy, Greece and Spain), or sometimes just PIGS (Portugal, Italy, Greece and Spain).

Punished by the weight of public-sector debt, poorly performing economies, increasing unemployment, decreasing tax income, and the subsequent downgrades on their debt by major ratings agencies, Portugal, Ireland, Italy, Greece, and Spain have threatened default on their debts.

European sovereign debt is entwined between member states and external lenders such as the United States, China, and Japan. One country's default on its debt could create a drastic and dramatic domino effect of defaulting countries, spreading financial mayhem in a viral environment. Consequently, Europe has been battling with the sovereign debt of individual countries and its overall debt position for much of the last twelve months as of December, 2011, and a viable solution that satisfies all the European nations or the international financial community still has not been ironed out.

Greece is, perhaps, the most prominent of the European nations that has received European Union bail-out money. To date, the country has received approximately €225 billion ($291 billion) in funds and is now struggling to impose a €28billion ($36 billion) austerity package of tax increases and spending cuts aimed at reducing its budget deficit of around 12 percent of the GDP. It is also in the process of implementing a €50 billion ($64 billion) privatization program.

Portugal requested around €80 billion ($104 billion) in funds in order to prop up its ailing finances in May, 2011. In return for these funds, it has implemented an austerity and privatization program similar to that of Greece, though these measures have not been received with such vitriol as in Greece, where the public has taken to demonstrating and rioting against European imposed austerity measures.

In late 2010, Ireland was also given €68 billion ($88 billion) to shore up its public sector finances and its ailing banking and financial sector as well as to meet its deficit until 2015. In order to receive the funds, however, Ireland agreed to use its public sector pension reserves to help meet its immediate needs. Ireland has four and a half years to repay the loans, whilst Greece has three years to do the same.

Spain and Italy have also been on the brink of requesting bailout funds for several months, though both have, thus far, managed to avoid the need to do so. However, the interest rates on their sovereign bonds have been moving between 6 percent and 7 percent for some time as the markets bet on the timing of such moves. It seems that, for now, the bailout funds extended to Ireland, Portugal, and Greece, in particular, as well as continuing moves by the ECB to shore up Europe's banking system have done the job intended and have averted contagion within Europe. It should be noted that Italy has a debt obligation coming due in the first six months of 2012 and about €312 billion ($88 billion) total coming due in 2012, and, dependent upon how this plays out, its finances might come under increased scrutiny.

## Potential Worldwide Effects of Collapse of the Eurozone

There are currently seventeen member states of the Eurozone. Current problems within the Eurozone have prompted many to predict that it will break up, either with some countries pulling out or under a complete collapse.

In both scenarios, it would likely follow that indebted countries would default on their debt as the perceived weaker nations would be unable to raise finance in the open markets to fund continued expenditure. With such interdependence on debt—with countries owning each other's debt and, in turn, being both a creditor and debtor—such an event would be likely to spread financial contagion rapidly from one country to another, with deep recession spreading rapidly. This could cause the Eurozone's banking system to collapse, and were this to happen, the repercussions would be felt around the world. Socio-economists believe that such a collapse would lead to rioting, political upheaval, and general unrest and have warned that an armed conflict within Europe's borders may be inevitable. Even Angela Merkel, Germany's current Chancellor, has said that the breakup of the European Union would leave Europe on the brink of war.

A collapse of the Eurozone may also lead to longer term problems for the US economy, notwithstanding pressure on the global banking system. The value of the dollar would likely increase, which will lead to exports falling over time as they become more expensive. This would put pressure on US companies, and unemployment would rise higher than the 8.6 percent advertised by politicians in December 2011. American banks lending to European companies and countries might also see defaults rise, which will put further pressure on the banking system in the United States and downward pressure on stock prices. Inevitably, such a course, if not corrected, might lead to a severe recession and possible worldwide depression not seen since the Great Depression in the 1930s.

## What Has Been Done? What Can Be Done?

As of December, 2011, The Eurozone member states have moved to prop up the most indebted nations with a series of bailouts. Until recently, non-member states such as the United Kingdom have committed funds to this process. But with their own sovereign debt problems and political pressure from a population suffering with governmental struggles to balance the books, such countries have begun to shy away from further subsidizing the overspending of other nations. The United Kingdom has refused to give any more money toward Eurozone bailout funds, and even Germany, when giving funds to the IMF in its recent efforts to raise more money, has done so on the provision that it is not used to bail out indebted Eurozone members.

The European Financial Stability Fund (EFSF) has also been set up to help Eurozone member states who are facing problems with sovereign debt and to provide capital to the financial sector of Europe's banks via loans to governments. This facility has commitments from EU members, the IMF, and other organizations totaling €780 billion (about $1,000 trillion) but is currently funded to lend up to €440 billion (about $569 billion). Negotiations are still in progress for further increases to the lending limits, as well. However, this overall ability could be under question if France's credit rating is cut, as Standard and Poor's have suggested. Such a move would cut the EFSF's lending capacity by around a third.

The ECB continues to buy bonds of the indebted Eurozone members, though under European law, its purchases are limited to a maximum of €20 billion per week. That is a total of a little under €1.1 trillion over the course of the next twelve months, and this compares to maturing debt of European sovereigns of €1.9 trillion in 2012.

The ECB has also recently loaned €487 billion to five hundred European banks at an interest rate of 1 percent for three years, in the hope that this money will filter through to the markets and help stimulate the economy.

At the same time, the ECB cut the level of cash reserves required to be held with it by the banks from 2 percent to 1 percent and increased the allowable collateral to receive emergency refinancing.

In efforts to reassure markets, the European Union has agreed to draft a new treaty that will lead to deeper economic integration in Europe. This is perhaps Europe's best chance of saving the Eurozone from collapse. The United Kingdom refused to sign the agreement, stating that there were issues of national sovereignty that it could not agree to give up, as well as the fact that they were not receiving adequate concessions from the European Union to justify entering into such an agreement. The agreement, if written into treaty, gives the European Union powers to place sanctions on countries whose budgets exceed 3 percent of their gross domestic product, though these will be averted if not approved by a majority. It also requires that budgets must be agreed upon with the European Union before being put into place.

In reality, coming to a final treaty solution may be the only way that the Eurozone and the euro can survive. However, achieving annual budget deficits of less than 3 percent will be a very tough task for member states; France, Portugal, Greece, Spain, Ireland, Italy, and Belgium all have budget deficits ranging between 4 percent and 32.4 percent of their GDP.

The Eurozone may need to become a tighter, more centrally controlled economic entity with greater political, fiscal, and monetary control ceded to a centralized parliament by member states in order to survive. However, this process in itself could lead to further political unrest as Europe's population is subjected to a lack of autonomous control by an unelected parliament. The Eurozone Experiment continues to be a fluid political and financial conundrum with its conclusion far from being written by the pages of time.

CHAPTER 13

# The Global Economic Shift

In the report "A Game of Catch Up" published December 17, 2011, by the *Economist* on the world economy is correct to note that the world went through a protracted divergence (West vs. East and South) over centuries, and the world is now re-converging. The divergence arose in response to the Industrial Revolution in Western Europe, where a dramatic escalation of industrial productivity enabled a country of such tiny population as Great Britain to out-produce the heavily populated countries of the East.(1)

## How the West Got Ahead

It was not only a matter of producing more commodities. It was also a matter of developing and producing the kind of productive capital that further accelerated the rise of output, in a self-reinforcing spiral of growth. Asia and everyone else dragged behind in the same old proven techniques, and a large gap—a divergence—soon took shape. The Western European and North American countries led the way and became the dynamic "developed world," persisting well into the twentieth century. The rest of the world either lagged behind or rode roughly on their coattails. But this was not to last forever.

The Industrial Revolution led to the Technological Revolution in the twentieth century. This had certain characteristics that would undermine the hegemony of the Western industrial giants. For centuries, a large industrial fortress (factory) could out-compete smaller upstart competitors through sheer force of mass production efficiencies (economies of scale). That efficiency was drawn from fixed product lines and from factories that could not readily be re-tooled. But new technology enabled efficiency at a smaller scale, made re-tooling easier so they could market variety, and deskilled much of the work, so that cheap labor was viable. Enhanced transportation and communication meant that these efficiencies could be achieved anywhere. And free trade in capital meant that jobs could be relocated anywhere, to seek the cheapest production costs. The entrenched advantages of big Western firms began to evaporate.

## The Convergence

The result has been a re-convergence of West-North and East-South. The poorer countries are now in a better position to obtain and adopt the new techniques and technologies. That, combined with their poor (hence cheap) labor forces, has enabled them to gain a new competitive edge in the twenty-first century—exactly at the time when Western countries were reaching the limits of their growth and beginning to stagnate. The gap has begun to close, at least for certain regions which have been able to mobilize the new technology; though there still remain many undeveloped regions that are not in a position to mobilize the capital and are still trapped in poverty.

But this transformation has created its own set of complexities. The developed countries still have developed entrepreneurial and financial infrastructure, which the developing world is slow to replicate. Many of them are still emerging from traditional cultures that are not business-oriented and cannot easily develop the required commercial institutions. This means that they often have to turn to Western financial markets and commercial services to support their endeavors. This creates an interesting paradox. Even as the United States is old and debt-ridden with slipping credit ratings and even as the developing countries are the ones that are strong on savings and zestful in their investments, the developing countries still turn to American treasury bills as the only reliable safe haven for their reserves. And even as the American financial sector is swinging through wild boom and bust cycles, developing countries still hang on to American dollars for security. However, once these developing countries' financial services mature, that dependence will cease to be necessary.

It was in the1980s that this new path began to emerge. Growth in the developed countries was flattening out, while certain developing countries were utilizing new technologies that contributed greatly to their rapid growths. As early as 1978, China was already realizing what looked like a sustainable high-growth rate. India as well as several other developing countries followed shortly afterward with impressive growth. This persistent growth differential has already started to reduce the income gap between developing and developed countries. As of this writing, China has already become the second largest economy in the world. The top developed countries are still leading in per capita output, and it will take a while to dislodge them—but China, Indonesia, India, and Brazil are nipping at their heels.

## Strategic Shift

An *Economist* article, "The Big Tilt – The rise of the East and what it means for business," identifies six primary impacts of the shift. First, referring to the recession, which began two years before the report was written, it was becoming apparent that Asia, largely China, was leading the world out of recession. Concerns have been raised about the effectiveness of the developed Western business model, and China, in particular, has been demonstrating a conservative stability, which may well have provided the weight to prevent a more serious system-wide failure.

In the current uncertain economic environment, major Western firms are rethinking their global strategies with a view to recentering their global strategy on Eastern supply chains' growing demands, as well. It is generally recognized that this is not merely a trend, but rather a fundamental rebalancing that is, in fact, due to accelerate. This redefining of the world economy is creating new opportunities—as well as new competition.

However, this rebalancing has also brought new problems for China. There are some growing concerns that China is in the midst of a long bubble based on unsustainable government stimulus and precarious financial speculation. Although China has shown a remarkable ability to weather some of these problems, this strategy simply cannot continue indefinitely. Its market growth looks more impressive in purchasing power parity (PPP) terms than at market exchange rates, and it is prudent to anticipate uneven growth and serious market adjustments in the medium term or perhaps short term. Yet, in relation to the rest of the world, China remains a strong behemoth positioned to be an ongoing source of stability and a viable contributor to global economic growth. Let us turn now to the second point in the economic shift discussion.

## Changes in Eastern and South America Regions

This discussion will focus on the internal shift that is taking place in the Eastern economies, specifically Asia and India, and the western hemisphere's south regions, specifically Brazil. These developments may appear new, but they have been the organic outgrowth of decades of current globalization strategies.

Naturally, after decades of growth based on exports to the West, the instability of the developed economies has sparked a turn toward serving the developing world's own domestic markets. The impact of that not only affects the importing sectors of the Western economies but also has repercussions on world currency markets as it makes China less obligated to keep the value of the Chinese yuan low. The combination of these effects together with the struggle to cope with declining growth have shocked Western countries out of the "Asia saves, we consume" model—and turned their attention to the massive debt load that has been accumulating for decades. Even more concerning for the developed countries is that their reduced consumption has only made a dent in the Asian world production machine, whose economic growth is expected to remain robust for some time.

Any realignment of production will not occur uniformly. Within Asia itself, the western shift of sourcing to cheaper countries is paralleled by an Asian shift of sourcing to even cheaper Asian countries such as Vietnam or Indonesia. And within Asian countries, as well, development is extremely uneven. And it is not only production that is being realigned in the East. To accomplish this systematically also requires a realignment of distribution, marketing, and pricing practices.

Western attention to Asian domestic demand is also growing, as expanding Asian markets are seen as new investment opportunities. The recent rise of the middle class in Asia has encouraged a shift in Western investment toward finished products for domestic markets. However, increased revenue in this area has not yet translated into great profitability, but rather a longer term investment in future market growth. Although middle-class markets in Asia are growing, they remain, in many instances, still far behind their counterparts in Western countries. This is due in part to these developing economies' need to re-tailor their products and their marketing to a different cultural environment.

Asian manufacturing is presenting a particular challenge to Western firms, as innovation creates increased cost savings on the same goods manufactured in the West at higher costs. This can have a positive effect in jolting Western firms out of a complacency born of previously captive domestic markets. However, these changes must be looked at positively to appreciate what is happening between the developed and developing economies. So while the East is exporting a degree of arguably needed dynamism to the West, the West still has significant influence, which is evident in the Asian preferences for Western brand names. This means that the Western world still has opportunities to compete globally, but change is clearly needed going forward.

## Savings and Capital

The third discussion point centers on the shift in Asian attitudes toward consumption instead of saving. It is well known that high household savings rates are deeply traditional in Asia, and this sentiment has also shaped similar views at the corporate level for many businesses, as well. Combine this with a relatively high aversion to risk, and the result is excessive corporate savings. That is, saving, rather than raising, capital. The Asian corporate sector, where one might expect a little dynamism and appreciation of risk, is holding back and saving. This strategy reigns because, for the most part, state-controlled enterprises need not aggressively maximize profit, and excessive regulation of capital flows also discourages many tentative ventures. However, the tide of capitalistic change has come to Asia.

Governments are now attempting to implement more highly developed financial markets to facilitate venture capital and to promote proactive investment projects. But attitudes that have been shaped for generations are still embedded in the system and have dampened these strategic changes.

It is thought that a move to a more freely traded Chinese currency may serve as a catalyst for greater investment. This has been both praised and critiqued as an expansion of Chinese influence on the global economic stage. Ambitious patriotism is a credible antidote to the saving reflex, but investors are still unsettled by the 2008 crisis and fall back on the fear of declining exports as the yuan rises. Meanwhile, the universities and the government are debating whether freedom from managing the Chinese yuan will enable better monetary policy for fighting inflation and whether that is compatible with the need to manage a threatened export sector and make the transition to more production for domestic markets.

## Changing Structures

The fourth discussion point in the global economic shift focuses on structural reformulations in business strategies. New business models are necessary, because the playing field has changed and is continuing to evolve as the day passes. Innovations in technology and other economic factors have been fostering a more level playing field. This is creating a convergence in the way firms operate. That is, firms in developing and developed countries are gradually becoming more similar in the ways they produce and the ways they do business. We used to have innovation in the developed countries and cheap unskilled labor in the developing countries. Currently, the developing world is producing is own centers for dynamic innovation and marketing with lower cost, skilled labor.

The developed countries, by contrast, are scrambling to keep their edge by improving their cost structures and embracing diversification. That is not to say that the West is losing. In fact, it is rising to the challenge to maintain the lead in many instances, but outsourcing for skilled labor and management is becoming a growing part of its strategy. Many Western firms are now consciously strategizing to play a major role in the tilt, though they are failing to address the fact that their domestic labor forces are losing out to the competition.

But there is more than just outsourcing involved. There are also major corporate restructuring shifts going on in the capital markets. Mergers and acquisitions are the name of the game currently, and these deals are not dominated by just Western firms. Some of the largest acquisitions nowadays are procured by Chinese firms, although the other BRIC (Brazil, Russia, India, and China) countries are getting into the game, as well.

The BRIC countries are effectively capturing the advantages that established Western capital can bring them. Fortunately for the Western establishment, the developing countries are still reliant on the developed world's financial institutions and capital markets. Indeed, the developed countries also have a stranglehold on the economic and, in some cases, material resources that the developing world needs. However, the wheels are in motion, and change is inevitable. Therefore, the developed world must also implement new strategies to deal with the apparent transformation on the economic horizon. It is a new game, and the rules are being presented and tested. Fortunately, or unfortunately, for both sides, the rules are still evolving, because the new global economic stage is not quite set yet. There are failures on both sides, tough lessons taught, and successes often skewed in the direction of change. With all the changes, many are looking to their business leaders and governments for guidance on this uncertain and often precarious journey of change.

## The Influence of the Political

This is as good a time as any to look at how politics are affecting the global economic shift. It has been evident that differences in political realities are important factors in economic development, as trade falls increasingly under the influence of regimes with varied governing policies and expectations. The free-wheeling capitalism of American ideology does not sit well with many third-world leaders and vice versa, but the dissimilar viewpoints are tolerated just enough to procure the necessary economic arrangements the regimes need in order to remain competitive and, in some cases, relevant.

In the case of China, its culture is very much into managed capitalism, with the state taking the lead (hence calling it socialist). In the case of other BRIC countries, they are into varieties of managed capitalism, with no strong attachment to free markets, with policy shaped largely by the corporate sector. None share the G7 countries' (Canada, France, Germany, Italy, Japan, United Kingdom, and United States) allegiance to free market capitalism.

The International Monetary Fund (IMF) is aggressively campaigning for free markets. But in practice, while it is possible for the IMF to coerce the weaker countries to comply, the big players only pay lip service and manage their economies as they see fit. On balance, developed Western governments and corporations will have to adapt to working with governments that are more intrusive than they are comfortable with—especially states which manage their capital flows in ways contrary to Western interests. But they are learning that the only effective way to manage the situation is to work with governments, not against them.

On the other side of the issue, state intervention is more often conducted for the benefit of vested interests than any commitment to the general public benefit. And if history can be a guide, this strategy oftentimes brings its ugly sisters corruption and inefficiency when they are least welcomed. So a balance has to be sought between fighting for efficient and ethical business dealings and accommodating political and corporate interests; the future of countries and their inhabitants depend on a viable long term solution.

## Cultural Challenges

A clear theme has been developing in these discussions, and that is that globalization involves much more than the removal of barriers and the broadening of trade. The structure of capital, the organization of industry, and the division of labor are being fundamentally transformed as new possibilities emerge. And in the process, disparate ways of doing business are merging uneasily. This points to the cultural challenges that are key to managing the integration successfully.

The sharpest cultural difference is that between a collaborative Western approach to management and a top-down approach in traditional countries. This applies not only to the written rules that shape business in different environments but even more to the unwritten rules and expectations in all aspects of the business. A full grasp of this matrix of behavior is impossible for outsiders to master by themselves. But it is possible to identify certain key behavioral expectations that may threaten to torpedo communication.

Every venture, therefore, needs its interpreter of cultural obstacles, and many global firms are beginning to recognize the need to develop this expertise. To this end, more attention must be paid to linguistic differences, since different languages (especially Asian) represent different ways of putting ideas together, and they are crucial pointers to the different understandings that separate cultures.

But success in foreign markets is not just a matter of hiring cultural experts to map a strategy. It requires attention to developing local leadership and labor market integration as well as cultural understanding and tolerance. A successful strategy requires long-term-focused decisions to make management at home highly familiar with the region, with as much hands-on experience as is practicable. It may even require encouraging regional leadership to take positions on the higher levels of central management as their qualifications develop, to broaden the culture of the organization as a whole. There is no perfect strategy, as these are uncertain times, but what is certain is that if no sincere attempt is made at integration and innovation, then failure is inevitable.

## Currency Issues

The last focus at this point will look at the issues relating to the change in the global reserve currency, a prestigious status that the greenback (US Dollar) has enjoyed since the signing of the Bretton Woods agreement after World War II in 1944. Prior to that, many different reserve currencies from various countries for many centuries went in and out of favor.

So what exactly is a reserve currency? A reserve currency is often held by a majority of financial institutions and banks around the world. This reserve currency usually gains this status because it has met certain "key criteria" and exhibited a proven historic stabilizer in the marketplace. To meet these key criteria, there must be a majority of financial securities denominated in that currency and a liquid market in that currency; the currency must also have a reputation as a safe haven based on the country's stability and capacity to fulfill financial obligations.

According to Barry Eichengreen of the *Wall Street Journal*, there are three factors that might cause a change in a reserve currency.

- **Technology:** it is easier to compare various currency prices with computers and even small handheld devices.
- **Viable alternatives:** the euro and China's yuan are taking on more prominent roles in the global markets.
- **Safe-haven status erosion:** with its federal debt level at 75 percent of the GDP, there is a growing fear that the government might lose its fiscal capacity to meet its global financial obligations. With trillions in deficits and a burgeoning debt obligation that must be met compounded with an economy

that refuses to get in gear, those fears might one day become a reality, unless changes are made to resolve these unsustainable liabilities.(3)

The Chinese RMB (yuan) has been in a semi-float now for years. But as with most other countries, China is managing its currency to keep it within certain bounds—primarily to keep it moderately growing to ease political pressures, while keeping it sufficiently high to maintain the stability of the export sector. China has a good case in claiming that sudden changes will be destabilizing not only domestically but internationally, as well.

Threats to the American dollar have not come primarily from China in the recent past. But the campaign to dethrone the dollar has been temporarily halted by the debt crisis and social unrest occurring in Europe and the Middle East. At this point, the greatest threat to the dollar's central position is the carefully managed rise of the Chinese RMB over the long term. The dollar still has a monopoly on the capital markets due to the sheer volume of securities that are denominated in this currency and the liquidity that derives from such an accomplishment.

The global economic shift, however, is a force that has yet to be contained. It may suffer setbacks, but the momentum is always in the direction of change. Therefore, if the developed countries and specifically the United States want to remain relevant and retain prominent roles in the global market, they, too, will have to change to build a stronger domestic foundation that can compete on the emerging global stage.

CHAPTER 14

# China: The Rise of an Empire

It is no secret that China is quickly climbing the ranks of the super economic powers and is challenging the United States and other developing countries for that top spot. China, one of the oldest civilizations on earth, has a long history filled with rises and declines in both power and influence. Today, this ancient giant sits poised to be the single greatest power on the planet, currently surpassing many other developed countries with its global economic influence and power. However, there are doubters that suggest that China is not ready to become the global superpower. They argue that while China has current economic strength, it is still weak due to its stranglehold on key areas such as domestic, social, economic, and political freedom. In addition, its dependence on the government for sustained economic growth also differs considerably from that of the Western powers.

However, past empires have relied on less civility in their quest to become a dominant force in the world. China arguably has a different social and economic culture compared to the West. Therefore, it might not be surprising if they are also building their empire in a non-Western tradition. In this piece, we will examine how China has fared so far in its empire building and discuss some of the key factors needed to build an empire, such as military power, raw materials, productive resources, a balance of trade between imports and exports, and energy needs.

There are many aspects of this global force of a country that need to be looked at and studied to get a good grasp on what the future may hold not only for China but for every other country on earth, as well. That is why we will endeavor to shed light on China's growth, what is driving it, its partners, the willingness or reluctance of those partners, its military buildup, and its acquisition and utilization of natural resources and energy domestically and internationally.

At the conclusion of reading this chapter, I am hoping that you, the reader, will grasp a better understanding of China's rise, or at the very least that you become aware of the fact that China is a real and formidable challenger to the United States's status as the largest global superpower.

### Criterion I: Military Power

Military prowess is arguably one of the first areas that must be looked at to determine the empire potential of any country. Most people think of the Chinese military as having an endless number of soldiers, primarily because of the huge population of the country. In fact, the People's Liberation Army (PLA) does have the largest number of military personnel in the world, with around 2.3 million in 2010, according to the International Institute for Strategic Studies (IISS). For comparison, the United States, with the second-largest standing military, had less than 1.6 million service members. Only India and Russia compare in numbers, each with more than one million military members.(1)

Even with this much manpower, the Chinese military only ranks second or third globally, depending on which source you rely on for this information. While there is much subjectivity involved in determining rank of military might, the website globalfirepower.com has undertaken the task by leaving out nuclear capabilities and using forty-five different factors such as active personnel, military equipment, technology, and access to resources along with applicable bonuses and penalties to create their ranking system. They list China as the number-three military in the world, behind the United States and Russia.(2)

Even further down the list is China's military budget in relation to GDP, where they ranked eighth in 2010, according to the IISS. A dramatic rise from the twenty-first ranking in military expenditures was noted in 2006, according to the Central Intelligence Agency website. However, its total assumed budget in dollars is second only to the US budget. The total military spending in the United States in 2010 was a little over 4.5 percent of the GDP, while China's spending was less than 1.5 percent of its GDP.

There is a significant difference in actual money spent, as well, with China spending nearly $79 billion versus the United States' $693 billion in the same year. It is important to note that in defense budgets as in any budget, the actual amount spent might vary considerably from the proposed budgeted amount. Also not surprising, there are usually increases in military expenditures across the globe over time due to new technology, maintenance, and adjustments to perceived threats in the global environment. That being said, in 2011, China raised its defense budget nearly 13 percent to $91 billion (601 billion yuan), while the United States raised its own budget to $725 billion.(3)

## The Budgetary Unknown

As mentioned above, the problem with all of these figures is that they are nothing more than educated guesses or official release numbers and are, therefore, likely far from reality for a variety of reasons. Beginning in the 1980s, the PLA began finding ways to find extra-budgetary means to add to the official spending budgets, obscuring the true military budget. This practice continued and increased throughout the following two decades. At this point in history, it is nearly impossible to know what the true figures are. It is likely that the true numbers are not even known by the Chinese government itself.

What is certain, however, is that the spending on defense has increased on average by over 10 percent annually for the past two decades. The reason that the percentage of GDP has remained so low is that the country as a whole has made a huge leap forward in modernization and industry in the same time period. It is traditional Eastern practice to move things along at a steady, long-term, coordinated pace, and that is exactly what China has been doing for over more than half a century. They have laid fifty-year-plus long-term modernization plans broken down into five-year milestones. The first five-year plan was initiated by Mao Zedong in 1953 and lasted until 1957. The country is currently in its twelfth five-year plan from 2011 to 2015.

Another factor in the increase in the military spending is the need to ensure that morale remains high for those serving in the military. For decades, there has been a concerted effort to modernize the military forces as the rest of the country also transforms. Military equipment, barracks, and living facilities have been adequately maintained and, in most cases, modernized.

In 2011, the pay and benefits to non-commissioned officers was expected to increase nearly 40 percent. The Chinese government could easily allocate more of its budget to the PLA, but it well understands that simply adding money and weapons is not the key to its modernization program. The long-term goal of the PLA, like most developed powers, is to train a smaller and more technically competent force and to employ new weaponry. The government is carefully and thoughtfully spending more funds on fewer troops, and the strategy appears to be working well.(4)

## Criterion II: Raw Materials and Productive Resources

The most alarming statistic concerning the growth China is experiencing is its consumption of the world's resources as well as its exporting practices concerning its native resources. The country has faced criticism in recent years over its exporting policies on many raw materials. The World Trade Organization (WTO) recently ruled that China's restrictions on the exports of nine raw materials (such as used in the steel and chemicals industries) violate global trade rules and give the behemoth an unfair advantage toward manufacturing within its borders. This ruling came on the heels of an eighteen-month investigation, which followed complaints from the United States, the European Union, and Mexico.

China is the top producer in the world of many widely used raw materials, including cadmium, gold, indium, iron ore, lime, lead, manganese, mercury, molybdenum, phosphate, salt, tin, tungsten, vanadium, and zinc. China had agreed to commitments for exports in its Protocol of Accession, which the WTO claims that the country violated in an egregious manner based on in its 315-page ruling on the matter.

Through its various quotas, export duties, and licensing procedures and rules, China has limited the export of these raw materials to a point that the global supply has taken a steep decline while the prices have skyrocketed in response to reduced supply. The WTO and complaining nations also claim that China has created an unfair incentive for manufacturing companies to move their facilities into China in order to gain access to the materials. Some of these coveted materials, such as silicon carbide and yellow phosphorus, are vital to the steel, aluminum, automotive, electrical, and chemicals industries.

## The Green Argument

China claims that the restrictions they have put in place are necessary for the conservation of the resources as well as lowering pollution through emissions in the country. China has never signed the Kyoto Protocol for global emission standards and is not known for its conservation efforts. In fact, the WTO's investigation claimed that China was unable to prove that their policies in this area had reduced or curtailed pollution.(5)

More recently, there have been complaints about China's exports of so-called "rare earth" elements, of which the country is the global supplier of over 95 percent. These rare earth elements are used not only in many green technologies such as wind turbines and hybrid cars but also in defense applications such as guided missiles. The global prices on these rare earth elements have gone up over 500 percent, and this is causing more bad sentiment between China and some of its major buyers of the elements, including the United States and Japan.

Some critics in the United States have suggested that the clean power movement led by solar power was severely impacted due to China's perceived unfair trade practices. These critics argue that China was able to dump cheaper solar-powered products on the American market because the government heavily subsidizes them. This practice along with the higher cost of the materials to produce these products essentially undermines American manufactures, leading to eventual bankruptcy since they are not competing on a level playing field.

China cannot use an environmental defense for its restrictions on the rare earth elements, as it has done little to curb the use domestically, making it fairly obvious that their goal is to keep the materials at home and undermine other manufacturers abroad. In the United States, some affected businesses are petitioning the government for relief from these trade practices. However, these trade practices are part of the reason that China has gained an advantage over the years. China understands that whoever controls the resources such as raw resources, energy, and labor will eventually control capital and become the dominant power in the global environment.

## Criteria III: Balance of Trade: Imports and Exports

Not surprisingly, the trade balance between China and other nations has grown in favor of China's exports over the years, exceeding even Japan's numbers at their height in 1986. Japan is one of the top importers of Chinese goods now, along with the United States, Hong Kong, South Korea, Taiwan, and Germany, according to 2010 figures. Even with China retaining the lion's share of exports to the world, its domestic consumption rates are also growing with the rapid industrialization taking place on the mainland. In 2011, the country's share of consumption in the GDP increased significantly after falling for ten consecutive years.

This shift signifies that a significant part of the domestic population is beginning to finally partake of the wealth that the country has been receiving, since China's economic power has grown dramatically through its leveraging of its market advantages as globalization brings other countries to its doorstep begging for lower cost goods and services. And like any rational market participant whose goal is to reduce costs and maximize profits, China will also do its part to help its fellow market participants, but not at its own detriment. Hence, the conflicts that keep reemerging as China exerts its dominance in various industries, which the global marketplace perpetuated through direct and indirect investments in pursuit of lower costs and higher profits.

The trade problems with other nations, real or perceived, may now be affecting the flow of direct foreign investment funds into the country. While

China is still considered by most to be a good place to send investment capital, in December of 2011, the inflow of foreign capital was down 65 percent from previous years. This has adversely impacted China's domestic housing market, since the funding, which has dried up, was a key driver in the housing market. China is normalizing in that aspect to the rest of the world, but it would rather not follow the financial missteps that the West has taken. For the time being, though, the fact remains that it is becoming increasingly difficult to obtain mortgage funds in mainland China.(6)

Truth be told, though, China still is very much dependent on the global economy to finance its interests. Its domestic consumption has not yet reached a level that can sustain any real economic independence from other countries. China's bread and butter are still exports, and that will not change in the foreseeable future. This is the engine that drives the global economy, and there is an interdependence between China and the rest of the developed world. However, the balance in the trade relationship is far from being equal.

For example, in 2010, the trade imbalance on goods with the United States was negative $273 billion, while China's total export trade balance was positive $183 billion in its favor for the same year. In the services sector, which is what America has shifted toward, the United States had a $7.5 billion trade surplus on services with China for the same year. This very small surplus reflects the trend in the trade imbalance and the reason for the ire of American businesses competing with China.

However, the future promises to bring forth changes according to China's economic strategy; as its population wealth increase, they will be able to rely more on imports from the rest of the world. It is assumed that China's goal is to spur more domestic consumption and rely less on exports, which would be good for the countries in the global economy who can export goods and services to it. Of course, like other developed countries, it will be looking at which country can provide the goods and services it wants and needs at reduced costs. Therefore, countries like the United States might still find it difficult to compete as China grooms other low-cost countries to provide the goods and services it needs.

As for China, this shift from mega world exporter to importer will not be easy to facilitate, even with a dramatic rise in domestic consumption. The Chinese government has many policies in place that will need to change prior to this scenario happening. These policies, which include subsidies for cheap labor, low interest rates, and an undervalued currency, are currently the foundation of China's economic strength. These changes will have to be implemented very meticulously in order to prevent Chinese industries from falling prey to the international markets and becoming unprofitable.

As part of China's domestic-shift agenda, employees will also have to be paid more if they are expected to buy more. The first rule of a legitimate consumer-based economy is that the consumer must have adequate wealth, whether perceived or real, in order for the system to be sustainable over the long term. However, for the system to remain functional, the following pitfalls must be avoided.

### How to Destroy a Consumer-Base Economy in 14 Steps

1. Create quarterly driven business plans rather than five-year plans
2. Create loopholes for the rich to evade taxes
3. Pass the costs of government subsidies and bailouts on to regular taxpayers
4. Allow too-big-to-fail banks to continue bad practices after bailouts
5. Outsource jobs for investment returns with no alternatives for workers
6. Do not provide adequate-paying jobs for economy consumers
7. Strip consumers of their retirement and savings
8. Destroy the housing market via fraud, schemes, and oversupply
9. Have student debt outpace salary increases
10. Have a stalemate in government so no fixes take place
11. Layoff private and public employees
12. Borrow more debt since there are no workers to pay taxes
13. Invest in other countries since domestic consumers have no money
14. Repeat previous steps until economy collapses

As you can see, many of these pitfalls have unfortunately become part of the American way of life. Fraud and unscrupulous business practices, lack of regulatory oversight, greed, a broken government, and outsourcing has effectively pulled the rug from under otherwise unsuspecting American consumers. The Chinese government must be much more diligent and attentive to the domestic economy if it is truly going to implement a consumer-based economy.

If China's industries were to falter, the government may be forced to jump in to save them, and other countries that will also be impacted and will need similar rescue packages. These are justifiable fears as to what could happen to the global economy if China's economy plummets.(7) It just might be the beginning of the end of the world as we know it. China's economic demise is a scenario nobody wants to see, especially when there is no long-term backup plan.

## Consumption, Consumption, Consumption

According to *CNN Money* last year, China is expected to build the equivalent of New York City ten times over during the next fifteen years. This is an amazing feat to imagine, but it explains why China surpassed the United States last year as the world's largest consumer of energy. The common thought that jumps out is that 1.3 billion people who are in the midst of modernizing would naturally use a lot of energy, but according to statistics from the US Department of Energy last year, China's industrial sector accounts for an amazing 70 percent of the country's energy consumption. By comparison, in the United States, only 33 percent of energy consumption is attributed to the industrial sector.(8)

This explains some other staggering numbers, as well. Building roads, skyscrapers, factories, and rail lines requires a lot of concrete, steel, glass, and chemicals. China consumes 50 percent of the world's concrete, and the numbers suggest that the consumption levels per capita are the highest the world has ever seen. China also consumes approximately one-third of the world's steel and aluminum, and its crude steel demand is expected to rise by 4 percent in 2012. China's factories are often less efficient than their Western counterparts, which could account for some of these numbers; however, most of the factories built in the last ten to fifteen years are just as efficient as those found elsewhere in the world.

## Criterion IV: Energy Needs

Energy is a vital part of becoming an empire, and a country without its own energy resources or uninhibited long-term access to energy resources will not succeed in its role as a dominant superpower. According to available data, China has both its own resources and access to international resources. While the rest of the world was letting their financial markets implode through destructive transactions, China was busy with productive transactions in line with its long-term plan of modernization.

China was once the primary exporter of oil in Asia, but in 1993, that role changed when they became a net importer of oil for the first time. Today, due in part to the growth and industrialization taking place there, China has become the second-largest consumer of oil in the world behind the United States. This is a role that can be reversed, which is evident in America, which has now become a net exporter of oil—a new phenomenon given its historical dependence on foreign oil. Some will argue that America was forced into this choice by a volatile political climate in the oil regions as well as China's insatiable appetite for energy. However, China, unlike the United States, has looked beyond the Middle East for its energy needs.

The global price of oil and gas has been affected to no small extent by China's need for the black gold in its industrial growth. However, China has also set up huge deals around the globe to ensure that it can get the amount it needs, leaving high prices in its wake as it consumes oil and secures foreign reserves for its future needs.

China, already the largest importer of Middle Eastern oil, is buying over 10 percent of the oil exported by Gulf States and has secured long-term contracts in the region. It is now also Iran's largest customer and accounts for 23 percent of Iran's oil exports. The import of crude to China is expected to climb by half a million barrels per day for the next five years, and it is expected to be the largest importer in the world, passing the United States by 2030.(9)

## The China-Africa Connection

As mentioned before, China has pursued far more countries for its energy needs than the United States has. China has invested heavily in Africa over the past decade, creating much criticism and drawing controversy from various parts of the world, both in favor and against these actions. In the years leading up to 2008, in fact, the trade value between China and Africa was increasing at a rate of 40 percent each year. The situation was described as a win-win situation by the Chinese government, but there were critics, as well. Many questioned the effects of cheap Chinese goods on the African market, with the British conservative author Peter Hitchens going so far as to accuse the Chinese of creating a "slave empire" on the African continent.(10) However, advocates considered the situation to be good for Africa, claiming that it might provide more access to world markets for the continent and move them more into the world economy.

China has also set up oil ties in Sudan, where it has had to protect its interests as the world community has stepped up pressure to stop the atrocities in Darfur, which China has allegedly turned a blind eye to. This has led human rights groups to call foul on these and similar Chinese trade policies where the human and social cost is neglected.

The trades have definitely worked to China's benefit; today, one-third of their imported oil comes from Africa, which holds only 9 to 10 percent of the world's reserves. The nation of Angola is among the top four suppliers of oil to China; this group also includes Saudi Arabia, Iran, and Russia.(11)

## China, the Middle East, and the United States

China does not have a long tradition of strategic interests in the Middle East, but as it continues to have increased need of imported oil, its interests there have naturally increased; most of China's imported oil, around 60 percent, comes from the region, and that percentage is expected only to rise. The ties between China and the Middle East continue to be problematic for the United States and its own relations with China. The United States is considered by many Chinese leaders to be a threat to China's long-term energy security. The reason for this is their perception that the United States aspires to exercise increased control over the Persian Gulf and the energy resources there.

China's relationship with countries such as Iran, which poses a threat to the West, is a conundrum that could lead to a less-than-desirable end. It is alleged that China feeds state sponsors of terrorism with cash and arms in return for their needed oil. In turn, these arms and cash are used against the United States, its interests, and its allies. The United States, on the other hand, relies on Chinese investment funds and exports and on oil from the turbulent Middle East region, notably countries unfriendly to the "friends" of China. This has become a dangerous economic and political game, which can have undesired results for all the participants. Clearly, a long-term solution is needed before the unthinkable happens.

China's dubious relations with oil producers are not limited to Iran and its friends. China also has its own friction with neighboring countries in Asia over oil exploration. There is continued tension with Japan over oil supplies from Russia as well as parts of the East China Sea. There are also disputes at the border of the countries in regards to resources on the line of demarcation. China also has disputes with several countries in the South China Sea, where it is exploring for oil.

## The China–Western Hemisphere Connection

China has also begun a strong push into the western hemisphere for oil deals, including deals with Argentina, Peru, Ecuador, and Brazil. The main push in South America is with Venezuela, the fourth-largest supplier to the United States. In addition, China is seeking ambitious deals with Canada, the number-one supplier of petroleum to the United States. All of these deals make strange bedfellows, and the longer there are differing interests and worldviews in these regions, the more dangerous tensions become.(12)

## China's Energy Merger and Acquisition Spree

China has been on a tear for a few years, sealing deals in the oil, gas, and nuclear sectors to ensure that they can continue their growth. Below are listed details on mergers-and-acquisitions activity and high-profile deals for the past couple of years.

### China's Sinopec Deals:

In January, 2012, China's Sinopec Group, a state-owned oil company, agreed to invest $2.2 billion for a third of US oil- and-gas-producer Devon Energy Corp's interest in five developing fields as part of a long-term partnership. One month earlier, in December, 2011, Sinopec increased its stake in the Australia Pacific LNG joint venture from 15 percent to 25 percent and agreed to buy 3.3 million more tons of liquefied natural gas per year through 2035 from the project.

Going back one more month, to November, 2011, Sinopec reached an agreement to acquire a 30-percent stake in Galp Brazil Services, a division of Galp Energia SGPS SA of Portugal, for $3.54 billion. In October, 2011, Sinopec signed a deal to buy Canadian oil-and-gas explorer Daylight Energy Ltd for $2.1 billion. Earlier in 2011, Sinopec acquired a 15-percent stake in the coal seam project owned by ConocoPhillips and Australia's Origin Energy Ltd.

Sinopec acquired an 80-percent stake in Pecten Cameroon Company from Royal Dutch Shell PLC for $538 million from its subsidiary Addax Petroleum in November, 2011. SIPC, a unit of Sinopec, purchased an 18-percent stake in Chevron Corp's Indonesian deep-water project for $680 million in October, 2011.

### China National Offshore Oil Corporation (CNOOC Group) Deals:

CNOOC Ltd, China's top offshore oil company, formed a joint venture with Canada's Nexen Inc. in the Gulf of Mexico in November, 2011. CNOOC owns a 20-percent stake in three exploration wells and a 10- to 25-percent stake in three others. In November, 2011, CNOOC completed a $2 billion acquisition of Opti Canada Ltd.

In October, 2010, CNOOC bought a 33.3-percent interest in Chesapeake Energy Corp's Eagle Ford Shale gas project in southern Texas for $1.1 billion, and in January 2011 it bought a 33.3-percent stake in the Chesapeake's leasehold acres in northeastern Colorado and southeastern Wyoming for $570 million.

### Other Notable Energy Deals:

PetroChina Company Ltd acquired a 50-percent stake in British chemical group Ineos's European refining business in July, 2011. China's Guangdong Nuclear Power Corp took over Australia's Kalahari Minerals PLC, the top shareholder in one of the world's largest uranium projects, for $991 million in December, 2011.

This is a representative, but incomplete list of China's deals in the last two years alone, and it doesn't even take into account the billions that China spent in the five or six years prior to 2010 acquiring holdings globally in gas, oil, nuclear power, and exploration. In 2005, CNOOC lost out on an $18.5 billion bid for Unocal to Chevron due largely to stiff political opposition, but this opposition has been loosened since the change in administration in the US government.

The question of government versus private sector investments and acquisitions is a moot one in the case of China. There is an assumption that the government directly or indirectly owns most of the businesses. Further, it is alleged that industries that are not strictly government owned or controlled are not entirely private, either, when compared to Western private industries, due to the nature of the Chinese political and governmental structure.

### Economic Growth and Long Term Plans

China's growth over the last twenty to thirty years is not a sudden, unplanned boom. The Chinese government has been very meticulous and patient in its planning, and the results of this are unmistakable. Yet even as far as they have come, the plans are not slowing in the slightest. Other than the stated wish to curb the country's growth slightly to avoid inflationary pressures, they are pushing ahead with long-term plans set up in five-year milestones.

The International Energy Agency (IEA) predicted in their World Energy Outlook 2010 report that China's energy demand will increase by 75 percent over the next twenty-five years and that this growth will represent over 30 percent of the global increase in energy consumption. A year earlier, the IEA predicted that the energy growth in China between 2007 and 2030 would be thirty-one times higher than that in the United States.

Although the global trend, in words at least, is to move away from fossil fuels and toward alternative energy sources, over 50 percent of the projected increase in energy consumption is expected to be in fossil fuels. Electricity is expected to grow faster than any other form of energy, with oil, natural gas, and coal also seeing significant rises in use. China currently uses more than three times the coal that the United States consumes. Because of the increase in fossil fuel use, carbon dioxide emissions are also expected to increase significantly, to the tune of 21 percent, much to the chagrin of the green police in modern industrial nations.

China set a goal to reduce its emissions in 2005, with that goal being a reduction between 40 percent and 45 percent by 2020. The interim goal was a 20 percent decrease by 2010, and they came close with reductions in the range of 16 percent, reversing their previously upward trend. This will be harder to maintain as they move forward, because the expected growth is so high. The extra electricity-generating capacity that they are expected to add by 2025 is equal to the United States's current generating capacity, and most of it will be coal fired.

China is also seeking to increase its nuclear power capacity. The country currently has more nuclear plants under construction than any other country. By 2020, China expects to rely on nuclear power for 7 percent of its total power capacity. That amount of nuclear energy will surpass the United States's current total nuclear capacity, which is the largest in the world. China has entered into roughly $20 billion worth of business contracts with France for plants and uranium mining, as France is the second-largest generator of nuclear power behind the United States.

In addition to nuclear power, China plans to increase hydroelectric power capacity as well as wind and solar energy power, but because of the limited capabilities of wind and solar, exploiting these will not help reduce their coal usage to any measurable extent.(13)

## A Brief Summary of China's Global Deals

China's growth and expected growth cannot be fueled from purely internal sources, as we have seen. In order to sustain their growth rate and prevent their economy from being derailed from its long-term trajectory, the country has aggressively and proactively sought out energy and resource deals with countries the globe over. In some of the cases, China has invested a substantial amount of capital to build up the infrastructure and hence stake its claim in the region. Many have compared these deals to the territorial acquisition of the colonial powers. However, advocates argue they are very different.

Below is a summary of deals that China has made with many other nations around the globe, similar to and, in some cases, overlapping with the list of oil deals given earlier. These deals are seen as a necessary course of action, and many argue that they only could have happened under a political system like China's. I argue it could happen under any political or economic system, but there needs to be, at a minimum, at least a five-year plan in place. Without long-term planning, the country only focuses on the short-term trends and is doomed to fail when the long-term realities materialize.

## Africa

As we saw earlier, China has been busy securing deals in Africa for oil, iron ore, metals, and other commodities, primarily through providing resource-backed development loans for countries to build roads, hospitals, and other infrastructure. In 2009, China surpassed the United States as the largest trade partner with Africa. China, in contrast to the West, has focused on trade and commercially justifiable investments instead of heavily subsidized loans and aid grants.

The Chinese also do not try to tell the African nations how they should run their countries, nor do they make loans that are contingent upon reforms in their governments, as the West often does. This has commercial upsides but also allows and enables atrocities such as the slaughters in the Sudan to continue. China's two-pronged approach in Africa and elsewhere has been to have companies seek out business contracts while the government simultaneously courts the countries with diplomacy, aid, and debt forgiveness. This approach thus far has been very effective.(14)

China has also invested over $80 billion in Sudan, but their traditional policy of non-interference has morphed into more of a diplomatic role since South Sudan seceded from Sudan in July of 2011, when China became the chief negotiator over oil rights between the two countries. This diplomacy was recently tested in January of 2012, when twenty-nine Chinese workers were kidnapped by rebels loyal to South Sudan in the Sudanese state of South Kordofan.

In Nigeria, China signed a $23 billion deal with the government in May of 2010, after the death of the former president of the country, to build three refineries in the country, which will have a combined capacity of 900,000 barrels per day when they are completed in 2015. However, Angola is China's largest African trading partner, with over $120 billion invested by China and over 1.5 billion barrels of oil negotiated.

## Canada

Since 2001, China has had agreements with Canada for energy help, with a joint group formed to oversee research, exchange of expertise, and cooperation between energy companies in the two countries. This agreement was renewed again in February of 2012. Over a two-day period, China signed not only deals between itself and the Canadian government but also more than twenty commercial business deals valued at $3 billion.

In 2009, PetroChina acquired a 60-percent stake in Athabasca Oil Sands Corps in Canada for $1.7 billion. Canada has the second largest oil reserves in the world, and the estimates for the oil sands that they planned to exploit were for as many as 5 billion barrels.(15) Also in 2009, Sinopec bought ConocoPhillips's stake in the huge Syncrude project in Canada's oil sands for $4.65 billion. This was China's largest investment in North America to date.

## Latin America

In December of 2010, the State Grid Corporation of China bought seven Brazilian power-transmission companies for nearly $1 billion, with thirty-year concessions to operate the power transmission infrastructure in the densely populated southeastern region of Brazil.

The same month, China Petrochemical Corporation bought Occidental Petroleum Corporation's Argentinian unit for $2.45 billion, only two weeks after CNOOC paid $7.06 billion to take full control of Pan American Energy, LLC, the country's second-biggest oil and gas producer. In March of 2010, CNOOC bought a 50-percent stake in Bridas Corporation in Argentina, which has oil and gas assets in Argentina, Bolivia, and Chile. In October, 2010, Sinopec agreed to form a $17.8 billion dollar joint venture with Spanish oil company Repsol to exploit Repsol's Brazilian oil deposits.

Venezuela has long been a major supplier of oil to the United States, but since Hugo Chavez became president around thirteen years ago, the amount has dropped steadily, although in small scale so far. China has become an increasingly larger purchaser of Venezuelan crude oil under the Chavez regime.

In 2006, an agreement was made between Chavez and China to nearly double the barrels per day supplied to China's growing country, and in 2007, a series of overlapping deals was agreed to, wherein China has supplied over $20 billion of a promised $30 billion to Chavez for funding of his politically popular, but financially unsustainable giveaway programs. This deal has been criticized as good for the Chavez government, but bad for Venezuela, and it is seen as unconstitutional, as well. The Venezuelan constitution expressly prohibits the country's oil reserves from serving as loan guarantees, which is exactly what has happened in the China agreements.(16)

In 1999, when Chavez took office, Venezuela was shipping 1.5 million barrels of crude per day to the United States. In 2010, that number had dropped to 988,000 barrels per day, and in 2011, it was down to 955,000 barrels per day. The number of refined oil products shipped from Venezuela to the United States has dropped even more steeply, from 288,000 barrels per day in 2005 to a mere 79,000 barrels per day in 2011.

### The Middle East

As we have already discussed, Iran is the number-one supplier of imported oil to China. The deals with Iran for oil and gas are valued at over $120 billion, with a potential for over 8 billion barrels of oil. However, Iran is not the only Middle Eastern country that China has entered into deals with to ensure its energy sustainability.

China has become one of the biggest economic beneficiaries of the toppled Saddam Hussein regime in Iraq by securing deals for around 17 billion barrels of oil valued at about $50 billion. China is now the top customer of OPEC, ousting the United States from that position. China also reached a deal with Afghanistan at the end of 2011, which would give China access to around 87 million barrels of oil in some northeastern provinces. In 2008, China negotiated for 18.7 million barrels with Yemen for around $465 million. China's Sinopec recently sealed an $8.5 billion deal with Saudi Arabia for a joint-venture oil refinery. Saudi Arabia supplies almost twice as much petroleum to China as Iran does.

### The United States

The deal mentioned earlier with Origin Energy of Australia for a twenty-year LNG deal was a joint venture with US Company ConocoPhillips, as well. Also discussed earlier were the China deals with both Chesapeake Energy and Devon Energy, both of which give China access to shale deposits in the United States.

### Russia

In 2009, China reached a deal with Russia to give them $25 billion in loans to help their cash-strapped economy in return for a twenty-five-year supply of oil at 300,000 barrels per day. This deal was not seen as one to last due to Russia's history with oil deals, specifically BP, but through some price disputes that were recently resolved, the agreement is still in place almost three years later.

## Conclusion

There is no doubt anywhere about China's expected growth throughout the next decade and beyond. The only questions seem to be if they will suffer under inflationary pressure from growing too fast or if they will be able to make the shift from exports to domestic consumption without significant financial and political difficulties. The real questions are if they will become the primary controller of oil and gas in the world through continued deals with other nations, and if they will be allowed to continue to do so seemingly without restrictions.

If China becomes the replacement for OPEC in the world, the global political and diplomatic landscape could likely look very different from what the world has ever seen in the past. China seems to be building its empire based on its traditions as well as utilizing knowledge and best practices that have served the Western world in its global rise. China also methodically and systematically integrated itself into the world economic engine so that most commerce must now pass through China, as it did centuries before. The empire of China is on the rise once again.

# SECTION 4

## State of Affairs

*"A man must always live by his work, and his wages must at least be sufficient to maintain him. They must even upon most occasions be somewhat more, otherwise it would be impossible for him to bring up a family, and the race of such workmen could not last beyond the first generation."*

-Adam Smith's *An Inquiry Into the Nature and Causes of the Wealth of Nations* (1776)

CHAPTER 15

# The Gig Economy: Age of the Independent Worker

A number of descriptive terms have been used to describe the impact of the shifting economic picture on workers including post cubicle, freelance economy, hustle economy, e-economy, 1099 economy, and creative economy. Yet the term that is increasingly being accepted by people is "gig economy." If you look up the word gig, it is originally associated with musicians doing performances by engagement. The lack of permanence in the work gives you a clue as to why the new economy is being called a gig economy. Workers are going from independent job to independent job to earn a living, and this approach is transforming the workplace and the economy.

The term gig economy is attributed to Tina Brown, a former editor of *Vanity Fair* and the *New Yorker*, who wrote a January 12, 2009, column in the *Daily Beast* called "The Gig Economy." She started the piece by saying, "No one I know has a job anymore. They've got gigs."(1) What had started out as a journalistic curiosity soon became a startling realization that the economy's labor force was and is being restructured for better or worse.

The main point of Brown's article was the surprising fact that so many people now have gigs rather than full-time jobs. These individuals will often work multiple one-time jobs that enable them to pay their rent and hang on to their cars or other property. The article acknowledges that gigs have been around probably since the dawn of man, but something is different now. What has changed is the fact that "gigs" used to refer to part-time work or supplemental income, and now the gig work has turned into a primary source of income for many households.

The gig economy, which arguably began with displaced and other type of workers trying to find ways to pay essential bills despite losing a job or being unable to find a job in the first place, has taken on a life of its own. Gig workers are now represented by consultants, freelancers, independent contractors, part-time workers, self-employed workers, and temporary workers as well as transitional workers. Now more than ever, the gig economy is representative of independent workers who tired of waiting for the economy to show signs of positive change. Instead, these individuals are choosing to work as freelancers or contractors for their careers rather than being dependent on traditional businesses for their income and benefits.

The demographics of the gig economy participants are also varied. Gig economy workers is not just the desperate unemployed worker or the community college student who is having trouble competing in the job market against four-year degrees holders. The gig economy is increasingly composed of college graduates who are often from elite schools and have well-accomplished backgrounds in a variety of fields. Many of these well-educated and experienced workers are either supporting themselves or generating additional income as freelance workers or doing contracted work in the gig economy.

In 2009, Tina Brown was focused on workers unable to find full-time work in a difficult economy. Unfortunately, very little real change has occurred to spark meaningful job growth since that period. As of early 2012, the economy is only now starting to show signs of a possible recovery. However, millions of workers have already transitioned to the gig economy, and its growth appears to be outpacing the traditional economy, as well. The result of this economic transition is that traditional careers might be phasing out and being replaced by a new labor structure. How do you survive in an economy where there are few jobs even if you have a degree from an elite school?

This question embodies the sentiments among the different demographics of the gig economy. It is important to note that not everybody feels the same about their gigs or the economy, for that matter. As Tina Brown writes, "Welcome to the age of Gigonomics." And unfortunately, in the gig economy as well as the traditional economy, there are negative and positive opinions about gigs.

You can actually divide gig workers into two different categories. There are those who *want* to work as freelancers and those who *have* to work as freelancers to make ends meet. The people who want to work as freelancers stand a good chance of developing successful businesses in the new economy. On the other hand, those who prefer to work in a structured environment for the traditional employer might not find freelance work rewarding. These individuals might see themselves as part of the collateral damage of some corporate world downsizing initiative. They see their participation in the gig economy as only a temporary stint until the traditional economy picks up again. However, with all the uncertainty and global changes, another question should be contemplated by these individuals: will the traditional job market ever exist again?

### Freelance Surge and the Art of Peer Production

It would be easy to attribute the trend toward self-employment to the recession. However, this is a trend that was developing long before the recession, due in large part to the emergence of continuous streams of technological innovations. The actual recent trend toward freelancing or independent work began with the introduction of the Internet and has only expanded in scope by the recession. The freelance-work market has surged due to technology and the ability to network with people around the globe. Previously, the main obstacles holding people back from self-employment were the cost of setting up a business, marketing goods and services, and connecting with the workforce. Once those barriers were eliminated, the opportunities naturally expanded.

Tina Brown's original article about the gig economy talked about people "pretending" to enjoy the freedom of freelancing or self-employment. She calls their love of freelance work a "cover story" for people who are unable to find a job. Yet, you have to wonder how many people have found the impetus and encouragement to do what they really wanted to do with their careers now that traditional long-term employment is becoming a relic of an older and less global economic landscape. One really should pause and consider carefully whether the gig economy is just the natural end result of an economic shift that has been occurring over the last one hundred years from agricultural to industrial and now technological focus.

The fact is that technology has displaced, replaced, and changed our notions of how the labor force should be structured compared to the last century. In our current technological age, it is estimated that as many as 42 million Americans are independent or part-time workers. Many of these people are also holding more than one job. They work multiple part-time jobs, work for multiple employers, use a diverse set of skills, and work odd hours. Completely turning the idea of employment upside down, these workers are survivors who just may be on the cusp of a new type of workforce that is ripe for expansion. In fact, the freelance workforce has been referred to as the "Industrial Revolution of our time" by one author, because the current trend represents such a massive change in how we define work and even the American dream.(2)

The industries that play a part in the gig economy also include just about any industry you can think of, thanks again to innovations in technology. Freelancers are found in industries like healthcare, publishing, consulting, biological or chemical engineering, software development, insurance, graphic design, and administrative support. In fact, technology has made many jobs adaptable to contingency employment using contracted labor. Being able to work from home is often possible today because much work can be transmitted using e-mail attachments, cloud computing, or remote access of office systems.

The truth is the gig economy has always been around, but due to a variety of factors such as a weak traditional economy and globalization, the participation rate has been rising at an increasing rate. As mentioned, some people are participating voluntarily while others are forced into doing freelance or contract work out of need. Employers and the government have used contracted workers for hundreds of years, especially at the professional level. Engineers, consultants, marketers, and other professionals have routinely worked on a contracted basis. However, technology has made it possible for a wider range of jobs to be done in the virtual workplace rather than in an office or specialized work environment. So now you find freelancers like accountants, technical writers, and software developers working right at home.

The gig economy runs concurrently with the traditional economy. In fact, it is not a separate economy, but rather one that is integrated with the traditional economy. The freelancer or self-employed person may produce his or her own products or services independent of a traditional business or may actually sell to a traditional corporation. For example, an accountant can do bookkeeping and tax preparation for private clients or contract services to a business.

It should be noted, however, that traditional companies hiring independent workers do not treat all the workers the same. Some workers fare well by gaining benefits comparable to full-time employees' benefits during their contracted period, while others do not get benefits and may not get paid for some jobs for long periods of time. For example, the traditional employer United Parcel Service (UPS) has long employed part-time workers; however, UPS differs from other traditional companies in that it offers full benefits and additional perks such as tuition reimbursement to its part-time workforce. Unfortunately, UPS's treatment of non-full-time workers is not the norm, but the exception to the way traditional businesses treat workers. The reality, as many have witnessed, can often be bleak for independent workers laboring for traditional employers.

## Independent Worker vs. Traditional Employee

So how does this new work model compare to the traditional work model? "Work is work," as some people would say. And they would be correct to a certain extent, since some characteristics of the two work models are the same. For example, a certified public accountant working for herself and the CPA working for a corporation would have the same credentials despite working from alternate economies. However, there are plenty of differences between the two work models.

Workers' backgrounds, demographics, education levels, and experience vary among independent workers, just like in the traditional economy. Workers come from all racial, ethnic, and gender categories and represent low-income high school graduates to well-educated and experienced workers. The type of work varies by worker classification and ranges from the professional level to part-time level. Contractors include people like accountants, consultants, landscapers, lawyers, musicians, web developers, writers, and photographers. Part-time work typically includes jobs like dog walkers, delivery personnel, gardeners, and fast food workers.

**Length of Employment/Employment Uncertainty** People working in traditional jobs used to have careers spanning over thirty or more years, and then they would retire with a decent pension. However, the length of employment and the certainty of that employment are changing. Some employees change jobs on an average of every four to five years. Today, the average traditional worker has about ten jobs over his or her work life.

In the gig economy, the independent worker has a series of jobs that range from one day to years depending on worker classification and the type of work. For example, a gardener may be hired to work for one day, while the engineer may work for two years on the same project. Increasingly, traditional jobs are becoming more uncertain due to layoffs and cutbacks, and the people in this group transition over to the gig economy or unemployment ranks if they cannot land jobs.

**Typical Job Duties** Typical job duties also fluctuate. The traditional job could have a set of job functions as outlined in the job description. Some contractors work in a single field or job, while others work on a variety of different projects and jobs.

**Earnings and Wages** Traditional employees may get paid a predetermined hourly rate or a salary and have opportunities for earning additional compensation in different ways, such as overtime, stock bonuses, stock ownership plans, and profit sharing. The gig economy participants may work on an hourly or contracted basis also, but additional compensation such as stock ownership or profit sharing opportunities are usually not available. The contracted or part-time rate varies based on the worker's classification and the length of employment contracts.

**Simultaneous Jobs and Quality of Work** For both the traditional worker and the gig worker, the quality of work completed tends to decrease when doing multiple projects in the span of time that would normally require full attention to a single project. While both workers might be required to perform simultaneous jobs, it may be more likely that gig workers will have to take on multiple jobs.

**Time Management** In traditional employment, time management is important to complete job duties and meet deadlines. For those that consistently fail to manage their time, the results can be demotion or job termination. In the gig economy, those who cannot manage their time or projects may see dire results, and costs can carry forward to potential new contracts or projects. A poor reputation as an independent worker can also lead to a lack of new opportunities.

**New Projects/Jobs** The typical employee at a business is often given duties or projects to complete that the company has already procured. In certain positions, like a salesperson, leads are given, and the employee has to close the deal in order to acquire the project.

In the gig economy, contractors have a variety of options for seeking new employment. They can work with a fee-based organization, secure work through non-fee-based networks, pursue work through job banks or agencies, get leads or make sales through a website, and so on. Independent workers cannot always count on someone to create jobs for them like in a traditional economy. They must seek out and often create their own opportunities.

In both the traditional and gig economies, additional educational or certification is required for certain types of jobs. For example, insurance salespersons, accountants, architects, engineers, and other professionals must have a license and/or degree or certification in order to secure certain jobs.

**Work Life Balance** Traditional employers offer vacation days as well as sick days that are paid or unpaid to offset the usually inflexible schedules. In traditional jobs, some employers expect employees they did not layoff to assume the duties of multiple laid-off employees. This may lead to an increase in hours and duties with the same or lower pay in certain cases.

One of the advantages of working in the gig economy includes having more flexibility in scheduling. However, on average, gig workers also tend to work more hours than traditional workers do.

**Health Insurance and Other Benefits** Traditional employment provides at least some minimum level of benefits or offers discounts for group benefits. These benefits include health insurance, disability and life insurance, pension plans, and education benefits. Gig economy participants must provide all of their own insurance or other benefits and or seek discounts through organizations covering self-employed workers.

**Retirement Programs** Generally, traditional employees have access to company-sponsored retirement programs whether 401(k), 403(b), or 457 plans. Some traditional programs allow employer-matching contributions. Gig economy workers pay for individual retirement plans that are available, and usually obtain these plans through programs offered by organizations that emulate traditional employer programs.

The simplified employee pension plan (SEP) allows either employers or the self-employed to contribute to a retirement account. The contribution is made directly to an individual retirement account or annuity (SEP-IRA). There are different kinds of IRAs based on their tax treatment, including the traditional IRA and Roth IRA. Gig economy participants, however, must pay their own fees and make their own contributions to maintain certain retirement programs; and that can be quite costly.

**Layoffs and Unemployment Benefits** Traditional employees are usually eligible for unemployment benefits if they are laid off or terminated from a job, because state law requires employers to pay into an unemployment fund for each employee. Some contractors and self-employed individuals may also be eligible to collect unemployment if they meet conditions as defined by applicable labor or employment laws. For example, they may be eligible if they fit certain state title classification requirements such as being long-term contractors or former military personnel. However, in most cases the self-employed are only eligible for unemployment compensation if they paid into the state fund for unemployment insurance. Some states offer self-employment assistance to qualified individuals. Since each state is different, if you are thinking you would qualify, you should contact your state office and confirm eligibility for these programs.

## Why is the Gig Economy participation rate increasing?

The gig economy is growing as a result of a number of factors. Those factors include technology, the recession that led to a reduction in the traditional workforce, globalization that caused a change in job structures, and a desire of workers to take control of their work life as job insecurity grows in traditional employment. In fact, some people choose to enter the gig economy because they believe that many of the benefits that used to come with traditional employment, like job security and guaranteed pension plans, are now gone, so they might as well work for themselves. Another reason for the growth in the gig economy is the fact that one person in a two-income household can now work from home using a computer and be able to take care of family at the same time.

So who exactly makes up the gig economy? It is an eclectic mix of people of all ages, genders, ethnicities, and races. Precise numbers are not maintained, but using US Bureau of Labor Statistics (BLS) gathered over the years, it is generally agreed that approximately one-third of the American workforce is in the gig economy as freelance or contracted workers. The BLS estimates that the labor force has grown from 154 million workers in 2008 to about 160 million workers in 2012. This means that the number of gig workers, as one-third of the American workforce, has also grown from about 50 million in 2008 to about 53 million in 2012. Again, these workers include consultants, freelancers, independent contractors, part-time workers, self-employed workers, temporary workers, and transitional workers.

The rapid increase in the gig economy participation rates is explained by many factors that were mentioned. However, besides the obvious reasons, like advancing technology, there are also business and market reasons that are contributing to the growth in the gig economy.

## Business Cycle: Recession

In other words, businesses and markets are driving the growth in the independent workforce. First is the fact the traditional economy is currently still at a low point in the business cycle, and it appears that a return to full economic growth is not expected for many years. The expectation of continued instability in the traditional labor market is leading people to depend on themselves for employment. Some of the millions of people in the gig economy will remain independent workers even after the economy normalizes. There are also freelancers who are in the gig economy because it provides temporary employment while the business cycle is at its low point. Once the economy picks up again and the job market expands, they will return to traditional employment.

The recession has led to many changes in the business world. Big name corporations that were viable before the recession went bankrupt due to things like low demand for goods and services, high costs of doing business, and failed marketing strategies. They include large employers like Borders, Circuit City, Marshall Field and Company, Washington Mutual, and KB Toys. Over eight million traditional jobs have been lost and are not being replaced. Two years after the official end of the Great Recession, the unemployment rate remains above 8 percent, forcing people to find alternative employment.

In addition, many of the replacement jobs that are being created are lower skilled and lower paying jobs than those that existed before the recession. New hires are being paid less. This is partly due to the massive loss of manufacturing jobs in the United States that traditionally paid good wages with good benefits attached. Instead of making goods, the economy is increasingly making value through financial products like derivatives or by creating lower paying service jobs.

The business foreclosures crossed industries, too, which indicates that there are other factors at play. The recession saw major chain bookstores, banks, clothing stores, electronics stores, and many others decide to close their doors over the last few years. This reflects the fact that many traditional firms still have not adapted to a flexible business model that can compete effectively in an increasingly global market environment. Consumers have many choices today due to technology, and businesses that fail to recognize changing consumer behaviors or increasing globalized competition are doomed to fail.

### Business Culture: Mismanagement and Failures

The traditional economy has also been roiled by business losses from failed investment ventures ushered in by Internet companies that do not add directly to their bottom lines, investment firms that steer some companies away from core business strategies, and poor managerial decisions encouraged by short-term earnings requirements of investors and Wall Street.

The gig economy is also being forced to grow due to the fact that some traditional employers lay off workers and rehire them as reclassified contractors or part-time workers. This is primarily so they do not have to pay benefits or so they can reduce the cost of benefits in addition to eliminating other rights the worker would have had as a full-time employee. Hiring contracted workers also gives the employer more flexibility in terms of labor-force expense management. Unlike full-time employees, independent or part-time workers can simply be told that they are no longer needed.

## Jaded Employees

Of course, these actions by traditional employers have created a suspicious workforce. Thousands of jaded employees are voluntarily leaving traditional employment in order to pursue more personally satisfying and fulfilling work and projects. They have that option because technology is providing the means to archive this independence and allowing them to work on jobs from around the globe without leaving the country. No matter what the reason is for joining the gig economy, the reality is that there are a lot of obstacles and challenges that are posed to this group of independent workers.

## Independent Workers' Critical Challenges and Solutions

Sara Horowitz, CEO of Freelancers Union, and other advocates are calling for reform to the nation's benefits, insurance, and tax systems in order to create a more level playing field for independent workers. Right now, they are penalized for being self-employed, because they often do not have access to affordable benefits like health insurance and unemployment insurance.

One of the problems with bringing about change to the traditional benefits market is that the government is not even counting independent workers right now—seriously. The number of gig workers must be pieced together by adding up different groups like entrepreneurs and part-time workers. Since the government does not recognize that one-third of the workforce is made up of gig workers, it does not make laws, regulations, or policies that recognize this economic component. Independent workers must muddle through a disparate private benefits market that is not friendly to those who work for themselves. The traditional economy ties one job to each worker, and that simply does not reflect the gig workforce. (3)

Here are a few of the challenges and solutions to this dilemma:

## Separate Jobs from Benefits

Problem: Linking benefits coverage based on a single employer cuts the gig worker out of the benefits system.
Solution: Decouple health insurance, unemployment insurance, and other benefits from traditional employers' control, and create portable and affordable benefits and insurance programs.

### Reform Unfair Tax Code

Problem: Gig workers are penalized because they must pay employee and employer payroll taxes.
Solution: Pay some taxes quarterly rather than annually and reduce the amount of the employee portion.

### Reform Work Conditions

Problem: It is currently difficult for independent workers to organize or form representative groups like traditional unions. This means gig workers are not represented by lobbyists, either, so their unified voices are not heard by government.
Solution: Create a governmental or private entity that can enforce and provide legal recourse for workers who are mistreated in a physical or online workplace or not paid for completed work.

### Increase Economies of Scale and Reduce Costs

Problem: Traditional employers enjoy economies of scale depending on their size.
Solution: Form an organized network that could aid in achieving some of the cost reductions that economies of scale provide. Gig workers could see a reduction in fees, resource costs, insurance premiums, manufacturing processes costs, etc.

## Organizational Efforts

So what exactly has been done so far in the private sector to fill the health and other benefits gaps that gig workers sometimes lack? Much of the effort to improve benefits accessibility for gig workers has been done by Freelancers Union. This group was started by Sara Horowitz in 2001 under the parent organization, Working Today, which is also a nonprofit organization she founded in 1995.

Freelancers Union is not a traditional union recognized by the government, so it does not have collective bargaining power to deal with issues like workers' rights, wages, or work conditions. It advocates for members on issues such as affordable insurance, taxation, and unpaid wages. The group is also a forum for independent workers interested in networking. The group has seen continuous growth over the years and now has over 171,000 members.

The Portable Benefits Network (PBN) created by Freelancers Union offers traditional insurance and other services at steep discounts. Freelancers Union was criticized by Congressional members and the public when it created its own for-profit Freelancers Insurance Company rather than providing discounts for traditional insurance. Though the co-op insurance company is a separate for-profit organization, it shares a board and employees with Freelancers Union. The co-op sells insurance to independent workers.

In early 2012, the US Department of Health and Human Services provided about $340 million in loans to Freelancers Union. The purpose of these loans was for Freelancers Union to establish insurance co-ops in three states as part of President Obama's healthcare reform efforts. This loan was not without controversy, however. Freelancers Union and the Democrats were accused of cronyism, because Freelancers Union had made a donation previously to the Democratic Party. However, Freelancers Union is only trying to make healthcare affordable for independent workers and small businesses.

Also, this was part of a larger initiative to provide $638 million in funding for healthcare co-operatives in eight states across the country that provides coverage to individuals and small businesses. So it is unclear what these political detractors were trying to accomplish by associating the loans to earlier donations, considering that many businesses and organizations make countless donations to many political parties. What they should be doing is insisting that the government do more to help the independent worker, because they might be part of that group in the future.

## Governmental Role and Functions in the Gig Economy

Consumer confidence is a significant driving force in any economy, and it determines whether individuals are going to willingly engage in economic activity such as buying goods and services. Consumer demand affects businesses and overall economic activity and can quickly make or break a business. During the financial collapse leading to the Great Recession of 2008 to 2010, the economy contracted as consumer confidence and demand dropped sharply. Since then, the government and taxpayers have spent trillions of dollars supporting economic policies designed to encourage consumer demand and keep the weakening economy afloat.

The government can have an enormous impact on the overall economy through legislation and policy implementation. For the economy to thrive, all of its components must be healthy. For example, one of the forces behind the sluggish recovery from the recession is the bottomed housing market. Until the housing market improves, the economy as a whole cannot improve.

The same is true of the job and labor market. If one-third of the workforce is working as independent workers, entrepreneurs, freelancers, or contract workers, then they must be encouraged and have access to support systems like those that the rest of the labor force does. Therefore, by enacting legislation and policies that promote economic security for independent workers, the government promotes a healthy gig economy that benefits society as a whole.

Following are a few ways the government can help in this endeavor:(4)

- Provide access to traditional job protections like unemployment insurance, health insurance, and retirement plans
- Enact tax laws to level the playing field between traditional and nontraditional employees
- Protect the rights of workers over the rights of corporations and businesses by decoupling household necessities such as insurance to make the access to benefits independent of the employee-employer relationship
- Grant independent workers the ability to organize in a meaningful way to address fair government and employer standards
- Provide more financial support for independent workers and entrepreneurs, since they are often the foundation of our economy

It is also important for the government to start maintaining meaningful data on independent workers to show accurate statistics about this group. The statistical information can then be used to formulate policies that address some of the issues concerning the gig workers. Because independent workers are a growing force in the US economy, it is to everyone's benefit to fully acknowledge and embrace them. As of right now, many gig economy participants are not even factored into the unemployment rate even when looking for traditional employment. Since they are not considered to be actively looking for work due to having a form of employment, they are left out of the statistics. This means that the unemployment rate should technically be higher than it is if some of the temporary jobs are not factored in—but politically, that will probably never happen whether there is a democrat or republican in office. It just does not make political sense.

## Future of the Gig Economy

How will the gig economy affect the traditional economy over the long term? Will it replace the traditional employment structure as globalization transforms economies globally and makes the workforce more decentralized?

These questions are not easy to answer. Though the gig workers account for one-third of the workforce, their lack of recognition as a group and the lack of hard data make it difficult to fully understand their economic impact. However, the current insufficiency of financial security is a serious barrier to self-employment. It is a sign of the job market's poor condition that so many people are working for themselves, despite the insecurity.

Independent workers and entrepreneurs support the economy in good times and bad, and more importantly, they create jobs when traditional companies fail to do so. In addition, the independent workers being hired by companies as contingent workers are now representing most professions, which means opportunities will grow as companies expand their use of contracted workers.(5)

If I were making a prediction about the direction of the traditional economy and the role of the gig economy, it would have to be that the gig economy will continue to grow rapidly. This is in response to two factors: Employers will continue to cut costs to remain competitive, requiring continued reductions in traditional labor costs. Globalization and technology will continue to drive changes in the way we have always done business.

Eventually, society will need to find a way to redefine "employment" and to develop adaptive laws and policies that embrace rather than exclude a large segment of the workforce. In the meantime, it might be a good idea to brush up on your gigonomics.

CHAPTER 16

# Technological Innovations in Commerce

Technology has been driving—and has been driven by—commerce, quite literally for centuries. We need only think of the results of key technological developments in history, from the successive adoption of bronze, iron, and steel for weapons to the ability to navigate across oceans to the Industrial Revolution to the adoption of the computer, to see massive, fundamental economic transformations.

Over the last twenty-five to thirty years, the widespread adoption first of the microcomputer in both home and business settings and then of the Internet—particularly broadband access—have both created new trends and accelerated the pace of change. Here, we will examine how these recent technological innovations have impacted commerce and what they are likely to mean for the future.

## Some Background

In the simplest terms, electronic commerce (inevitably abbreviated to e-commerce) is merely the transaction of business via electronic data—a succinct definition courtesy of the *Economist*.(1) But we have been conditioned since the advent of the Internet to associate the *e* with all things web-based, and indeed, electronic data is far less powerful without a network to move it quickly, easily, and almost instantaneously from place to place.

The credit card, for example, would be a much less useful innovation absent the ability to verify available credit and prevent fraud at the point of sale. Few card issuers would be willing to take on the tremendous risks that would result in such a situation, and rates would inevitably be much higher. While pre-Internet card transactions certainly existed, they were slower, thanks to the need to dial directly into the appropriate computer system; they were also more expensive and much less ubiquitous—no card terminals for taxicabs, mall kiosks, or sidewalk vendors. The Internet, especially in conjunction with data-capable mobile phone networks, has changed that.

Technology (and henceforth that term will be a blanket reference to the combination of computer, wireless, and Internet technologies) has made commerce faster and cheaper. The *Economist* points to a 1999 study by Forrester Research that used stock trading as one example of this impact. Before online trading, an equity trade cost an average of $100. Afterward, the cost fell to about $15.(2) Since 1999, it has fallen even further; many online brokers now offer commission rates for standard trades that are under $10.

The same technology has radically reduced many costs for businesses. In banking, for example, if we set the cost of a face-to-face transaction with a teller at a completely fictional and simplified-for-our-purposes cost of $1, a telephone transaction would cost about $0.50, and an ATM transaction would cost about $0.25. The cost of an Internet transaction would then probably be about $0.01.(3) It is easy to see why banks are doing their best to discourage customers from setting foot inside the lobby of the local branch. Sustainable cost reduction is a significant incentive that directly impacts future profitability.

At the same time, technology has opened up markets that were not previously available to companies, at least not without a tremendous expansion of their footprint. Amazon has no need to build a global network of stores to sell books (and now so much more) to customers worldwide, and one need only look at the 2011 bankruptcy of Borders, which was forced to liquidate its remaining 399 stores after a bankruptcy court auction attracted little in the way of bids, to see the efficacy of the new business model versus the old.(4)

It is not only access to customers that has benefitted from technology, as the example of bank transaction costs demonstrated. The concept of "just in time" (JIT) logistics is one that could not be fully realized in the absence of new technologies.

For any firm that holds inventory, its stockpile of raw materials or finished goods represents money held hostage. Not only is it held hostage, it is also subject to shrinkage (loss due to damage, spoilage, or theft) and even obsolescence in some cases. The ideal, of course, would be to have on hand only what is actually needed to fill customer orders or, in the case of a retail store, keep the sales floor shelves stocked.

The first industry to move to JIT replenishment was manufacturing—Toyota was the first, as the practice originated in Japan in the 1950s. It saw widespread adoption by manufacturers in the 1970s.(5) At that time, it required dedicated systems that interconnected manufacturers, component suppliers, and raw material sources in order to feed parts and materials to the assembly line only as they were required by production needs. The practice benefitted the companies all along the supply chain, since they all gained predictability and had no need to maintain large inventories as a hedge against unexpected demand.

Technology—combined with such innovations as the widespread use of optical barcode scanning and now radio-frequency identification (RFID) tags—not only made JIT cheaper and more effective but also allowed its practical application in a wider range of industries. Retailers like Wal-Mart were quick to adopt the practice, especially since it integrated quite naturally with existing point-of-sale barcode scanning.

JIT has benefitted every industry that has adopted it, but it has proved a particular boon to logistics companies like FedEx and UPS. These companies adopted systems that allow near-real-time tracking of shipments and became major partners in JIT inventory and logistics management for many businesses. To their credit, these types of time-critical services have allowed these traditional shippers to provide more than just parcel delivery. They are on pace to outcompete the US Postal Service, and some suggest they will usher in the demise of the service, which is desperately lagging behind in providing comparable services.

### Competing on the Global Stage

Much has been made over the past two decades of how large businesses are squeezing out small businesses and "mom and pop" shops. Wal-Mart has been continually vilified in this regard, and even the romantic comedy *You've Got Mail* pitted the heartless corporate chain bookstore against a small local bookshop. Some industries have seen small businesses shaken out by the larger enterprises. However, thanks to technology, smaller businesses are finding new ways to survive and even compete against their bigger counterparts. The proper use of technology indeed has the potential to catapult small companies higher up the economic food chain than they would otherwise be. The twin facts that a brick-and-mortar location is no longer a necessity and that the Internet allows a business to reach customers anywhere mean that a niche business—even a highly specialized niche business—can now thrive. That's not to say that being "found" on the Internet is always easy, but an entire industry devoted to search engine optimization has now sprung up to facilitate these solutions, as well.

Technology doesn't provide only downstream access to customers. Small businesses can also benefit from upstream access to suppliers. Sites like Alibaba.com provide a forum in which suppliers of any size located anywhere in the world, can offer their products to buyers of any size located anywhere in the world. A small home-based Internet retailer in the United States can find products at a lower wholesale cost from a manufacturer that might be located in Vietnam or Malaysia.

You should not assume that consumers are predisposed toward online retailers located in their own country, either. BorderJump, an international e-commerce facilitator, surveyed 7,600 Latin American and Caribbean consumers, a majority of whom said they preferred US e-commerce sites over those tailored specifically for their home country.(7) Fully three-quarters of US online retailers were selling abroad in 2009, and of those, 14.5 percent generated more than a quarter of total sales from outside the United States.(8)

This trend has created yet another business niche: the third-party provider of payment and/or shipping services for international customers. While an existing payment processing platform on an e-commerce website might be sufficient for processing payments from abroad (assuming it integrates a currency converter, which many do not), fulfillment is another matter entirely. Dealing with the customs and postal regulations and taxes that vary from country to country, to say nothing of understanding the best means of assuring delivery once the merchandise enters the destination country, is a highly specialized set of tasks best handled by an expert in the field. Such companies also offer websites tailored to the country in question, as well.

## Regulatory Environment

What governments love most about commerce, in any form, is the fact that it generates tax revenues. Commerce, by its very nature, also produces legal disputes. Both of these issues become more complicated in an e-commerce environment, particularly when that environment crosses national borders.

One of the most contentious and publicly debated issues in the United States has been the collection of state and local sales taxes on online purchases. A 1992 Supreme Court decision, Quill v. North Dakota, exempted retailers from having to collect sales taxes in states where they had no physical presence (the legal term for which is nexus). That has led to the public perception that Internet purchases are not subject to sales tax, which is not true.

The mere fact that retailers are not required to collect the sales tax does not mean the purchase is entirely exempt from it. State laws require the person or entity making the purchase to pay the appropriate sales tax directly, and many states that levy income taxes include a line on individual income tax returns for the reporting of any such sales taxes owed. In reality, few people actually report and pay what they owe, and enforcement is practically impossible.

The Supreme Court did note in its Quill v. North Dakota decision that Congress has the authority to change the treatment of nexus and require the collection of sales taxes, but to date, that has not occurred. State and local governments complain that they lose substantial revenues to online retailing; a University of Tennessee study concluded that the amount lost was $7.7 billion in 2008.(9) Other concerns include the competitive disadvantage that local businesses suffer, since their prices will be higher by at least the 4 percent to 9 percent that is typical for sales tax; the loss of vital revenue to schools, law enforcement, infrastructure, and other services supported by sales taxes; and the regressive nature of online sales tax evasion since it favors those with computers, Internet access, and credit cards.(10)

Another common, if understandable, myth centers on the Internet Tax Freedom Act (ITFA), which was passed in 1998 with a three-year term and extended to 2003 and again to 2007. The ITFA prohibited new (but not preexisting) state and local taxes on Internet access and "multiple or discriminatory" taxes imposed on Internet commerce. It did not, however, void traditional state and local taxing authority.(11)

Businesses that operate online, whether partially or entirely, are subject to essentially the same regulations as traditional brick-and-mortar firms. Licenses, fees, taxes, and applicable laws are generally determined by the state and locale in which the company is domiciled. This has been the subject of debate as the concept of nexus has been scrutinized by states seeking tax revenue. It has also led to such conflicts as California modifying its sales tax legislation to impose it on companies with "subsidiaries or affiliated companies" within its borders; in response, Amazon claimed that its business unit that developed the Kindle—which is located in California—is a division separate from its e-commerce operations.(12)

The United Nations has identified the significant legal issues affecting transnational e-commerce as jurisdiction, choice of law, and dispute resolution mechanisms. Some of these become even thornier in the case of purely digital transactions that involve no physical product, which are becoming increasingly common. It is also a major concern in the case of deliberate fraud, when the perpetrators may base themselves in a country that has little in the way of enforcement or international cooperation mechanisms.

More broadly, technology raises questions of contract law (purely electronic signatures, for example), electronic recordkeeping, and even the nature of an appropriate chain of evidence in the case of civil disputes or criminal prosecution. The United States addressed many of these issues in 2000 with the E-Sign Act, and the UN offers model legislation governing e-commerce, e-signatures, and electronic contracting.

Finally, technology has created huge issues of intellectual property protection, exemplified by the very-public debates and civil legal actions over music and movie file sharing and widespread piracy of software in particular, with China being one of the worst offenders. The ability to protect purely digital intellectual property is another niche business opportunity, though the battle against piracy represents an ongoing "arms race," and the challenge has perplexed even the likes of Microsoft.

## Emerging Mobile Technologies

One of the greatest challenges of e-commerce is the speed with which the environment changes. Moreover, because the marketplace is global, an innovation that is just now taking hold in certain countries may have already been superseded in others or may be unavailable in certain markets because the necessary infrastructure doesn't yet exist (a data-capable mobile phone network, for example).

A major rapidly developing trend is mobile technology and mobile e-commerce, spurred by the proliferation of smart phones and high-speed data networks. This mobile Internet emphasis has three main consequences for e-commerce:

**The need to develop mobile platform-friendly websites.** An e-commerce site that is difficult to use from a phone or tablet will quickly be discarded in favor of a site that is easier to use.

**The ability to integrate GPS-based location data.** Knowing where a consumer is right now allows targeted advertisements, discount offers, and other real-time promotion strategies. It also raises significant privacy issues.

**A move toward mobile-device-based payments.** Appropriate software and encryption systems permit the mobile device to be used for payment, further advancing cashless payments but also creating security concerns.

Contactless transactions such as those based on a mobile device use technologies like near-field communication (NFC), which is fast and secure.

Beyond cashless payments, NFC supports information interchange, coupons and loyalty programs, and even access control. It is an open-standards system with built-in support for a variety of security schemas.(13)

## Cashless System

Technology is rapidly bringing us toward a cashless system. Debit cards are now routinely used for transactions of nominal value, for example, and J.P. Morgan Chase recently debuted its QuickPay system, which allows a Chase account holder to send money to any individual who has a mobile number or e-mail address and a US bank account. It is this ability to pay a person—who is obviously not capable of processing a credit or debit card transaction—that had been one of the main obstacles to a cashless transaction system, though companies like PayPal had already started breaking down those barriers.

The major remaining obstacle, however, is the "unbanked," the substantial number of people who do not have any sort of bank account. Companies like Wal-Mart that deal extensively with this group of consumers have introduced innovations like debit cards that are not linked to a bank account, so options do exist for those willing to use them. Objections to disenfranchising the unbanked, however, are likely to remain the most significant roadblock on the path to a cashless system—and overcoming this disenfranchisement represents a significant business opportunity.

Unfortunately, the inherent distrust that some people have of the banking system has only been exacerbated by the 2008 financial crisis and the ongoing troubles in Europe. This distrust and the need to create a decentralized payment system have led to some intriguing innovations. One such innovation is the bitcoin, a purely digital currency. While the technical workings of the bitcoin are complex and highly technical, involving public-key encryption, hashing algorithms, and digests, the underlying principle is actually something that can be embraced by individuals such as economist Milton Friedman.

Friedman once called for the abolition of the US Federal Reserve, saying that it should be replaced by an automated system capable of increasing the money supply at a fixed and predetermined rate.(14) Such a system would eliminate inflation. The bitcoin, which achieves this goal, was created in 2009 by a programmer working under the assumed name Satoshi Nakamoto. It operates on a peer-to-peer network (think of file-sharing services like BitTorrent) that enables irreversible payments and is based on nodes broadcasting to the network which then records them in a public history that essentially verifies the validity of all circulating bitcoins. This "currency" is normally stored in a virtual wallet on the owner's hard drive, though it can also be forwarded to an exchange (which functions in many respects like a bank) or even converted to paper form.

A fundamental difference from traditional currency is that bitcoins are created at a fixed rate, which is actually set to slow over time. The current creation rate averages 300 bitcoins per hour, but that will fall by half in 2013, by half again in 2017, and so forth every four years.(15) In this way, the currency avoids the need for a virtual mint or central bank, which is what governs the supply of a physical currency.

Ironically enough, it is the lack of any central governing authority that makes the bitcoin unattractive to many people. While its proponents trumpet the very fact that there is no central bank controlling the bitcoin (and diluting its value through such actions as the Federal Reserve's quantitative easing programs), most people are uncomfortable with the concept of a currency that is not underwritten by some central authority and exists only in the sometimes obscure world of the Internet. The world, it seems, is not ready for a "community-based" currency.

## Digital Manufacturing

Another emerging technology with the potential to fundamentally alter a long-standing pillar of commerce—manufacturing—is the 3D printer. Known informally as the RepRap, which is short for "replicating rapid prototyper," this device has a thermoplastic extruder at its heart. Driven by software, it can produce essentially any component (within size limits imposed by the printer, of course) that can be replicated in plastic. In fact, the RepRap is even capable of self-replication, though certain components cannot be made of plastic. The basic concept for RepRap is that its design and supporting software can be distributed online, and a single printer can in turn produce more printers. These RepRep machines are continuously bringing new innovations to this niche industry. The RepRap has developed a cult following and has inspired many innovations that have gone beyond its original plastic replications. The goal for this group is to be able to create a machine that can replicate itself by manufacturing all its parts, including plastic, metal, and other components. This may seem like science fiction today, but it is becoming a reality thanks to these individuals' ingenuity, open-source programs, and technical ability.

This is merely the latest form of decentralized manufacturing. While there are certain manufacturing processes that require heavy equipment or specialized environments (think of steel production or microprocessor manufacturing), many common consumer goods are composed of fairly simple materials that can be assembled relatively easily. Combined with powerful computer-assisted design (CAD) software, appropriate equipment can be used in remote locations or non-commercial environments to manufacture a wide range of products that might not otherwise reach that market. It also presents the opportunity to offer an unprecedented level of customization for many goods.

## Conclusion

Technology—particularly the wide-ranging and nearly instantaneous communication provided by the Internet and the massive calculating power offered by modern computers—continues to change commerce, and at a steadily-increasing pace. It has in many ways democratized commerce, enabling a single small shop to potentially buy or sell globally, and unchaining tremendous manufacturing power from the massive and expensive factory of the nineteenth and twentieth centuries. These changes—and those yet to come—will be detrimental to some businesses but will create many more opportunities for the savvy investor and entrepreneur.

# SECTION 5
## Solutions for a Better Tomorrow

*"Your imagination and your initiative, and your indignation will determine whether we build a society where progress is the servant of our needs, or a society where old values and new visions are buried under unbridled growth. For in your time we have the opportunity to move not only toward the rich society and the powerful society, but upward to the Great Society."*

-President Lyndon B. Johnson, "The Great Society" (1964)

CHAPTER 17

# Government Financial Tools and Effect on Behavior

Federal, state, and local governments are three of the most powerful influences in our lives, and how these entities wield that influence determines public and business behavior in many instances. One of the ways influential power is exercised is through the passage of financial laws, regulations, tax credits, and grants. These financial tools are often viewed merely as laws, but they drive people and businesses to act in a certain way every day. Another way to state this is that the government uses financial tools to achieve policy outcomes.

Financial tools used by the government to influence public and business behavior can be thought of as incentives or as punishments. There are incentives to act a certain way, but there are penalties when behavior does not meet government expectations. In fact, imposing financial penalties is the primary strategy used to motivate people and businesses to act in a certain way.

The desired behaviors government tries to control through financial tools can be sorted into three main categories: behaviors that promote an orderly society, behaviors that promote the well-being of society's members, and behaviors that are culturally considered to be ethical.

For example, there are parking fines to ensure that vehicles park in certain places and do not present risks to other drivers, which contributes to an orderly society. There are taxes on cigarettes intended to discourage smoking and promote citizen well-being, while also reducing public healthcare costs. Corporate fines encourage ethical business behavior with the intent of minimizing victimization of consumers and investors.

Considering the many goals of government in just this one area of affecting public and business behaviors, it is not surprising that there are tens of thousands of laws passed already. In fact, it was reported by analysts that 40,000 new federal and state bills went into effect January 1, 2012.

(1) Many of these laws include fines and penalties intended to promote certain behaviors. For example, a new federal law imposes trucker and bus driver fines of up to $2,700 if the driver uses a hand-held cell phone while driving.(2) Obviously, the intent of the law is to discourage commercial drivers from getting distracted while talking on cell phones.

Do these financial tools work? The answer is not simple. In many cases, they do, but when businesses fail to adhere to the laws, the results can be astonishingly disastrous. In the following discussion, we will review the types of financial tools used to affect public and business behavior and then discuss the success and failures that mark government's efforts.

### Affecting Public Behavior

The methods used to influence public behavior may have a significant influence on business behavior. Public and business behaviors are often intertwined. For example, if tax breaks are given to homeowners to encourage buying homes in an area in need of revitalization, it is quite possible new businesses will open in the same area. The business is relying on free enterprise to generate revenue and create profits, but it is the government's use of tax tools that drives the economic engine.

However, the government does attempt to direct public behavior with consumer-specific financial policies. The plan is simple: use money to underlay consumer decisions. When the government adds, raises, or lowers taxes, consumers are faced with making choices and determining breakeven points. For example, you have probably heard a smoker say after a tobacco tax increase is passed: "If cigarettes get any more expensive, I will have to quit smoking."

A number of financial policy tools are used to modify behavior, and the goal is to modify it to suit the best interests of the public. Behaviors are influenced in the hope of conferring benefits that can be social, economic, or community based. One of the modern day challenges has been finding ways to engage the public so that the policies are effective. Governments can pass laws every day, but if the public does not take them seriously or is not concerned about issues or outcomes, then the incentives and penalties will not be effective.

### Taxes and Tax Credits

Taxes top the list of policy tools used to influence public behaviors. The taxes are sometimes used alone in that they are added to products at the manufacturing or retail levels, thus driving product costs up. In some cases, the tax increases are used in conjunction with other tools. A good example is taxes on tobacco coupled with public service marketing campaigns that show pictures of cancerous lungs. However, there is no doubt that raising tobacco taxes is the most important policy tool government can use to reduce smoking rates.(3)

There are a host of direct taxes and tax credits that impact behavior to some degree. Tobacco taxes are just one type of direct tax that is labeled a "sin tax." Sin taxes are taxes on services or products that are considered unhealthy for the individual or for the public in general. In the case of tobacco use, smoking causes cancer in smokers, but second-hand smoke can also harm non-smokers.

Another sin tax is the tax on alcohol. Like the tobacco tax, an increase in an alcohol tax is passed on to consumers as a price increase. There have been numerous studies done that attempt to measure consumer responses to price changes in alcohol and tobacco use. The problem is that there are usually several reasons at play at the same time. Though there is evidence that a tax increase can discourage alcohol use by some people or lead to modified drinking habits through selection of products with lower alcohol, other factors influencing alcohol consumption include age, drinking culture, income, availability, and lifestyle. Also, there is evidence that taxation does not influence those consumers most likely to abuse alcohol or who indulge in risky drinking patterns, like students and young adults.(4)

Another tax used to reduce consumption is the gasoline tax. The higher the price of a gallon of gas, the less gasoline is used. However, the reduced gasoline consumption is not necessarily due to driving fewer miles. In fact, the research reports that the total number of miles driven by consumers is not responsive to the price of gas. A 10-percent increase in gas prices, which can include gas price and taxes, only reduces the vehicle miles traveled by no more than 0.3 percent.(5) This is due to a migration to more fuel efficient vehicles that enable the consumer to drive the same number of miles while using less gasoline.

The government gets additional benefits by raising gas taxes which benefit consumers, should they change their behaviors. These benefits include less traffic congestion, less dependence on foreign oil, less use of non-renewable resources, less pollution, and fewer car accidents.

Another type of tax is the luxury tax, which is assessed on expensive items like cars and boats. The purpose of the tax is to alter consumption of certain items. For example, some larger expensive cars get less gas mileage than smaller cars. The luxury tax discourages purchase of these vehicles—unless money is no object to the consumer. The Internal Revenue Service points out that the luxury tax generates additional revenue for the government, but if it gets too steep, people will simply stop buying the products assessed with this tax.

Tax credits and tax deductions are also used as incentives to encourage consumers to purchase products. There are a number of energy-related tax incentives in the form of credits and rebates that have been authorized by law for the purchase of energy efficient windows and heating and air conditioning systems, additional home insulation, and alternative energy water heaters.

A new, innovative tax is the "bag fee." This tax is a small fee that is charged for each plastic bag used at grocery stores and retail establishments. The purpose of the fee is to encourage consumers to use reusable bags so that pollution is reduced and landfill waste is reduced. The revenue from this tax is supposed to be used for environmental cleanup purpose.

Even the mortgage interest deduction homeowners are allowed to take when they itemize on their tax returns was intended to promote home ownership. However, as the number of people unable to itemize grows, there has also been a decline in terms of the influence that this deduction has on homeownership rates.

The list of taxes imposed by government over the years to change consumer behavior is long. However, more than taxes are used as financial tools.

### Tickets, Fines and Penalties

When you see the blue lines in a parking lot and a sign with a silhouette of a person in a wheelchair, it is clear that parking spot is reserved for the disabled. You could park there, but in doing so, there are two consequences. The first consequence is that a parking ticket will be issued. The second consequence is the fact that you will probably have to endure the wrath of fellow consumers. As a result of this knowledge, you find another parking spot. Without really thinking about it, you were just influenced by the government.

Fines, penalties, and tickets are financial tools used to modify consumer behavior in the same way taxes do. There is an endless array of fines authorized by law, enforced by the police or other legal entities, and often imposed through ticket writing. There are fines to discourage things like:

- Speeding
- Drinking and driving
- Driving without a seatbelt
- Littering
- Driving with small children in the front seat

- Disturbing the peace
- Scalping sports tickets
- Driving without passengers in motor pool lanes
- Public drunkenness
- Watering lawns during a drought
- Texting while driving
- Building too close to a property boundary

## Special Rates, Offers, and Financial Incentives

Not all government financial tools that affect behavior are negative as evident in taxes, tickets, and fines. There are also policy tools that are positive incentives. The tax rebates for the purchase of energy efficient appliances are incentives to act in a socially beneficial manner rather than a punishment for acting inappropriately.

The Congressional Budget Office has also studied how financial incentives can motivate people to act in a way that promotes good health. These include higher taxes on unhealthy foods and products so that the consumer is financially motivated to consider the higher cost of an unhealthy purchase rather than making an impulse purchase based on cravings only. As the cost of unhealthy products increases there has been a noticeable decline in overall sales of these products. In fact, it has given many who always wanted to change their unhealthy lifestyle the push to quit some of their bad purchasing habits and look for alternative goods to purchase instead. Government agencies are implementing various financial incentives along with counseling and clinical interventions to better address health issues like obesity, diabetes, and drug abuse.(6)

Rising healthcare costs is an important issue in the United States that politicians and consumers are grappling with on a regular basis. The Affordable Health Care law that becomes fully effective January 1, 2014, is one of the newest laws passed that involves the use of financial tools to influence consumer behavior. US citizens will be required to have healthcare coverage, and those whose income qualifies will be subsidized. The law is meant to ensure that all Americans have access to healthcare, which will lead to two major benefits. First, people will be able to get the medical care they need, and as a result, there will eventually be a decline in rates of obesity, high blood pressure, diabetes, and so on. Second, the amount spent on healthcare is predicted to decrease as a result of a healthy citizenry.

In fact, the government built incentives for businesses into the healthcare law. For example, employers will be able to give workers incentives worth 30 percent to 50 percent of their healthcare premiums if they participate in wellness programs. These government-authorized incentives are expected to change consumer behavior in a positive way. The healthcare law will be an interesting experiment in what is being called "behavioral economics." The insurance mandate requiring everyone to buy health insurance is supported by a financial penalty for not buying the insurance. There are differing opinions as to whether the mandate will be successful. Dr. Alan Garber at Stanford University sums it up well by saying, "Behavioral incentives can be powerful, but they are unlikely to overcome a powerful financial incentive." In other words, people may decide to pay the annual penalty rather than pay a monthly health insurance premium. Financial penalties can backfire, as has been proven in the past. When copayments are too high, people simply stop buying many of their prescriptions.(7)

One other financial incentive the government has used to influence public behavior is reduced public transportation fares. This incentive is typically used in large cities where vehicle congestion is a problem and bus or rail services are available.

Much more could be written about financial programs like welfare, unemployment, and criminal fines. The government relies heavily on money to guide the public's behavior. It is not just the public's behavior that is influenced by government financial policy tools. Business behavior is also affected by taxes, fines, settlements, and subsidies.

## Affecting Business Behavior

The government's direct influence on business behavior may be too little or too much, depending on your viewpoint. However, one thing is certain: the government wields a lot of power that is used to direct and control the actions of businesses. The power lies in the government's ability to make laws and regulations and its ability to assess fines and penalties if those laws are violated. For example, regulations prevent collusive behavior for price setting purposes and to increase product choices in the marketplace. Businesses that are caught colluding are subject to severe penalties.

Unlike the public, businesses have greater mobility and flexibility. Corporations move their headquarters, plants, and offices based solely on tax incentives offered in some cases. Yet, like the public incentives, there are tax incentives to promote positive behavior and financial penalties when business behavior is illegal.

## Taxes, Tax Credits and Tax Breaks

Taxes and tax credits can have a major impact on business behavior. For example:

- Property taxes influence business location decisions
- Capital gains taxes impact investment decisions
- Tax credits promote hiring people from certain groups (i.e., veterans, disabled, minorities, and ex-felons), leading to job creation
- Tax credits and subsidies encourage business development
- Sales taxes influence product and service pricing
- Tax credits encourage business expansion into particular locations

Property tax has been reported to have a negative impact on new business startups. The Tax Foundation states that, "The ideal tax system, whether at the local, state, or federal level, is simple, transparent, stable, neutral to business activity, and pro-growth. In such an ideal system, individuals and businesses would spend a minimum amount of resources to comply with the tax system, understand the true cost of the tax system, base their economic decisions solely on the merits of the transactions without regard to tax implications, and not have the tax system impede their growth and prosperity."(8)

Tax decisions are made at the federal, state, and local levels and can cause businesses to manage a complex balancing act. They are also used in a variety of other ways. For example, in 1995, the excise taxes on fuels containing ethanol were reduced to promote production and consumption.

Taxes are certainly not the only factor considered in business decisions, but they are a major one. The ultimate goal of government in relation to business is to promote business activity (thus the Tax Foundation's pro-growth statement), but the government also encourages ethical behavior. Throughout the history of the United States, the government has had to issue fines and order settlements because businesses have failed to follow the law or act honestly.

## Corporate Welfare

Tax breaks fall under corporate welfare, which is the term used for special treatment allowed to businesses to give them a competitive advantage. These are government financial tools that include grants, subsidies, tax credits, and loan guarantees. They have an enormous influence on corporate behavior in the following ways:

- Subsidies encourage domestic firms to expand overseas
- Tariffs restrict imports, leading to greater domestic production and new business startups
- Loan guarantees fund plant expansions
- Grants promote businesses' willingness to invest in research and development

Opponents of corporate welfare believe that these financial tools tend to promote the development of overgrown corporations with too much governmental influence. Some criticize such policies because they feel that the government interferes in the free market and creates a deregulated business environment where competition is oftentimes eliminated.

### Fines and Settlements

As mentioned earlier, many government laws are designed to regulate corporate behavior. There are thousands of laws covering everything from marketing and advertising practices to financial reporting. There are also a number of agencies responsible for auditing and monitoring business activity to ensure compliance.

In 1999, Hoffman-LaRoche was charged a $500 million fine for price-fixing. But since then, the fines for business fraud or deceptive practices have grown significantly in size. They include:

- Healthcare Company - HCA (2000): $1.7 billion
- Citigroup (2005): $2 billion for accounting fraud
- Enron (2005): $1.52 billion for investor fraud
- American Electric Power (2007): $4.6 billion for pollution
- Pfizer (2009): $2.3 billion for deceptive drug marketing practices
- Eli Lilly (2009): $1.415 billion for deceptive drug marketing practices
- British Petroleum (2011): $20 billion escrow account for gulf liability claims
- GlaxoSmithKline (2011): $3 billion for deceptive drug marketing
- Abbott Laboratories (2011): $1.3 billion for patent infringement
- Bank of America (2011): $20 billion settlement for faulty mortgages

Many of the top fines have been assessed against drug manufacturers and oil and gas companies. During the 2008 recession, there were a number of financial institutions investigated and fined. In 2011, Goldman Sachs was fined $550 million for fraudulent mortgage investments. Also in 2011, Citigroup was fined $258 million for fraud, also involving mortgage securities, and $725,000 for research reports deemed misleading. However, there are still more multi-billion-dollar settlements yet to be made with Wells Fargo and J.P. Morgan Chase similar to the one Bank of America agreed to.(9)

## Success or Failure Can Be Difficult to Measure

The government has successfully used financial tools in a number of areas. For example, fewer people smoke cigarettes today than they did ten years ago. In 2001, a Gallup poll indicated that 22 percent to 28 percent of people smoked. In 2008, only 21 percent smoked.(10)

Though alcohol-impaired driving is still a problem in the United States, the statistics show signs of progress. The Centers for Disease Control figures report that there were 30 percent fewer episodes involving alcohol-impaired driving in 2010 compared to 2006. In addition, road fatalities involving alcohol have dropped dramatically.(11) Other successes are found in statistics like the following: the use of car seats has reduced children's deaths due to vehicle collisions by 50 percent since 1975.(12)

Tax incentives have worked well for many states trying to attract new business. Just recently, Boeing agreed to build a new plant in South Carolina after being offered $900 million in tax incentives.

The reason so many people are angry at these recently fined financial institutions is that many of those same firms have been fined in the past for other, similar fraudulent activities. For example, Citigroup/Salomon Smith Barney agreed to a $400 million settlement in 2003 for its role in the Enron scandal. Citigroup, like so many financial firms, has a long history of fines levied by the Security and Exchange Commission and court settlements. Bank of America has also paid fines in the past to settle illegal trading and accounting misdeeds. In addition, the fines that have been assessed may seem large, but in comparison to bank profits, those fines are insignificant and are often factored into management decision-making as just another cost of doing business.

In other words, passing a law and making something financially beneficial or disadvantageous is not an automatic formula for initiating behavioral change. Humans are complex, and each person relies on a unique decision-making process, which may or may not be rational.

The tax on alcohol has not stopped people from drinking alcohol or driving while drunk. People are still driving without their seatbelts, speeding, and texting while driving. Despite all the studies, there is no way to know conclusively how many people have changed their behavior due to taxes and tickets or other financial incentives and penalties imposed by government.

Government policies rely on incentives, but a good economist considers both intended and unintended consequences. For example, promoting the use of ethanol in fuel shifted the production of corn crops for food to production of corn crops for fuel. It is estimated that two out of every ten ears of corn are now used for food, and the other eight are used for ethanol and animal feed, with ethanol exceeding feed.(10) There is also concern that the competition for usage of crops will be detrimental to the food supply in the future.

Financial tools do work at the federal, state, and local levels. Public and business behavior is motivated by governmental financial policies. That is one reason so many laws are passed with fines, taxes, and fees included. The success of fines and fees in changing behavior is evident in the fact that more are proposed all the time. For example, there has been discussion on imposing a "fat tax" on unhealthy foods high in fats and sugar. Proponents believe that this tax will improve the public's heath by discouraging people from buying these low-nutrition foods. However, such a tax will also lower business revenues due to lower sales on those same products.

Changing public and business behavior is not easy. It can take decades, as the statistics have shown. It also takes careful planning to institute laws and regulations that bring intended consequences. While there have been documented failed behavioral policies, there are clearly some behavioral policies that have benefited and changed society for the better.

CHAPTER 18

# Alternatives to Layoffs: Managing People in a Tough Economy

If you are hungry for a daily dose of doom and gloom, just take a look at what current reporters, bloggers, and economists have to say about the present and future employment picture.

"Putting pressure on an already lousy job market, the mass layoff is making a comeback. In the past few months, Cisco, Lockheed Martin, Bank of America, and Sterling Savings announced a combined 23,000 in job cuts," economist Howard Davidowitz tells *The Daily Ticker*. Meanwhile, state and local governments have cut 142,000 jobs in recent months, and Wall Street is braced for another round of cutbacks. A few weeks ago, Goldman Sachs announced plans to let go 1,000 fixed-income traders. Although the economy has shown signs of recovering, the underlying uncertainty that still exists continues to make layoffs an option for many public and private organizations. While layoffs seem to be the strategy of choice for many companies these days, some businesses choose to do things differently.

## Corporation vs. Small Business Layoffs

There are pros and cons to layoffs, of course, but in a tough economy, the corporate behemoths seem to speak the loudest. By eliminating unneeded levels of management, they say, layoffs will flatten the corporate structure. This will improve communication, both internally and externally, get employees more involved, and expedite decision-making. Showing bankers and investors a lean and mean organization will increase shareholder value. And for many firms, showing competitive quarterly earnings numbers has now become central to their corporate culture and overall business strategy.

Arguments against wholesale layoffs are heard more often in smaller businesses or privately held companies whose growth and goals are not directly tied to stock prices or the opinions of Wall Street. These long-term-focused businesses fear that the quality of products and services will deteriorate if employee morale drops. This is a commonsense notion and a justified perception based on the empirical evidence. It is difficult for employees who feel betrayed, frightened, uncertain about their job security, or even angry after demonstrating consistent peak performance. Low morale contributes to increased tardiness, absenteeism, and turnover. It may even affect healthcare costs due to increased stress and exhausting work schedules.

Layoffs are not limited to the private sector, though. There has also been an increase in layoffs from the public sector. However, government layoffs come about from a variety of factors that are quite different from those that exist in the corporate or small business environment. Primarily, government entities reduce their workforces due to political pressures and/or decreasing tax revenues. Their layoff processes are, by necessity, more public and, therefore, more subject to scrutiny and comment than those of privately held businesses. When public layoffs do occur, they are usually met with passionate debate on both sides as to why this is a necessary course of action. Although these layoffs might be announced far in advance, they are still surprising to the public when they finally do occur, because of the direct impact that these decisions have on their daily lives and the hope that they would not actually occur.

Regardless of reasons for and opinions about layoffs, when it comes time to do the deed, the methods of implementing layoffs vary widely. It does not matter so much whether the company is large or small. In fact, a lot of the decisions depend upon management philosophy and ethical standards. Some large firms, fearing rumors will affect stock price and employee morale, will keep planned layoffs a secret, and they are not above lying about imminent reductions in their labor force until the very last legal minute. The fear that they may lose good employees who will jump ship rather than be let go is what often prompts the secrecy strategy. The environment that is fostered at these types of organizations is thus one of distrust and often cynicism between management and staff.

A more humane approach is taken by some companies and is generally more prevalent in small businesses for sometimes obvious reasons. In a smaller firm, the workforce is more like a family, and there is often a degree of compassion for the impact layoffs will have on workers' families and the community. Because it is possible for employees at major corporations to not know each other, most care less about the lives that are being affected by management decisions; this is often not the case at smaller firms. In fact, it can be quite difficult to be callous and calculating in life-changing decisions when you have to face friends and workers who are also impacted by these very decisions. It is especially difficult when these businesses are an integral part of the community where more than just an office space is shared.

It is clear, then, how and why employee-reduction programs differ between large and small firms and across the public and private sectors, as well. Let us compare the implementation of these strategies, looking first at the major corporation. In the corporate boardrooms, often with an exclusive group of executives, lawyers, and accountants assembled, letters and severance agreements are discussed, drafted, and legally scrutinized. This is considered a necessary precaution. Some firms will often go further and require employees to sign agreements not to sue in order to receive severance packages. Sometimes, outplacement counselors or firms are also retained to assist employees in navigating the unemployment waters. News releases to commercial and financial media are reviewed and legally revised as needed. When all is in order, the dramatic announcement is made, often in one mass meeting or in various small group or department settings. In extreme cases, stories are told of employees being terminated by voice mail or text message. All in all, the process can be quite nerve-racking, considering that the rumors and leaks usually precede these announcements months before the event.

In a small business, by contrast, the process is often more personal and sometimes even more emotional. The owner or owners may struggle long and hard to avoid the inevitable. Often, owners will share business realities with key subordinates or with the whole staff in order to lay the groundwork and allow time to absorb the impact. Early retirement may be offered to older workers, or other forms of voluntary separation may be suggested. When layoffs are done, it is more likely a one-on-one or two-on-one event, with the manager and possibly a human resources representative communicating directly and personally with each affected employee. In general, alternatives to layoffs are explored and exhausted before a decision is made to lay off employees at smaller firms.

## The Long Term Impact of Layoffs

Conventional wisdom would seem to say that when a company gets shaky due to lagging sales and/or rising costs, cutting the size of the workforce to reduce fat and eliminate deadwood is a customary and successful response. A research study published in Human Resource Management shows evidence which suggests that just the opposite might be true.

The study tracks the financial performance of Fortune 100 companies over a five-year period—two years prior to the layoffs, the year of the layoffs, and two years following the layoffs. The results indicate that financial performance did not improve—it got worse. There are some very telling reasons why this occurs.

Often, when layoffs are announced by a publicly held company, the stock price will take an immediate upward jump. However, on a number of occasions, stock prices increased after the announcement of a reduction in force, only to later slide back to their former levels or even lower. Possibly, Wall Street reacts negatively because investors fear a long-term adverse effect from layoffs or, even worse, because layoffs may be viewed as a signal that a company's underlying financial problems are real. Although the short-term gains might be applauded by investors who want to profit and then move on to other investments, in the long term, the company may suffer. Those investing in the business rather than its share price realize clearly the effects that layoffs have on the workforce. And as the number or frequency of layoffs increases, investors justifiably get nervous about whether the business's long-term viability might also be at risk.

## First to Fire, First to Rehire

While there is no substantial body of research that proves that one particular type or size of company will fire or rehire more quickly than another, anecdotal evidence would seem to support the trickle-down theory. For example, if a major automobile plant lays off a thousand workers, that will eventually impact suppliers, transportation workers, the local government, and enrollment in local schools—like a string of dominoes, falling one by one. Depending on the length or permanence of the downturn, small businesses will close and population will decline. Real estate values will plummet, and foreclosures will increase.

If things begin to turn around and the auto plant begins hiring, over time, business will begin to pick up at local coffee shops and restaurants. People will move back into town, school enrollment will increase, and more teachers will be hired. The upswing, however, is likely to be slower and less dramatic than the downturn because of the uncertainty that usually still permeates the markets. Even though small firms might see an uptick in orders and productivity, they might still be hesitant to hire new employees for fear that the trend might not be sustainable. And these smaller firms are often justified in maintaining their current positions in an environment where some larger corporations on which they are dependent continue to make sporadic cuts in labor force and other business costs.

### Considering Alternative Strategies

Given that the layoff process is not enjoyable for anyone (with the possible exception of fans of Donald Trump's semi-reality shows), are there alternative strategies that might eliminate, or at least delay, a wholesale layoff? Let us consider some practical alternatives to a complete termination.

**Freezes** The first, and often the easiest, step an employer can take to avoid layoffs is to institute a hiring freeze. This means that no new employees will be brought onboard, and anyone who resigns or retires will not be replaced. A salary and benefit freeze is another option. However, a wage freeze needs to be communicated skillfully. The employer should promise to review this decision periodically and provide a time frame in which employees can expect updates and changes to such a policy.

**Furloughs** A furlough is basically a mandatory period of time off work without pay. This may range from an occasional random day or two to a specific day or days each month to a shortened work week. While it may not be greeted with joy, it is viewed by most employees as better than losing a job altogether. The downside of a furlough is that while employees are working fewer hours, the workload remains the same. Customer service may suffer if customers experience longer wait times or must deal with employees they are not used to. Internally, teamwork may be affected, and productivity may slow down. However, a sense of job security will be established, which can have far-reaching upsides throughout the economy and lead to increased consumer confidence and an uptick in economic activity.

**Reduce or Eliminate Temporaries** Contract or temporary workers are often brought on to deal with work overload or special projects. Some firms might look at each of these situations carefully and reduce or eliminate the use of temporaries unless they are essential to the core business operation.

**Incentivize Layoffs** Offering early retirement to older workers is a fairly common strategy in lean times. Buying out employee contracts and encouraging voluntary layoffs also fit into this category. However, there may be a short-term negative financial impact to voluntary terminations if the company must spend a large chunk of money all at once when people leave. Unless this is part of a long-term strategy for the business, it should be carefully considered. Yes, there might be lower cost labor, especially when retiring higher paid employees, but remember that years of experience are also retiring with these individuals. So if there are no viable replacements for these individuals, then it just should not be an option, especially if younger employees are planning on leaving as soon as the economy gets better.

**Reduce Hours, Pay, or Benefits** When employees consider the possibility of losing a job altogether, losing a few hours a week or taking a pay cut may be reasonable alternatives. Again, if the goal is providing a form of job security, then this is a good option. However, if this strategy is adopted, it needs to be done across the board. Nothing could be worse for morale than rank-and-file employees watching their paychecks shrink while top management receives a salary increase or big bonuses in the aftermath.

The current downturn has affected virtually every sector of the economy. Layoffs in some companies and industries will continue to be inevitable. However, there are a number of alternative strategies that can be successful in either avoiding or delaying the layoff option. When alternative strategies are employed, businesses should consider the downside risks of each one. They should communicate openly with both employees and the public—not just in the beginning, but throughout the process. And if layoffs must occur, they should be handled with as much frankness and compassion as possible. Placing people before profits in the short term will generally pay-off in the long term by enhancing morale, the business's reputation, and the bottom line.

## An Anecdote from Overseas

PBS *NewsHour* journalist Margaret Warner recently did a report about how some German companies were doing well in the midst of a weak global economy. There were many reasons as to why some firms were doing well. Some attributed it to the euro currency and competitive advantages that were realized in using the newer currency versus the old official deutsche mark. Some suggested that it was the heavy investments in research and development that gave them their competitive edge. Others suggested that it was the German work ethic, ingenuity, and the pursuit of doing a little bit better than previous generations. Some suggested that it was the small and medium-sized family firms that allowed Germany to be so successful, even in a global downturn. In fact, many reasons were given by different businesses, but were instructing was what was said by a couple of companies in regards to the treatment of employees and layoffs specifically.

One company in particular, Trumpf, discussed the success they had in pursuing alternatives to layoffs. This specialized metals company discussed how important it was for them to retain their employees, who were loyal and well skilled due to the company's continuous training program, even in the economic downturn. Instead of layoffs, Trumpf turned to a German program called Kurzarbeit, which subsidizes employers who are planning on keeping their workforce employed. The program does not pay to keep workers on, but is used to provide additional funding in conjunction with other cost-saving wage measures a company can undertake. In Trumpf's case, they reduced pay as well as work hours, but provided employees training on their days off, which kept the workforce's skills current.

These choices proved to be a winning strategy for the company. As the economy begun to recover, it was poised to take advantage of the growing demand for its products and outpace its competitors who had not utilized similar strategies. The company's management stresses that because they dealt with specialized goods, if they had done large-scale layoffs, then they might have had to endure a lag in terms of getting the workforce up to top efficiency.

Trumpf's vice chairman, Peter Leibinger, remarked that, "The desire for security and safety is the most, so to speak, the strongest driver in German culture."(1) These should not be just German qualities. These are qualities that individuals in any economy can appreciate and governments should strive to encourage.

Companies that lay off workers have to go and rehire the necessary employees who might have to be completely trained to the businesses' practices, deal with rehires who might have to be retrained, or lose skilled employees to their competition. Layoffs might seem like an optimal strategy in the short term because of the immediate effects on the bottom line; however, long-term cost and competitiveness may outweigh the short-term gains.

Another key point is that although every individual business must ultimately choose the best strategy for its operating costs, profit targets, and long term goals, there is another consideration. In an ideal economy, instead of layoffs, businesses will implement cost-effective measures to reduce employee schedules and wages. In doing so, they will provide a sense of security to workers, thereby raising the level of consumer confidence in the economy. The benefit of this will more than likely be an uptick or stable aggregate demand rather than the usual decline in demand after layoffs. This will be beneficial to suppliers who might have a higher level of consumers buying their goods and services compared to heavy buildup in inventory if mass layoffs were the strategy of choice.

So, yes, each firm can do what is best for it in the short term, but it is obvious that their collective actions dictate consumer confidence, aggregate demand, and the eventual impact on the economy. So it might prove to be a successful and worthwhile strategy if there were incentives for businesses to keep their labor forces employed—which will reap great rewards for society and the economy. If the government, businesses, and educational groups collaborated to figure out a viable short-term solution, as in Germany, instead of layoffs, then this might end up saving taxpayers billions in tenuous simulative monetary policies, safety-net payments, and deficit expenditures.

CHAPTER 19

# Large Corporations vs. Small Businesses

For many years, the debate has roared on with regard to which is better—big companies or small companies? In the early 1900s, as innovation thrust forward and corporations began to grow, it seemed that large companies were "in," providing lifetime employment for many and a great deal of benefits to surrounding communities—including smaller businesses. However, today, things have definitely changed.

## Are Large or Small Companies Better for Local Economies and the Nation as a Whole?

When trying to determine whether large or small companies are better for local economies, one need only to look at the value that they bring to the communities in which they are located. For example, while many feel that the Wal-Marts of the world create jobs, oftentimes, these jobs come at a price—and that price usually entails a decline in the surrounding local businesses. Therefore, to say that large companies are better would simply not be the case, as these corporations tend to snuff out the mom-and-pop organizations that are usually the pillars of the communities in which they are located.

In fact, despite the fact that Wal-Mart employs approximately one percent of the entire United States population, it is truly the small, locally owned companies that have the most positive effects on their communities. According to a recent Penn State study, smaller, locally owned businesses actually provide a much higher long-term economic growth. The study goes on to say that not only are small businesses good for local economies, but that large corporations are bad. This is because these companies oftentimes have internal systems for services such as their legal, maintenance, accounting, and supply that are not always based in the same county—or even in the same state.(1)

When taking into consideration the nation as a whole, one of the biggest factors here is the fact that because many large corporations do not pay taxes, it could essentially be said that it is small companies that are fueling the majority of federal tax revenue.(2)

## The Good, the Bad, and the Ugly of Big and Small

Certainly, there are both benefits and drawbacks to big and small companies. In some ways, the pros and cons of each can be dependent upon whose view it is being taken from.

Large corporations can provide many benefits to their customers, their communities, and their governments. Some of the advantages of large companies come in the form of:

- Enabling cheaper prices due to economies of scale
- Creating jobs for a large number of employees
- Offering faster production of products, which can also lead to larger amounts of supply
- Providing competition, which could lead to lower prices for consumers
- Contributing a depth of resources

In addition, large US companies have long helped in strengthening the overall national economy. They do so in a variety of ways, including through capital investment and research and development and by supporting good-paying jobs. The global engagement of large companies also helps in strengthening the nation's economy.(3)

With these benefits, however, also come some drawbacks. These can include:

- The squeezing out of small businesses that compete for the same consumer—especially when the goods or services that are produced are chosen primarily based on price
- Pollution caused when manufacturing various products in the cases of some large companies
- The potential for holding influence over political parties with large contributions
- Devastating aftershocks to the local community if the big company goes under

Small companies also have their strengths and weaknesses. Some of the strong points include:

- The contribution these entities make to local economies
- Innovation, as on a percentage basis, small companies are responsible for more technology-based patents than are large companies
- The maintenance of jobs in the local community, although they do outsource
- Bold culture, often taken from the personality of the small business owners—which is, in many cases, risk oriented, innovative, and decisive
- Flexibility in tough economies, which enables small business to quickly make changes in order to stay afloat

Small businesses were responsible for nearly 50 percent of the total payroll employment in the United States in 2007. In addition, they were responsible for nearly 60 million of the 120.6 million total payroll jobs in that same year. In fact, small companies are accountable for approximately 44 percent of total private payout.(4)

Some small company negatives, however, can include:

- Trouble attracting talent, because larger companies, due to their larger resources, tend to fare better at attracting and keeping talented employees
- Difficulty attracting capital because of small size, lack of collateral, or smaller market share
- Smaller budgets that come along with smaller companies and can be especially negative in rough economic times when the company needs additional reserves in order to get through an economic downturn.(5)

### The Benefit to Local Economies

When it comes to benefitting local economies, small companies appear to be the clear winner. In fact, a case cited by *The Andersonville Study of Retail Economics* showed that when comparing ten locally owned businesses in various industries with ten national chains that competed in the same categories, small companies came out ahead. The study indicated that when $100 was spent at one of the local independent businesses, it created $68 in additional local economic activity. However, when that same $100 was spent at a large chain store, it would only produce $43 in that same local economic activity.(6)

In the jobs category, small business is again the winner. In fact, many seem to think that small business is the true engine of job creation. It has been shown that in the past decade, small companies and local service providers have actually created in excess of 60 percent of the net private sector jobs.(7)

## Big or Small—Who Pays More to Uncle Sam, and Who Does Not?

Small companies—especially those that are classified as sole proprietorships—certainly come out on top when it comes to who pays the most, as a percentage, in taxes. As sole proprietors, for example, these business owners are taxed at their individual tax rate—sometimes paying out more than half of their income in taxes. Conversely, almost two-thirds of United States corporations pay no federal taxes at all.(8)

It does seem, though, that large corporations are the frontrunners in avoiding taxation. In looking at corporate taxes as a percentage of federal revenue, these numbers have fallen by nearly two-thirds in just over fifty years—weighing in at 27.3 percent in 1955, but less than 9 percent in 2010. Corporate taxes as a percentage of GDP have also taken a nosedive, falling from over 4 percent in 1955 to just over 1 percent in 2010.(9)

How do corporations accomplish this feat? The Government Accountability Office, or GAO, reports that some corporations report no income before deducting expenses. Other large companies state that they have no net income after they have deducted their expenses. Either way, these companies are reporting no tax liability.(10)

## The Effect on Each Other—Which is Best?

Overall, both large and small companies can essentially have an effect on each other. The truth is that no business operates in a vacuum, and because of this, both large and small businesses can have an overall effect on the local and national economy. This being said, both large and small businesses have also helped in strengthening the US economy as well as each other.(11)

One of the most important connections that big and small companies have to each other is in the supply chain, where both types of companies sell to each other. According to a recent survey, the United States parent operations of the typical US multinational company purchases both goods and services from over 6,000 US small businesses. In addition, it purchases approximately $3 billion of inputs from these small business suppliers.

Overall, large corporations rely on their small business suppliers for just fewer than 25 percent of their total input purchases. Therefore, both small and large businesses are critically important, especially when partnering for the production of goods and services.(12)

CHAPTER 20

# Government Partnerships

With the surge in large company layoffs over the past few years, a large number of former employees have now become employers—even if that means running a one-person operation. Few in the United States are unfamiliar with the big company bailouts and the countless dollars that have been thrust upon large corporations. According to *New York Times* tallies as of July, 2011, the government had made commitments of about $12.2 trillion and spent $2.5 trillion. This amount, which included the initial $700 billion Troubled Asset Relief Program (TARP), was signed into law by President George W. Bush in 2008 and was more than monies set aside for small business bailouts.

As a matter of fact, even well-intentioned programs like the $200 billion Term Asset-Backed Securities Loan Facility (TALF), which was supposed to spur small business lending, only used about $43 billion of its intended funds for small business. And, unfortunately, this program did not directly lend to small business, but rather the funds were provided to securities issuers who were to make loans.

Clearly, small business lending is far from where it needs to be. So that brings to mind a question: what about the little guys? Why should the government invest more in small business and entrepreneurs?

While government regulations can be a good thing, they can also hinder certain areas—specifically in terms of small business. In the past, small business growth and development stalled—and profits lessened—due to government compliance. Oftentimes, laws can actually hurt companies by raising the cost of doing business and costing small businesses more than larger companies.

Although small businesses tend to give back and enrich communities more than their larger counterparts, it is more often big corporations that have been "bailed out" and given government incentives. This can be especially tough for small companies during economic crises such as that of the past several years (since the 2007 financial crisis began).

Yet there is very good reason why the government should actually be paying more attention to and offering small business assistance. According to the Small Business Administration (SBA), the smaller the business, the more patents per employee that are filed.(1) This essentially supports the theory that small businesses innovate at a faster rate than large businesses do.

Some of these small businesses' technological innovative patents include the following areas:

- Biotechnology
- Pharmaceuticals
- Communications, including the Internet and telecommunications
- Power Systems
- Medical Instruments(2)

It is clear that entrepreneurs span various industries. This group is almost always the first to discover an emerging technology before larger, cumbersome corporations do. The usual scenario is that a smaller, more creative, and more flexible firm will create an innovative technology or intellectual property. Then that innovation will be acquired by a larger firm, which often has better means to expand on the smaller firm's ideas.

For years, there has been an ongoing debate as to why the government should invest more in small businesses and entrepreneurs. Many of the proponents of this debate usually give the following reasons that support this idea. More government investment has the potential for leveraging into additional innovative programs. Governmental support could be the incentive that can attract additional partners or participants such as investors, universities, and even larger businesses.

Investment capital from the government also encourages entrepreneurs and small businesses to invest more in research and development (R&D). Increases in R&D can generally lead to faster discoveries and more innovative ideas. Financial backing from the government also creates a less conservative and more liberal environment where riskier, but potentially more rewarding ideas can be tested without the unnecessary fear of failure, allowing these firms to move forward.(3) Sometimes, it is in the failure of ideas that lessons are learned and better, successful innovations are created.

It is fair to say that with the government support, some entrepreneurs might be tempted to take on additional risks that they otherwise might not if it was their own capital at stake, but the potential for new innovations generally outweighs this risk. Also, since the government regularly tries to stimulate economic activity, they might very well benefit from entrepreneurial funding, which is known to stimulate economic activity through the creation of new jobs.

### Moving Forward With New Legislation

One of the ways that government can promote the growth and success of new businesses is through the passage of the Business Incubator Promotion Act, legislation that has been put together and reintroduced by United States Senator Sherrod Brown of Ohio. Through this act, the government would both create and support business incubators throughout the United States, accomplishing two primary goals. The first, to provide resources for such entities to operate and expand their assistance to small businesses; and the second, to help ensure those communities that have been hit hard economically would have access to federal resources via the US Commerce Department's Economic Development Agency.(4) In doing so, this legislation could essentially help in the creation of higher skilled and higher wage jobs as well as providing incentives to create products in America and export them worldwide.(5)

### How Small Business and Entrepreneurs Compare to the Big Guys

Within the argument regarding why the government should invest more in small businesses is the comparison of how small businesses fare in relation to large corporations. With all the incentives and governmental credits that larger business get, it might be argued that they are clearly more beneficial to the government and hence the public than are smaller businesses. This could very well be the case, but let us take a closer look at how small and larger businesses stack up in terms of their access to capital and their impact on society.

### Access to Capital

Access to capital is one of the areas in which small business owners and entrepreneurs lag far behind their larger corporate counterparts. Because many traditional lenders are wary of offering loans or other forms of capital prior to seeing a "track record" or substantial collateral, smaller businesses are often forced to turn to alternative funding sources. This unfortunate scenario is also compounded by the fact that they also are often charged higher interest rates, required to allocate equity for funding, or required to give up control of their companies in exchange for capital investments.

In comparison to smaller business, larger businesses generally have much more opportunity for financing. Typically, funding for larger companies can be obtained from a variety of external sources such as creditors, debt holders, equity investors, hybrid equity-debt investors, and even the government.

One of the most compelling examples of how small business loses out to big is in the disbursement of bailout funds from the government in the recent economic downturn. Over half of the $4 billion in federal funds that was originally earmarked for small business lending was actually used as repayment for the bailout funds that were received by many of the large banks in the Troubled Asset Relief Program, or TARP.(6)

In yet another case of small business funds misallocation, the Small Business Lending Fund, created for the purpose of raising capital at smaller banks—the primary funding source for small businesses—was used instead by banks to help in paying down the high cost of TARP debt. The TARP programs, as it turns out, actually did a much better job of assisting firms on Wall Street than it did solving the issues faced by small businesses.(7)

In addition, the 2008 creation of the Term Asset Backed Securities Loan Facility, TALF, was also meant to support lending to both households and to small businesses. With this program, the government had initially agreed to offer up to $20 billion in funds for such relief. Yet, here too, taxpayers and small business actually ended up shouldering much of the burden to instead bail out bigger corporations.(8)

These financial missteps by those that are supposed to be helping small businesses are inexcusable considering that larger businesses generally get preferential financial assistance from the government. These large companies may even obtain additional funds or save money, due to government programs that are offered to subsidize a certain industry or sector of the economy. For instance, the government may provide benefits to companies that work in various environmental programs, or it could subsidize companies who hire local job seekers.(9)

Smaller businesses conversely are often left to come up with creative financing via personal loans, home equity lines of credit, or small bank loans—that is, if they are able to qualify. In other instances, small business owners and entrepreneurs often provide their own seed or expansion capital via the savings or retirement account funds of the owner or partners.

Whether it is a large or small business, the government should take a more active role to ensure that businesses that are good for society have adequate financial resources available. In providing financial support to any and all businesses with positive growth opportunities, the financial sector and the government can help develop the overall economy.(10)

There are some avenues for small business to access capital. For example, the SBA has always been an available resource to such firms. The venture capital offered by the Small Business Administration funded over 1,300 small companies' needs in 2010 alone.

Small business incubators have also played a large hand in assisting small companies with both capital as well as mentorship. These entities, with the purpose of helping the "little guy" to survive and thrive during its startup phase, have become immensely popular—especially over the past dozen years.

In using the combination of help and funding, these incubator programs work with entrepreneurs and small business owners to help them to build their product or service offering as well as to learn necessary business skills such as managing cash flow and marketing.(11)

Many of the sponsors of business incubator programs are individuals as well as government organizations. One example of how these programs are working successfully is in New York, where incubators are even broken down into very specific industry sectors such as arts, fashion, general startups, kitchen, and technology.(12) The incubators have been so successful that New York, like other forward-looking governments around the country, is expanding these programs in hopes of creating long-term economic growth stimulators.

Other city and state government entities not yet on board this trend should pay attention as it is proven how small businesses can attain success in this manner. In fact, according to a study for the US Department of Commerce Economic Development Administration in 2009, it was discovered that business incubators actually create up to twenty times more jobs than traditional community infrastructure projects—and they do so with a much lower cost per job.(13)

## Employment

When it comes to hiring, small businesses are actually doing the hiring, while large companies are disproportionately lagging behind in this vitally important issue. In many cases, small businesses are referred to as the engine of job creation. Over the past ten years, it has been the smaller companies, service providers, and those entities referred to as mom-and-pop operations that have created over 60 percent of the net private sector jobs.(14)

To be fair, as a group, smaller businesses fare much better in creating jobs, but it is important to note that the potential to hire does vary among the different types of small businesses. For example, the corner drugstore may create only a handful of jobs throughout the entire life of the business, whereas other innovative businesses, particularly those in the technology arena, may have explosive job growth within a relatively short period of time. Of course, if the business fails and there are no resources to support the venture, then those same jobs might also be destroyed. In an ideal society, this would be an opportunity for the government to step in and do a thorough analysis to determine whether there is ample benefit to society in rescuing these businesses and saving those jobs that would otherwise be lost.

## Taxes

Overall, it would appear that small businesses and entrepreneurs pay a larger percentage of their income to taxes. But be advised that even among the various small businesses, the amount of taxes paid can also vary depending on how the small business is set up. For example, sole proprietorships are taxed at the individual's personal income tax rate—which is often higher than rates paid by corporations.

An article in the *New York Times* mentions that the Government Accountability Office (GAO), the investigative arm of Congress, reported that "two out of every three United States corporations paid no federal income taxes from 1998 through 2005."(15) Overall, it seems clear that federal taxes have essentially shifted in scale from corporations to individuals.

In order to reduce their tax liability even more, some large corporations set up headquarters in offshore locations. By setting up an offshore corporation, companies are able to save a great deal in the taxes that are paid as well as receive additional incentives.

These "tax havens" are typically small countries with very little other resources except the tax incentives that they offer to individuals, investors, corporations, and often creative business ventures that are seeking tax shelters. Some examples include the Bahamas, where there is no personal income tax, inheritance tax, or capital gains tax, and even the United States Virgin Islands, where companies are offered a 90-percent exemption on income tax and possibly even a 100-percent exemption for those who qualify.(16)

While companies both large and small are increasingly forming offshore corporations, it tends to be the larger ones that are more often taking advantage of this loophole. According to a new report, thirty of America's most profitable companies actually paid "less than zero" in income tax between the years of 2008 and 2011 by utilizing offshore formations.(17)

Although tax incentives are offered to both the small and the large, overall, it still appears that federal taxes have shifted in scale from the large corporation to the small business owner, while the bulk of capital continues to go into the coffers of the larger enterprises. By keeping more of the funds that are earmarked for small business assistance in the small business arena, the government would benefit significantly in not only helping small business to grow but also in keeping more of its taxable revenue within the United States.

### Community Value

It could also be argued that locally owned businesses tend to generate much greater benefits for the local economy than large corporations and national chains do. A case cited by The Andersonville Study of Retail Economics showed that when comparing ten locally owned businesses in various industries with ten national chains that competed in the same categories, when $100 was spent at one of the neighborhood's independent businesses, it created $68 in additional local economic activity. If that same $100 were to be spent at the chain store, it would only produce $43.(18) It used to be that owners and employees of local businesses would spend a greater proportion of their earnings within the community, thereby enabling the other businesses to prosper, as well, but with the emergence of discount retailers, that trend has changed markedly. The unfortunate scenario is that the community is so busy chasing the lower cost goods and services that the bigger corporations offer, they fail to see their own local economy deteriorating until it is often too late.

### Innovations

With today's fast-moving technology industry, many new innovations are being created each and every day. It is the power to harness the current technologies to create new and innovative technologies that will ultimately boost economic productivity and job growth. It is not enough to simply remake the same product line for decades while your competitors are inventing exciting products. However, that is what some large corporations do. Some of these archaic-minded businesses spend more money on marketing, trying to convince consumers to buy their product, than on research and development to invest in something new. Others will created a litany of patents on their existing products or intellectually property, either to stall their competition or to simply make some additional revenue when new and market-impacting quality, creative ideas are lacking. The wiser among this group will at least invest in or partner with a smaller firm with the hopes of capitalizing on any new innovations, and according to the statistics, this is generally a sound strategy.

The Small Business Administration has reported that small businesses lead large corporations in number of patents per employee—in some cases, producing more than ten times the patents per employee than larger corporations. And although smaller firms are granted only 8 percent of all patents, they do receive 24 percent of all patents that are issued in the top one hundred emerging technologies. More importantly, these patents that are issued to small companies are much more focused on specific types of innovations that usually have a higher impact and result in a higher return.(19)

## Outsourcing

Although once thought of as only used by large companies, outsourcing has begun to trickle down to small businesses, as well. Many companies, both large and small, are now taking advantage of the widening wage gap between Americans and those in poor or developing countries.(20)

The reasoning behind outsourcing differs a great deal between large and small companies. For instance, large companies often turn to outsourcing in order to cut costs, while small companies and entrepreneurs look to this process for completing tasks that just simply cannot be performed in-house. These functions can include accounting, payroll processing, distribution, and a variety of other tasks that provide significant cost savings that might be needed by some small businesses just to stay afloat.

In fact, there are many reasons that smaller companies may turn to outsourcing more often than their larger competitors do. The most important being that smaller companies can use outsourcing to help in leveling the playing field with bigger companies. This is significant because, without outsourcing, smaller entities typically cannot afford to match the in-house support that large corporations have. By outsourcing, smaller companies can gain access to the same economies of scale, expertise, and overall efficiency that larger companies possess.(21)

So while the government bails out large corporations and entities that Wall Street deems "too big to fail," let us hope that they do not forget the smaller businesses that make up Main Street. If small businesses as a group fail, then it is inevitable that our local economies will also fail and so, too, will our national economy.

CHAPTER 21

# America Competing in the Global Economy

As the global economy shifts, there are a number of different changes taking place. Some nations have been catalysts in such forward movements, while others have made the necessary adjustments in order to simply keep up. Without significant improvement, however, still others may soon be left behind.

Certainly, competition requires a nation to have strengths in a number of different categories. One of the measures of economic strength can be seen in the trade balance of a country. The trade account indicates whether a country is a net importer of goods or services or net exporter of goods and services. The United States currently has a trade imbalance. According to the US Census Bureau and the US Bureau of Economic Analysis, in 2011, exports of goods and services were at $2,103.1 billion and imports of goods and services were at $2,661.1 billion, resulting in a goods and services deficit of $558 billion. The data shows irrefutably that America is a net exporter of goods and services in the global economy.

Yet given the current state of certain key industries in the United States, it raises an important question: how can the United States increase its domestic economy while continuing to successfully compete globally? This is a difficult question, but one that needs to be examined. We will examine this topic by focusing on a few key themes.

These topics are all vitally important to preparing and staying competitive in the global economy. The information that will be presented shortly is relevant to individuals, employers, entrepreneurs, education institutions, and the government, as well. The world is changing, and you can learn how to best position yourself to take advantage of these changes, or you can remain uninformed and just hope for the best.

## Education and Focused Training

With the expansion of globalization over the years along with multinational business activity, a great deal of debate has evolved over how the United States will continue to be seen as a viable global competitor. One successful way to do so arguably begins with the education and training of the workers in a variety of industries as well as in providing incentives for potential employees to enter specific fields. This strategy can be effective considering that over the past several years, a majority of employers have reported that the skills required to perform certain jobs have increased. However, the availability of workers with the desired skill sets has decreased.

This is especially true in technological fields as well as emerging industries. In general, jobs that are built upon the foundation of science, technology, engineering, or mathematics (STEM) have seen the largest mismatches between available positions and potential workers with available skill sets.

Globalization has also led to dramatic changes in the overall structure of the workforce itself. As outsourcing continues its expansion through the domestic economy, it is no longer necessary for employees to be in the same time zone or even country. These changes can be attributed to the fact that businesses are looking for lower labor costs to offset declining expenses and profits; however, there is another reason. Some employers recognize that the skill-sets gap might persist for some time and therefore take the necessary precautions, such as outsourcing, in order to remain globally competitive. The silver lining in all of this is that many employers are increasing their spending on education and training programs.(1)

## Keeping Key Fields Filled by Current and Future Labor Force

The labor force participation rate is a primary component in long-term economic success. In fact, the "wealth of nations" is considered to be a function of the opportunities that are created for both current and future generations.

Without good jobs available, the United States will not be able to sustain growth in its own economy domestically or be able to compete as it used to on the global level now or in the future. If America wants to return to its days of global economic dominance, there are difficult, but not impossible ways that this can be achieved. Some options include:

**Financial Incentives to Pursuing Certain Fields** The US government offers a number of programs, credits, and other incentives for companies to partake in certain activities and key future industries, such as clean energy. This initiative is already working in selected fields through programs like the Advanced Biofuel Product Grants and Loan Guarantees, the Idle Reduction Equipment Excise Tax Exemption, and the Value-Added Producer Grants.(2)

**Government Credits on Debt That is Taken On in Specific Ventures** When the private sector is unable or unwilling to take on ventures that will serve the public good, the government can step in to help with funding on a variety of levels, including credits to decrease debt. In terms of profit, these ventures might be unattractive in the short term for traditional private investment firms, but the long-term benefits to society and the economy should convince the government to invest. For example, for companies that are modifying production models to be more environmentally friendly, the government currently offers credits on debt that is undertaken to accomplish such activity.

**Government Financial and Tax Incentives in Key Industries** In addition to other incentives, the government can offer businesses more tax breaks for participating in or moving forward with certain projects that will help them not only to become more efficient but also more competitive overall in the domestic and the global marketplaces. Currently, there are incentives in place such as the Biodiesel Income Tax Credit, the Fuel Cell Motor Vehicle Tax Credit, and the Small Agri-Biodiesel Producer Tax Credit.(3)

**Private Incentives Such as Training Programs with Guarantee of a Job Once Complete** Private companies can also offer incentives to entice potential future employees to key industries of the future. This can be a solo effort where the employer brings in its own trainers, or it can be a partnership. Partnerships can be established and marketed with local educational institutions. These types of partnerships can be rewarding for the program participants, educational institutions, and the employer, as well. The employers benefit further in having lower initial training costs and the reassurance that these potential employees are trained to meet their business requirements. And if there are no jobs available locally, these participants' training can be practically used in the national or global network for that field. And although they cannot offer a guarantee of long-term job security, private sector jobs do have other incentives that include potentially lucrative starting salaries, depending on industry merit-based promotions and salary raises as well as a chance to be on a more level playing field with current employees.

## Product Quality

Certainly, product quality has a very large impact on how the United States competes in its domestic economy and the broader global economy. Even though the service sector accounts for approximately 70 percent of all economic activity in the United States, the manufacturing sector still accounts for nearly 12 percent of the country's output. This divergent trend has been forecasted to increase on the side of the service industry over the long term. There are many that perpetuate the belief that manufacturing will be obsolete in the future United States for a variety of reason. However, the transformation brought on by globalization might derail that notion if America's global dominance decreases. The overall health of the United States and any sustainable nations' economy is fairly dependent on manufacturing. The right mix of goods and services created domestically adds immeasurable value and security to a nation and its long-term prosperity. It has been argued that a nation without a manufacturing base is doomed to an inevitable economic and societal failure. This is, in essence, because of the manufacturing sector's ability to create tangible goods and jobs, and, therefore, tax revenues and profits. If the right goods are being produced, the manufacturing sector will also tend to support the economy through the ups and downs of the business cycle.

This is in stark contrast to the service sector that sometimes offers unessential services that are often discarded by consumers as soon as the market heads downward. It is therefore prudent to find the right balance between domestic production and global demand. For the United States, the ability to compete globally is very dependent upon the purchase of US-made products.(4)

## Better or Worse Than In the Past?

In the past, American-made products carried the reputation of being of a higher quality. However, over the years, this has changed somewhat as the business strategy and culture has changed at even some of the most respected firms. And the level of decline compared to earlier periods can be astonishing, depending upon the product and industry sector that is being considered.

For example, years ago, Asian-made products like electronics carried the stigma of being considered "cheap." Some of the worst offenders were of poor quality, were inexpensive, and were often unsafe for consumers. However, today, the situation seems to be remarkably different for some Asian-made goods.

American-made products are attempting a comeback, though. For example, whereas American-made vehicles have been thought of as being "gas guzzlers," today US auto manufacturers have risen in the global ranks in terms of product quality and have even surpassed many of the foreign-made vehicles for their quality, features, and environmental friendliness. To remain competitive in manufacturing over the long term, businesses need to strike a balance between low cost and high quality.

### How Products Production Compare Domestically and Globally

One of the major obstacles in terms of global competition is the United States's huge manufacturing trade deficits. These trade deficits underscore the fact that America's overseas product sales are not keeping pace with the level of purchases that the United States is making from abroad. Imports of goods exceed exports of goods. According to the US Census Bureau and the US Bureau of Economic Analysis 2011 reports, exported goods were $1,498.2 billion and imported goods were $2,235.3 billion. The resulting balance is an overall goods deficit of $737.1 billion.

According to the report, increases in goods exported compared to the previous year included: industrial supplies and materials, capital goods, automotive vehicles, automotive parts, automotive engines, foods, feeds, beverages, and consumer goods. The report also found similar increases in imports of those same goods compared to the previous year.(5)

Thus, the overall effect is a depressed demand for manufactured offerings from the United States, and this, in turn, prevents United States manufacturers from maintaining the workforce needed to achieve a healthier growth in the economy.

In this case, a larger and faster growing manufacturing sector would help to restart a healthy cycle for the US economy. So many times, we look for abstract answers to economic problems instead of focusing on the tangible practical solutions. These real solutions might include construction of needed infrastructure or the manufacture of necessary goods that provide jobs and stimulate productive and sustainable economic activity. These tactics would subsequently help in spurring more consumers' spending and a greater demand for US-made goods.(6)

### Positive Quality Changes

One of the most positive changes in product quality can be seen in the American automobile industry. After decades of producing disappointing vehicles, American automakers have begun to earn higher scores than overseas automakers. This has been stated in J.D. Power surveys of both quality and owner satisfaction.(7)

After many years of purchasing better made and longer lasting imports, the American car buyer is finally seeing the improvements in domestically made vehicles. This has also led to sales increases of US-manufactured vehicles.

This re-emergence of quality did not happen overnight, however. It has taken decades for some American manufacturers to finally realize that just because something is "made in America" does not mean that Americans should buy it. Thankfully, we still live in a free society where consumers can make choices on what goods and services they can buy. Yes, there are limitations, and sometimes the choices are really not that great, but it is still better than in other countries. It is because of the freedom of choice that the free market system was able to work, and consumers chose the better quality product when given similar prices.

The loss of significant market share coupled with deteriorated profits pushed many American manufactures to reassess their business strategy. Those that chose to compete are doing so and are actually doing a better job than expected. The success stories are the businesses that are competing to deliver quality products rather than just producing cheap products that simply meet the minimum legal, safety, and quality standards of the nation. So to be fair and encourage the process of positive change, do not just buy American because the goods are made in America. Rather, buy American because it competes with or is better than the other products on the market. If the American product is of a significantly poorer quality, then you are better off buying a non-American brand—to do otherwise would be to the detriment of the long-term prosperity of the nation, just for a few short-term gains.

## Negative Quality Changes

Along with the positive changes in certain US industries come some negatives in other sectors that have pushed some of the American-made products far behind overseas competitors' offerings. Those that have chosen to embrace negative quality changes are often doing so because they cannot compete on anything but price. These types of businesses need to focus more on research and development to better differentiate their products from the many other options that consumers have.

If the markets are unfairly being flooded by cheap, poor-quality foreign goods, that is negatively impacting the nation's businesses and a society has a right and, in some cases, an obligation to petition its government. The wronged businesses also have a right to seek some form of relief from the government, whether it is legal or economic considerations to help it compete better. If the business just cannot compete because of lack of managerial expertise, adequate resources, or ingenuity, then its fate must be left for the market to decide. If this same business is attempting to circumvent the market's weeding-out process in order to hawk its goods or services to unwitting consumers, then the governments have an obligation to protect the nation. It is a common fact that after emerging as unique on the markets, some products will become commoditized or commonplace over time as other firms create similar or better products. Therefore, a society should reward or incentivize businesses to take chances on new products by giving them a grace period to dominate the markets, but this should be a short grace period.

The grace period should not be looked at as an unlimited period where the business can force a monopoly on the markets and, in essence, just be able to print money over the long-term existence for the product. By adhering to such a principle, the markets will not be as efficient or productive as they could be. This would create an environment where firms will just try to look for long shots in order to monopolize the markets rather than compete on quality and other factors in the free markets.

The grace period should, therefore, be a time for the product's originator to recoup some of the cost and strengthen finances to overcome the flood of competition that will be coming. Competition is an inevitable and important factor in a free market economy, and we should protect that principle rather than discard it in the face of innovation. There are better, more creative ways to protect and incentivize entrepreneurs and innovative risk takers. Getting rid of their competition for long periods of time is not the model that should be followed for the long-term prosperity of a nation.

The technology sector is infamous for creating an innovation and then commoditizing it in due period. One such area is the electronics industry. In fact, according to a recent survey in a top electronics industry magazine, the *Electronic Engineering Times*, respondents felt that the quality of electronics products produced in the United States is unfortunately deteriorating.

This downfall may be attributed to a growing issue in both private and public companies that is resulting in not just dissatisfaction from the customer but also frustration on the part of the engineers that is due primarily to pressures on cost reduction as well as time to market. The overall consensus is that many United States companies do not give their engineers enough time to truly put quality into the products and the documentation that they work on—and the quality initiatives that are undertaken at electronics companies are often required to show a return within one year or less.(8)

Over 60 percent of the *Electronic Engineering Times* customer respondents stated that product quality in US-made goods is actually worsening. In this case, many companies are actually going overseas in order to meet a price point rather than a quality point with their products. (9) Firms should only go overseas if they can experience cost savings and still create quality goods and services that benefits the society in the long term. If these firms are outsourcing jobs, which generally has a negative domestic impact, and are then expecting these same domestic consumers to buy cheap, poorer quality products, then such an enterprise should be encouraged to engage in more productive practices that benefit the nation. If the industry as whole needs help, then a think tank should convene to see what can be done domestically to help such a company compete effectively domestically and globally. If just one firm with implicit monopolistic powers is having a detrimental and counterproductive impact on the domestic economy, then this firm's practices should be corrected to bring it more in line with free market practices that will benefit the nation over the longer term.

Source: Electronic Engineering Times

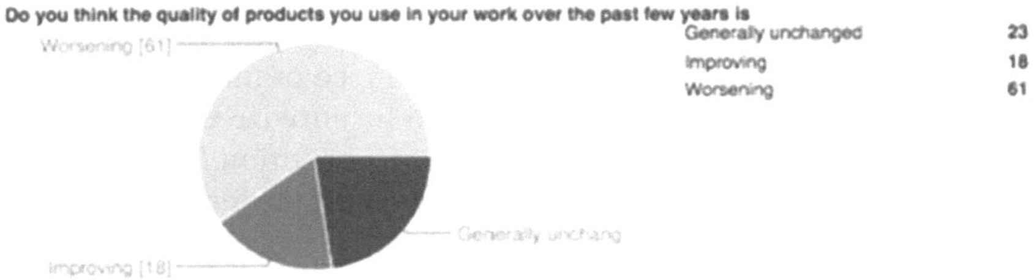


**Source: Electronic Engineering Times**

## Customer Service

It is no secret that in order to be a long-term success in business, it is imperative to have an effective customer service team. This is the rule and not an exception. Customers are part of any economic enterprise whether that business wants to acknowledge its customer service obligation or not. On the domestic front, if consumers are purchasing from United States suppliers and retailers, many businesses will be providing some form of customer service.

In contrast, many imported products offer little or no technical help with their goods. In addition, when customer support is offered, it is typically difficult for US customers to take advantage of that service due to language barriers and time differences.(10) Customer service may not be at the top of the list for the first-time customer, but it will be a factor for repeat buyers. And successful businesses remain viable over the long term because of repeat purchases. Therefore, it is important to have an effective customer service team.

The *Electronic Engineering Times* has also recently reported that despite worsening product quality in American-made products, it was felt that the poor quality may not be such an issue if customer service were better. Over half of the survey respondents stated that companies do not offer enough support and quality in their products.(11) This can make competing in the global market difficult unless these issues are properly addressed.

### Is the Customer Still Always Right?

One of the primary issues in failing customer service in the United States is that the customer no longer feels that they are always right or that they even have any right to address grievances. In today's economy, companies have had to find ways to save in nearly every capacity, just to stay open for business. Unfortunately, one such area that has been cut back on is customer services. Due to automation and impersonal tactics, not only do customers feel that they are not right, but in many cases, they are not even heard at all.

### Customer Service and Cost Savings

Many companies are realizing cost savings through the outsourcing of their customer service departments. The cost to keep an in-house customer service department—including computers, phones, and rent—can be expensive for companies. Many businesses have already realized that significant cost savings can be achieved when these functions are outsourced, effectively passing most of the overhead costs onto a third party.

Companies have also cut back on their customer services costs by automating the process. Although these automated systems can speed up the process of answering customer questions and taking care of other simple tasks in many ways, many customers become frustrated with the "maze" and seemingly "endless loops" they are placed in when attempting to resolve their issues through an automated system.

Likewise, while most companies now possess an online presence with answers to common customer questions or frequently asked questions (FAQ), these online help centers will often have a forum and community sections where users will attempt to solve each other's problems or at least discuss their grievances. If not properly executed, however, these help systems can prove to be disastrous. That is why better online help centers have an option to contact a live person. It seems that written explanations cannot take the place of a live representative.

While cost savings can be realized by doing less in-house customer service with live interaction, it is important for companies to exercise caution when outsourcing these activities. This is because companies must ensure that the representatives provide value to the customers and create long-term or repeat buyers. Otherwise, the company may be less able to compete either domestically or globally due to its inept customer service.

Companies must keep in mind that they typically get what they pay for. Today's customers expect quality products as well as excellent customer service. Ignoring this could quickly bring a company into the red.

## What About Advertising?

If customers are satisfied with a company's product offerings as well as with the customer service that they received, they are more likely to tell other potential customers about their experience. For years, word-of-mouth advertising has been a very solid way to attract customers. However, this can work in reverse, too, if a customer has a negative experience. These customers can actually be a nightmare for businesses, because bad online news travels faster than offline news, and dissatisfied customers are usually looking to air their grievances in the wake of a poor product experience and a poorer customer service experience. A business should not underestimate the power of the Internet when it comes to customer service and its goods or services. With today's Internet, word travels fast. Even on social networks such as Facebook and Twitter, a customer's experience with a particular company can become known in a matter of minutes, thus either strengthening or damaging a company's reputation within a very short period of time.

More successful companies take their customer service seriously and even have a presence on social media sites, as well. There are, however, some unscrupulous companies that hide behind aliases in forums, chat rooms, and social media sites, ready to counteract negative publicity. This strategy often backfires and can actually create more problems and bad publicity when others are alerted to the business's practices. It might serve these businesses better if they took the cost of hiding their otherwise poor customer service and invested in a quality customer service team, even if it is third party based.

Word-of-mouth advertising through these social networks has, in many cases, actually taken the place of traditional advertising. And overall, promoting product offerings in this way can be further reaching as well as much less costly for companies than the purchase of traditional advertising sources.

Overall, in order to successfully compete in the global marketplace, companies must continue to make the customer the primary focus over product offerings. One of the biggest reasons for this is that the option pool for products has only gotten larger over the years. Today, potential customers can purchase locally or online—thus giving them many more choices, even for the most basic products.

Combining the increased options with the need to be budget conscious, companies will likely find that all but the most loyal customers are on the hunt for the perfect buying experience. This includes great product quality, low cost, and excellent customer service. If the marketplace is efficient, it will eventually get rid of the businesses that have poor quality products or careless customer service—or both.

## Technological Changes

Business investment in technology has increased a great deal over the past few decades. Technology has also increased the demand for those workers who possess good communication as well as STEM skills (science, technology, engineering, or math skills). Yet the impact of technology has not been uniform across the board. In fact, it tends to vary somewhat by both occupation and industry as well as among different organizations within the same industry.(12) What is clear, however, is that the businesses choosing to invest in new technologies and processes usually fare better than their competitors who do not make these investments.

The United States has had a mixed reaction to its investment in technology. For example, those industries that have invested the most in technology also have the highest demand for skilled workers. These industries, in turn, will pay higher wages to workers than other industries.(13) However, some businesses that rely on technology are focused on the productivity gains that can be achieved with new and emerging technologies. In most cases, when given the option between hiring new workers and investing in productive technologies, these businesses often find the latter option to be the winning choice. In many industries, technology is not simply an input into the production function; it actually changes the production function. It does so by affecting the organization and essentially expanding the types of possible outputs. Therefore, those organizations choosing more traditional work methods are less apt to have invested in technology—and thus produce products that are less customized.(14) Technology gives businesses productive options that were not possible with a traditional workforce.

Even in this economic downturn, businesses are still taking the opportunities to invest when the opportunity presents itself. And these investments are not limited to the giant corporations. According to a recent report, "America's Economic Engine—Competing in Uncertain Times," done by the major management consultant Deloitte, mid-market companies or businesses with annual revenues below $1 billion are investing in technology because it directly impacts their productivity and their bottom line. The Deloitte report also goes on to discuss the fact that companies are indeed pursuing these technologies because they cut down on costs and create less reliance on unskilled labor and more need for a skilled labor force.

The economy is still at a low point in the business cycle, but these types of companies will be poised to take advantage of increasing consumer demands as the economy strengthens. If history is a guide, then these businesses that have gotten leaner through their cost cutting and productivity enhancements will eventually pass those savings on in the form of new hiring as the economy heats up again.

The future impact of technology on the labor force will, in large part, depend upon whether or not more organizations choose to adopt the strategy of customization in response to the new technologies that are available to them. In addition, competitive pressure is very likely to change the structure of many workplace organizations.(15) The question that is yet to be answered concerns what exactly the future American workplace will look like, considering the increasing number of outsourced employees and resources, investments in productive technologies, and a labor force that is clearly not prepared for the global transformation that is occurring.

### The Downfall of an Inflexible Company

In our recent economic history, we have many case studies of what has occurred to businesses that were slow to adapt to the changing economic environment. In some instances, companies that were highly successful—and profitable—got caught relying too much on old technologies which led to their demise. One infamous example is what occurred at Eastman Kodak Company (Kodak).

At one time, Kodak was the undisputed king of the photographic equipment world, with over 80 percent of the market under its control by the 1980s. However, by the mid-1980s, approximately one hundred years after George Eastman invented the paper-based film, the digital revolution was beginning. Kodak, however, decided that this new technology would be a passing fad and erroneously did not change its business strategy. Ironically, Kodak did invest in the digital technology with collaboration from computer behemoths like Apple and Microsoft; however, the company felt that the world would not be switching away from traditional film because of its ubiquity in society. Kodak continued to fall further and further behind its competitors by sticking to its old-school philosophy and failing to realize that there was not a sustainable future market for the products it still wanted to sell.

Rather than moving forward into this new age, Kodak focused more on making some unwise acquisitions of other businesses that did not help them progress, and by the mid-1990s, when the company was forced by its digital competitors to keep up with the new technologies, it was apparent that they were lagging behind. The consumer digital tech business was growing, and competition was fiercer than Kodak's executives could have imagined.

In the early 2000s, Kodak ramped up its digital camera production and actually reached the number-one domestic spot with strong United States sales by 2005. However, once again, Kodak appeared to get complacent in its underestimation of the digital camera market. The digital camera industry only became more competitive with strong participation from the international manufacturers, essentially turning the digital camera into a commodity in a short period. By 2010, Kodak was ranked seventh in the domestic camera market with a little less than 9-percent market share. To make matters worse, Kodak was now facing competition from other technological devices such as camera phones, tablets, and other portable devices. It seemed that its business model was failing.

Whether vying for territory in the digital camera or other graphics markets such as printing, Kodak was, in fact, too late to own any facet of the market and continued to fall further behind the other now well-established players. The company soon realized that the investment that would be required to even ramp up in various markets would generate a debt load that would eventually outpace the company's ability to generate revenue. The company is now facing bankruptcy.(16)

The story of Kodak foreshadows the unfortunate tale of many of America's industrial-based organizations. By being inflexible, these once-large business icons are unable to keep up with the shifts and turns of new technology and its inevitable competition, until it is usually too late. Some of the companies that do fail were dominant in their industries and generated billions in revenues before their economic future was turned on its head by emerging technologies. In business schools across the country, these firms now serve as case studies in what not to do in the face of a changing business environment.

However, while these old lessons are being taught about the past, new business models are also facing challenges as they try to understand and deal with the effects of the global transformation. If history is a guide, then the firms that emerge after the global economic transition will more than likely be the flexible companies who adapted to the changing world rather than holding on to archaic practices that society is phasing away from. Successful companies will recognize they are not immune from change and will deal with the internal and external issues that will affect their long term viability.

## Research and Development Investment

Although technological innovations have been taking place for the past few decades, the United States is still just now at the beginning of an extremely innovative technological period in history. With this in mind, it is important to ensure that new technological advancements and the companies that support them are able to move forward successfully. Research and development investment is the key to the long-term sustainability of any business. If a company does not invest in newer technologies, productivity processes, or products, then it becomes dependent on the weaknesses of its competitors to survive. And given the level of investments in R&D, a business will be making a grave mistake in not making significant contributions to this area.

A free market economy ensures that competition will always be around. A company might get an edge by discovering or creating some new innovations or product, but if they are profitable, these achievements are rarely unchallenged. As long as there are profits to be made and the demand expected to be more than fleeting, competitors will find a way to create similar or better goods and services. It is, therefore, imperative that a company keeps investing heavily in its R&D department no matter how large its current market share. A company that becomes complacent with its current goods and services will surely become irrelevant in the marketplace.

### Key Industries of the Future

For those companies willing to adapt to changing technology, there are a number of key areas that are open for future leadership—and profit. This includes clean energy and technology innovations.

### Clean Energy

Revenue growth in the primary clean energy sectors of wind, solar, fuel cells, and bio-fuels has gone up tremendously over the past several years and is predicted to triple over the next decade.(17) This means that investment capital has been pouring into the sector as the demand for products such as photovoltaic panels are in high demand. Companies that focus on wind energy are also seeing the benefits of the clean power movement.

### Technological Innovations

The possibilities in future technological innovations are virtually limitless. Just some predictions include new satellites, computers, and high tech measuring equipment to learn more about the Earth's weather patterns. Environmentally friendly home designs will help entire cities stay cool in warm weather along with reducing carbon footprints. In addition, hydrogen fuel cells may likely be powering homes, offices, and vehicles much more efficiently.(18)

### How the Government is Making Sure the United States is Competitive in These Areas

Both the US government and many of the companies themselves are making investments in future key industries such as clean energy. The US government understands the many negative consequences that are associated with using traditional energy. And, while many of the other advanced nations worldwide are producing over half of their electricity from renewable sources, the United States is still far behind.(19)

In order to help in catching up, the government offers a number of incentives to encourage the development of solar energy as well as encouragement for other programs like environmentally friendly product creation. In addition, laws and regulations have also been passed in many of the areas that are instrumental to future development.

Some of the government incentives include:

- Advanced Biofuel Production Grants and Loan Guarantees
- Advanced Energy Research Project Grants
- Volumetric Ethanol Excise Tax Credit (VEETC)
- Biodiesel Education Grants
- Biodiesel Income Tax Credit
- Improved Energy Technology Loans
- Value-Added-Producer Grants
- State Energy Program Funding
- Clean Construction USA(20)

Examples of just some of the US government mandated laws and regulations include:

- Vehicle Incremental Cost Allocation
- Renewable Fuel Standard (RFS) Program
- Fuel Economy Test Procedures and Labeling
- Import Duty for Fuel Ethanol(21)

In addition to investment and incentives from the government, companies themselves are also making inroads to key industries of the future. And, in many cases, these companies are not just investing as a philanthropic effort, but rather as part of their long-term business strategy.

One example of this is Google. In 2010, Google invested over $900 million in clean energy projects such as wind, solar, and transmission in order to make itself a more sustainable company.(22)

One reason for this is that Google is working on more efficient data center operations. It plans to achieve this goal by procuring clean power for its data centers as well as investing in additional clean energy projects in other areas.

The company feels that clean energy will be the primary energy source of the future. The investments made by the company today are essentially tied to specific projects that are slated to bring in a steady stream of long-term revenues. Another reason or bonus for these initiatives is to receive government credits that offset some of the costs of these investments. Google hopes to become eligible for government credits in these areas that will help to offset their federal corporate tax obligations.(23)

Some of yesterday's industries have followed in Kodak's footsteps, refusing to keep up with the times, and in many cases, by the time they realize their mistake, it is too late. Although some of the gravest situations require bankruptcy and then a major overhaul or reorganization, there are firms that can avoid this fate if they take steps to correct their failing strategies.

## How You CAN Teach an Old Company New Competitive Strategies

Having a competitive advantage is healthy for most companies; however, it can also be costly and dangerous if the company is not up to par in its technology, manufacturing, and operations. How a company handles its competitive advantage and its movement into the future can be a direct link to its ultimate success or failure. There are several ways that companies must keep up, or they will be left behind.

**Defining the Overall Mission** Companies must be clear about where they wish to stand in the marketplace. Without a clearly defined purpose for their product offering, customers will tend to shy away—especially if it is evident that the company is lagging behind in technology and/or in the products that it produces.

**Defining Competitors** The strengths, weaknesses, and capabilities of competitors must be researched and then improved upon.

**Identifying Customers** Companies must also keep in mind the end user for their offerings. Without keeping up with current demand, products can become outdated and essentially obsolete.

**Differentiating Product Offering** Companies must also give customers a reason to choose their product over their competitors' offerings. While a lower price is certainly one way to bring in customers, this model is not sustainable for long-term success. Differentiation can also include superior customer service as well as offering a quality product.

**Using Advanced Technologies** By investing in newer or updated technology, companies will be much more apt to successfully move into the future. One such example is in the manufacturing sector. By utilizing more advanced technology in product production, companies are likely to lower their cost per unit in the long run while also lessening the product's time to market. Thus, it is imperative to not remain complacent. Otherwise, competitors are likely to improve upon current technology and to surpass others in the global marketplace.

**Pricing Correctly** Here again, although lower price can initially bring in customers, it cannot sustain success for the long term. Companies must find a price point that allows quality manufacturing while still giving the customer a good value for their dollar.

**Marketing Strategically** In order to stay at the forefront of customers' minds, companies need to sustain a strategic marketing initiative both domestically and globally for their best competitive advantage.

Once this is accomplished, the company must continue to maintain its competitive edge—both domestically and globally. Some of the ways in which to do so includes keeping up with supply and demand while staying in good shape financially. A large part of continued growth and competitiveness involves keeping up with changes and trends in the overall marketplace. In addition, it may be necessary for the company to expand—and if so, does the company possess the financial resources as well as the human capital in order to do so?

### Business Culture

Remaining competitive in the global economy—where some of the developing countries like India and China are growing twice as fast as the United States—will depend on a business resources, strategies, and also in large part on national policies that are made in the United States.(24) Sometimes, national policies can be difficult to change even with the enlistment of powerful lobbying groups in the legislative capital. Lobbying tends to resolve general industry concerns that enable the survival of the group. However, businesses will have to look at their individual business cultures to ensure adaptability with globalization and to affect change.

### What Exactly Is America's Corporate Business Culture?

A company's business culture is essentially the behaviors and the beliefs at work in determining how a company's employees and its management interact and handle its outside business transactions. In many cases, business culture is not actually written or even defined; it is instead implied.(25)

As corporate business culture relates to the United States as a whole, especially over the past few years, overall corporate culture has been primarily viewed as one of greed—especially in light of overpaid CEOs, mass layoffs of "bottom rung" employees, and not-so-ethical tactics that at times seem to be the norm rather than the exception. In the short term, it seems that it is the businesses that show the world their worst side that are reaping immense profits and market share. But this behavior really is not sustainable for a business or a nation over the long term. In fact, those companies that have sustained winning cultures, ethical behaviors, solid relationships with customers, and good product values have been able to persevere and develop strong competitive advantages over the long term.

In addition, some companies that have slipped have been able to right themselves by refocusing on corporate culture. For instance, there is a case to be made regarding IBM's near demise in the 1990s. IBM's attitude at that time was that it was the "best of the best." However, when it stopped being flexible, it began to quickly lose customers to its competitors. By reversing that attitude, the company was eventually able to repair its customer relationships.(26)

## Moving Away From Creative Accounting

Other ways in which companies may have harmed the view of corporate culture in America today include the movement from traditional "bottom line" accounting to one of "creative accounting." Some of the creative accounting methods used by some firms were so complex and perplexing that it was difficult to even recognize what line of business these firms were actually in. Not to mention the fact that it made it difficult to compare to other firms in the same industry. These firms focused more on managing the market perception of their earnings than on the long-term sustainability of their core business policies.

Nowhere was this more evident than in the demise of Enron. This company went from focusing on its main business lines of providing energy and some commodities to its customers to essentially promoting, trading, and pursuing deals as if it were an investment firm. Enron used numerous limited liability special purpose entities or vehicles (SPV) in order to conduct its various investment ventures in the deregulated energy environment so these deals would not appear directly on the parent company balance sheet. Unfortunately, when trades or business ventures failed, the managers felt that they had to hide this information from investors and began engaging in financial statements schemes. The company ushered in its demise by initiating various creative accounting schemes that did not mesh with its economic realities. One of its infamous accounting strategies included adding expected future revenues to its current income figures.

When these pie-in-the-sky revenues were not actually realized, the company was left with enormous losses, a tumbling stock price, frustrated customers, and eventually an internal collapse that left employees without income or retirement savings.(27) Subsequent investigations by the government showed numerous instances of fraud, insider trading, and other deceptive practices that were beyond just creative accounting. The scandals at Enron and other companies led to a public outcry and a major push to overhaul the accounting practices standards and industry.

Another area that saw various levels of creative accounting was that of debt or leveraging. When used wisely, debt can allow a business to pursue investment opportunities that would otherwise be off-limits without issuing new shares and thereby diluting the existing shares and driving down the share price. However, the level of debt or leveraging is monitored very closely by investors and creditors because of the perceived increase in risk or liability. Financial leverage can raise the scale of business activity to generate potentially larger profits. However, it can also magnify a business's potential losses if the venture does not pan out. In addition, too much leverage can even have an impact on a company's stockholders in that the use of excessive debt can increase the risk of creditors claiming repayment as well as leading to a lower appraisal of a company's asset value.(28)

It is also important to focus more on the traditional bottom line, income over expenses, rather than taking unnecessary risks through unsound investments or high-debt levels. By also staying on track with investments and practices that reflect the business's core operational models, companies will be better able to sustain operations over the long term as well as be in a better position to compete in the domestic and global marketplace.

## Moving Away From a Share Price Focus or Short Term Focus Model

Over the past couple of decades, United States companies—unlike their European counterparts—have been sacrificing long-term opportunities for short-term results.(29) In fact, starting with the dot-com era of the 1990s and continuing to our present day, a great deal of executive compensation is directly related to a company's short-term performance, which is reflected in the company's stock share price.

This results in a lot of pressure for management to deliver results on a quarterly basis rather than on providing long-term value. But this focus on the short term can also lead to other significant problems for companies, because the level of increases that seems to be required from quarter to quarter might not be sustainable. This unfortunately leads to various creative accounting schemes, unnecessary risks into investments that might not be related to the core business lines, and other methods of managing quarterly earnings so that they are just better than the market's expectations.

In addition, uncertain market forces created by emerging technology and globalization are constantly changing the economic environment. These unexpected changes can easily derail a company's short-term efforts to creatively manage their earnings. More importantly, they might be more susceptible to these market forces than a company that is more long-term focused. A long-term-focused company is prepared to make the necessary investments that will sustain it over the long haul, even if it means that it will be less profitable over the next few quarters. The gains will be smaller in the short term, but those investors that are onboard with the business will reap larger gains over the long haul. After all, investing should not be like going down to the casino. Sometimes it takes time to build a good business.

## Moving Away From Tax Avoidance

Policy makers in the United States understand the effects of their legislative decisions on the American business as well as on the nation's overall ability to remain a global economic leader. However, they rarely agree on how to accomplish this goal. One such area that has always drawn passionate debate from businesses and the taxpayers has been in regards to the US and international tax codes. Currently, reforms proposed by the current Obama administration in Washington are suggesting a minimum tax that corporations should be paying across the board, including foreign subsidies. This is an effort to bring back over $90 billion a year that the United States loses to offshore tax entities. Not surprisingly, these reforms have been met with strong opposition by those who want to protect the corporate right to pursue tax havens.

It has been suggested that the current tax laws actually create incentives for companies to base their operations in other countries where they are able to minimize taxes. However, the reality is that for the companies based in the United States and paying the higher taxes, it becomes much more difficult to compete.(30) In these cases, the companies are paying higher taxes within the US borders even though they are creating jobs in the United States. These loyal American businesses actually have to work harder to compete since they are paying a much higher tax than the businesses that have forsaken their patriotic duty to this country by not paying their fair share of their businesses tax debt. Not surprisingly, this has sparked renewed debates and various proposals among industry lobbyists and US lawmakers in their effort to push back against the administration's tax and other business reforms.

Republican Ways and Means Committee Chairman Dave Camp proposed an ambitious global tax solution that will be on par with the rest of the developed world. Under the Camp Proposal, as it is called, the current global corporate tax system should be replaced with a fairer territorial tax to enable the United States to remain competitive with other countries. Within this new system, the corporate tax rate will effectively decrease from about 35 percent to 25 percent. The territorial taxation system works by allowing taxation only in the specific nation where the income is earned instead of being double taxed. Camp suggests that foreign income earned by a corporation's foreign subsidiary should be exempt from US taxes rather than being taxed in the foreign country and then in the United States. Currently, these foreign subsidiaries' income is not subject to taxation here in the United States, but is tax deferred until it is brought back to the United States.

Additionally, Camp also suggests that corporations that want to repatriate foreign profits should be allowed to transfer those earnings back to the United States, but at a low tax rate of 1.25 percent. Currently, repatriated profits are taxed at the full corporate tax rate, which is reduced by foreign credits deductions. Therefore, most companies do not repatriate these earnings, choosing instead to keep trillions of dollars offshore. Of course, there are critics accusing Camp of wanting to ensure that offshore countries remain a viable tax haven for businesses.

Others suggest that the United States should place its focus on trying to attract foreign direct investment whereby foreign companies could not only employ United States citizens but also pay United States taxes.(31) This again calls for lowering its current business tax system.

Because 2012 is an election year in the United States, it is very unlikely that any tax reforms will be enacted. There are too many special interests that will blockade any significant legislation. This is unfortunate, considering that America does need its multinational businesses to contribute more to the tax base. It is bad enough that some are increasingly shifting jobs overseas, but to compound these actions with an almost defiant stance on paying taxes is astonishing. America should create incentives and policies to foster global competiveness, but businesses should also look at the long-term prosperity of the nation in the decisions they make. Does the nation really benefit in avoiding taxation—or is the burden just redistributed to others who are not getting foreign tax credits and other incentives geared toward corporations? United States policy makers must look at the US tax code through a more global lens and consider how to more effectively position the US economy to compete better in domestically as well as globally.(32)

## Embracing a Nation's Long-Term Goals

A business that chooses to have factories built or to utilize facilities in another country is not necessarily bad for the long-term prosperity of a nation. Having factories in other countries is good for the nation if the revenues or profits that are made as a result of the cost savings are benefitting the homeland. If the domestic economy is benefitting from the cost savings in the form of other nonmanufacturing jobs that are created or if those monies are reinvested in another fashion so that it benefits the domestic economy, then that business is beneficial to the nation.

Businesses also benefit the nation if taxes are levied and paid to the nation in a manner that adds to the tax base and can allow that country to fund its expenditures without relying heavily on foreign investments to sustain its domestic budgets. If the business is avoiding or paying fewer taxes than expected, then it is an enterprise that is against the long-terms goals of the nation and indeed might be avoiding other responsibilities that might prove beneficial to the nation over the long term, as well.

Even when an enterprise is engaged in business practices that do not benefit the nation directly, it might still be beneficial to the domestic economy. If the activity of the business is actually creating productive jobs and otherwise stimulating greater economic activity, then it is of benefit to the nation and to society as a whole. Immediate action needs to be taken to correct a business's economic wrongdoings if the enterprise is not stimulating positive productive economic activity and is engaging in practices that are actually destroying the long-term prosperity of the nation.

## Moving Away from Company's Short term Focus Layoff Policies

In times of economic challenges, companies often seek to cut costs through employee layoffs. This, however, may or may not always be cost effective in either the short or the long term. Finding and training good employees is a company expense in and of itself. And even the talk of potential layoffs tends to reduce employee morale and consumer confidence levels, essentially putting the company at a disadvantage even prior to the actual layoff.

Therefore, when a company succeeds in hiring and training a good employee, letting go of the employee may end up being more costly over the long term even though it solves a short-term revenue issue. Should business pick up, former employees have oftentimes found employment elsewhere, leading their original employer to resort to the necessary task and expense of finding and training new employees. There are some alternatives that companies should consider prior to moving forward with letting go of good, quality employees—no matter how bleak the current revenue situation is.

**Postponing Other Major Expenditures** One such solution is the postponement of high-dollar company purchases, thus saving dollars in other areas. In addition, a restriction in business-related travel and re-evaluating the costs of any work being outsourced may also save company funds in lieu of an employee layoff.

**Instituting a Wage Freeze** Many employees are agreeable to a wage freeze when it is compared to a total layoff. This could also include cutting back on or completely eliminating overtime as well as freezing or cutting back on the amount of employer contributions to employee retirement plans.

**Reduce Working Hours** An employer could reduce the working hours of employees or even take those who are full-time workers to a part-time status. Here, too, many workers would prefer working some hours to working none at all.(33)

## Moving Away from Layoffs and Rehiring as Part-time Workers

Another trend that is gaining traction in this economic downturn is the practice of laying off workers only to rehire them with reclassified job titles. For example, in some cases, teachers are laid off then rehired at a later period, often with less than 50 percent in pay and little or no benefits. The employers can achieve this because these rehires are now reclassified as part time or substitute employees.

This is a very demoralizing practice that needs to be stopped. Yes, a job is better than no job, but there is a better way to achieve much more desirable results. That is, assuming that the goal in the first place was not malicious. If the former assumption is incorrect, then these practices should be re-examined.

If, however, the goal of these businesses and organizations is indeed to lower costs in order to deal with the weakening economy, then there is a plethora of creative downsizing ideas that I have discussed in detail in this book. One of the options that could have been utilized is allowing those employees to keep their full-time status and scale back the pay scale and other benefits to bring them more in line with cost that strengthens rather than weakens the economy to go through the economic downturn. A status change sends the wrong message to the labor force.

The underlying goal of any employer considering creative downsizing is to give the employee a sense of economic security. By not laying off the employee, but instead looking at cost saving options, the employers show that they value their employees enough to consider them in a long-term mutual relationship that can weather the good and bad economies. These types of strategies boost consumer confidence and often lead to quicker economic recoveries as individual workers see themselves as part of the engine that drives the nation rather than just an expendable cog in the wheel that can be discarded at a moment's notice.

A free economic society that believes that long-term prosperity of a nation should not only be sought but should also be found to be desirable for the nation. The cost of not adhering to such a system of economic consideration is often redistributed to the majority with no economic benefit. In fact, this type of counterproductive enterprise that selfishly robs a society of its short-term wealth and long-term prosperity will do everything in its power to preserve its way of life. It stops at nothing to prevent its extinction, including deceptively using the very same legal system, legislature, regulatory groups, and even the masses that unwittingly might protect these rogue enterprises at the detriment of their own long-term prosperity. It is, therefore, prudent for a nation that wants to prosper in the long term to be vigilant at the individual, the community, and the national level to counteract the seemingly vast war chest of these destructive businesses.

### Government Partnership

In many ways, the government has a lot at stake in ensuring that US businesses remain competitive. This can only be achieved if concessions are made by both businesses as well as the government. This goal can be reached via a form of partnership such as offering grants and other incentives to companies in certain industries as well as through various types of regulation that relate to pricing, monopolization, and consumer protections. It is in everyone's interest to have competitive businesses that can add to the tax base and prosperity of the nation. Therefore, the government should do whatever is necessary to create a more level playing field for its businesses so they can compete more effectively in the global marketplace.

The government has already established policies to ensure that many businesses run on a level playing field. Some of these policies included the deregulation of various businesses such as the railroad, airline, telecommunications, and finance industries. This is in addition to domestically enforcing limitations on the business practices of monopolies that reduces overall competition and fairness in the marketplace. Sometimes, however, there are new problems that are created when the government attempts to create a level playing field for fairer competition.

### Reform in the Enforcement of Regulations

For the most part, government regulations have had many positive effects on business. Over the years, newer and more reformed regulations have come into play. In fact, in early 2012, President Obama outlined a plan to create a twenty-first century system of regulation whereby the public health and welfare are still protected while still promoting economic growth, competitiveness, job creation, and overall growth.

While some regulatory enforcement can actually penalize offenders in various regulated areas, it can often become more than just the cost of doing business for a more compliant company. These proposed reforms by the administration attempt to reduce some of the downside for compliant companies. Some of the reformed twenty-first regulations include: the removal of unnecessary reporting and regulatory requirements on hospitals and other healthcare providers by the Department of Health and Human Services; the filing of a suit by the Department of Labor that will simplify and improve hazard warnings for workers; and the elimination of unnecessary regulation in the railroad industry by the Department of Transportation.(34) These reforms will not be perfect, but they are necessary steps that should be taken to reduce or even stop compliant firms from being penalized in the marketplace.

## Economic Planning Board

One suggestion is to form a permanent economic planning committee that will serve the good of a nation while respecting the rights and motivations of businesses. By creating an environment that encourages economic planning, companies can become more productive as well as more competitive both domestically and globally. The economic planning will consist of both the control and the direction of economic activity not by the government, but along with it.

Some have feared and oftentimes justifiably criticized governments that are too involved in the functioning of the economic markets and societal issues. The goal here will not be to have the government control the society or businesses. Instead, the goal will be to ensure that a non-political group that has the long-term prosperity of the nation as its benchmark will work together to achieve this goal. Ideally, the economic planning committee should consist of equal representation from the government, private sector, and the academic arena. In bringing together various legislative, empirical, and theoretical viewpoints, the hope is that the committee will work together in reviewing economic issues as well as providing practical solutions that will make the nation competitive domestically and globally.

## The Bottom Line

Nurturing continued innovation in the United States is one of the most important factors in keeping America competitive in the global economy. According to Forbes, the US is still one of the best places worldwide to start and run a business although it came in at number ten in their ranking system. Canada was number one.(35)

| Forbes Best Countries for Business (2010)* | | |
|---|---|---|
| **Rank** | **Country** | **Brief Description** |
| 1 | Canada | Market oriented economic system that complements its high tech industrial society |
| 2 | New Zealand | Free market economy that competes globally |
| 3 | Hong Kong | Free market economy that is dependent on foreign trade and finance |
| 4 | Ireland | Foreign trade dependent economy |
| 5 | Denmark | Market economy with worldwide industries in high tech agriculture, pharmaceuticals, maritime shipping and renewable energy |
| 6 | Singapore | Highly developed free market economy |
| 7 | Sweden | Status as a peaceful and neutral country complements its high tech capitalism and extensive welfare benefits |
| 8 | Norway | Prosperous welfare capitalism that relies on the free markets and government intervention |
| 9 | United Kingdom | Leading trading power and global financial center |
| 10 | United States | Largest and technologically powerful economy in world |
| | | |
| *Metrics include: property rights, innovation, taxes, technology, corruption, freedom (personal, trade and monetary), red tape, investor protection and stock market performance | | |
| **Source: Forbes** | | |

However, the United States is arguably still one of the best places worldwide to start and run a business despite its many shortcomings and obstacles it needs to overcome. Therefore, it is imperative that a business do everything in its power to help create a healthy and competitive business environment, which can increase long-term prosperity for everyone.

The best way a business can remain or become globally competitive is to adapt strategically to the winds of change sweeping throughout the world. The successful enterprise will not just aim to capitalize on short-term fluctuations in the economic environment but also position itself to reap the long-term benefits that will be good for its shareholders, customers, and the nation's prosperity. In this regard, both the public and the private sector along with governmental support need to push for and embrace the necessary polices and reforms to achieve these long-term goals.

# Selected References and Resources

## SECTION 1: Economic Crisis

### Reaction to the Financial Crisis

**Selected Resources:**

USA Today article

Seeking Alpha website

National Public Radio (NPR)

"What Fed's 'Operation Twist' means for you," by Dave Carpenter, Associated Press, 9/22/2011. http://www.usatoday.com/money/economy/story/2011-09-22/Fed-Consumer/50511514/1

James Kwak, "Treasury Insider's View of the Financial Crisis," The Baseline Scenario, (April 21, 2009). http://seekingalpha.com/article/132130-treasury-insider-s-view-of-the-financial-crisis

Jacob Goldstein, "Fed's 'Operation Twist,' Explained in 4 Easy Steps," NPR.org, (September 21, 2011). http://m.npr.org/story/140643696

"The Financial Crisis: A Timeline of Events and Policy Actions," Federal Reserve Bank of St. Louis. http://timeline.stlouisfed.org/

## Citation(s):


1. Greg Gardner, "Rattner: Taxpayers will lose $14B on auto bailouts," Detroit Free Press, USA Today Money 12/16/2011. http://www.usatoday.com/money/autos/story/2011-12-16/auto-bailout-taxpayer-cost/52007784/1
2. Charles Lane, "GM should buy back U.S. taxpayers' shares," Washington Post Opinions, 12/5/2011. http://www.washingtonpost.com/opinions/gm-should-buy-back-us-taxpayers-shares/2011/12/05/gIQAvC7rXO_story.html
3. "Report: Big Bank Bonuses in 2011," (November 2011) http://www.newbottomline.com/report_big_bank_bonuses_in_2011.
4. Monika Mitchell, "The Federal Reserve: Helping the Rich Get Richer," Huffington Post (November 30, 2011). http://www.huffingtonpost.com/monika-mitchell/federal-reserve-big-bank-loans_b_1118876.html
5. Charles Gasparino, "Break Up the Banks: The Fed Must End 'Too Big to Fail,'" New York Post Opinion Column, (December 21, 2011). http://www.nypost.com/p/news/opinion/opedcolumnists/break_up_the_banks_j3vm2GlC4JIbIKmcH2sT0H
6. "Vickers report on banks to be accepted in full – Cable," BBC News – Business Section, (December 18, 2011). http://www.bbc.co.uk/news/business-16235636
7. "Jon Huntsman Would Break Up Big Banks, Wants Tough Settlement for Mortgage Fraud," Huffington Post, (November 29, 2011). http://www.huffingtonpost.com/2011/11/29/jon-huntsman-would-break-up-big-banks_n_1118518.html
8. "International regulatory framework for banks (Basel III), "Bank for International Settlements (BIS). http://www.bis.org/bcbs/basel3.htm
9. Dave Clarke, "Fed Bank Capital, Liquidity Proposal Follows Basel," Reuters, (December 20, 2011). http://www.reuters.com/article/2011/12/20/us-fed-banks-idUSTRE7BJ1OM20111220
10. "Andrew Jackson, Veto Message," The Founders' Constitution, Volume 3, Article 1, Section 8, Clause 18, Document 20. http://press-pubs.uchicago.edu/founders/documents/a1_8_18s20.html

**Selected Resources:**

CNNMoney.com's bailout tracker http://money.cnn.com/news/storysupplement/economy/bailouttracker

Morgan Stanley Speculating to Brink of Collapse Got $107 Billion from Fed http://www.bloomberg.com/news/2011-08-22/morgan-stanley-at-brink-of-collapse-got-107b-from-fed.html

Richardson, James D., comp. A Compilation of the Messages and Papers of the Presidents, 1789--1897. 10 vols. Washington, D.C.: Government Printing Office, 1896--99.

## Wall Street Fines and Settlements

**Citation(s):**

1. The Distribution of Fraud Enforcement. (2007, February). Cardozo Law Review, 28 (4), pp. 1593-1597.
2. Terrorist Financing. (2008, February 29). Retrieved from Financial Action Task Force - Groupe d'action financiere: http://www.fatf-gafi.org/dataoecd/28/43/40285899.pdf
3. Criminal Investigations. (2010). Retrieved from United States Secret Service: http://www.secretservice.gov/criminal.shtml
4. The Investor's Advocate: How the SEC Protects Investors, Maintains Integrity, and Facilitates Capital Formation. (2011, October 24). Retrieved from U.S. Securities and Exchange Commission: http://www.sec.gov/about/whatwedo.shtml
5. Toby J. Bishop and Frank E. Hydoski, (2009). Corporate Resiliency: Managing the Growing Risk of Fraud and Corruption, Hoboken, New Jersey: John Wiley & Sons.
6. George Santayana, (1905) Reason in Common Sense, volume 1 of The Life of Reason.
7. Dennis Moberg and Edward Romar, (2003). WorldCom, Retrieved from Santa Clara University: http://www.scu.edu/ethics/dialogue/candc/cases/worldcom.html
8. April 15, 1922 - Senate Investigates the "Teapot Dome" Scandal. (2011). Retrieved from United States Senate: http://www.senate.gov/artandhistory/history/minute/Senate_Investigates_the_Teapot_Dome_Scandal.htm

9. Timothy Curry and Lynn Shibut. "The Cost of the Savings and Loan Crisis: Truth and Consequences," p26. http://www.fdic.gov/bank/analytical/banking/2000dec/brv13n2_2.pdf
10. SEC Charges Goldman Sachs With Fraud in Structuring and Marketing of CDO Tied to Subprime Mortgages. (2010, April 16). Retrieved from U.S. Securities and Exchange Commission: http://sec.gov/news/press/2010/2010-59.htm
11. "Judge Rejects An S.E.C. Deal With Citigroup," (2011, November 29), The New York Times, p. A1.
12. One of Nation's Top Investment Firms Settle Enforcement Actions Involving Conflicts of Interest Between Research and Investment Banking. (2003, April 28). Retrieved from U.S. Securities and Exchange Commission: http://www.sec.gov/news/press/2003-54.htm

**Selected Resources:**

Public Law 107–204—JULY 30, 2002 ("Sarbanes- Oxley Act of 2002") http://www.sec.gov/about/laws/soa2002.pdf

## Flash Crashes: High Frequency Trading

**Citation(s):**

1. The Distribution of Fraud Enforcement. (2007, February). Cardozo Law Review, 28 (4), pp. 1593-1597.
2. Terrorist Financing. (2008, February 29). Retrieved from Financial Action Task Force - Groupe d'action financiere: http://www.fatf-gafi.org/dataoecd/28/43/40285899.pdf
3. Criminal Investigations. (2010). Retrieved from United States Secret Service: http://www.secretservice.gov/criminal.shtml
4. The Investor's Advocate: How the SEC Protects Investors, Maintains Integrity, and Facilitates Capital Formation. (2011, October 24). Retrieved from U.S. Securities and Exchange Commission: http://www.sec.gov/about/whatwedo.shtml
5. Toby J. Bishop and Frank E. Hydoski, (2009). Corporate Resiliency: Managing the Growing Risk of Fraud and Corruption, Hoboken, New Jersey: John Wiley & Sons.
6. George Santayana, (1905) Reason in Common Sense, volume 1 of The Life of Reason.

7. Dennis Moberg and Edward Romar, (2003). WorldCom, Retrieved from Santa Clara University: http://www.scu.edu/ethics/dialogue/candc/cases/worldcom.html
8. April 15, 1922 - Senate Investigates the "Teapot Dome" Scandal. (2011). Retrieved from United States Senate: http://www.senate.gov/artandhistory/history/minute/Senate_Investigates_the_Teapot_Dome_Scandal.htm
9. Timothy Curry and Lynn Shibut. "The Cost of the Savings and Loan Crisis: Truth and Consequences," p26. http://www.fdic.gov/bank/analytical/banking/2000dec/brv13n2_2.pdf
10. SEC Charges Goldman Sachs With Fraud in Structuring and Marketing of CDO Tied to Subprime Mortgages. (2010, April 16). Retrieved from U.S. Securities and Exchange Commission: http://sec.gov/news/press/2010/2010-59.htm
11. "Judge Rejects An S.E.C. Deal With Citigroup," (2011, November 29), The New York Times, p. A1.
12. One of Nation's Top Investment Firms Settle Enforcement Actions Involving Conflicts of Interest Between Research and Investment Banking. (2003, April 28). Retrieved from U.S. Securities and Exchange Commission: http://www.sec.gov/news/press/2003-54.htm

**Selected Resources:**

Public Law 107–204—JULY 30, 2002 ("Sarbanes- Oxley Act of 2002") http://www.sec.gov/about/laws/soa2002.pdf

## SECTION 2: Business as Usual

### Gramm-Leach-Bliley Act

**Citation(s):**

1. Lori Enos, (2000, September 08), FTC Lowers Boom on Net Porn Scammers, Retrieved from E-Commerce Times: http://www.ecommercetimes.com/story/4233.html
2. Melanie L. Fein, (December 2000), Securities Activities, New York: Wolters Kluwer Law & Business, p3: 65-66.

3. "Minnesota Sues U.S. Bank on Privacy Data," (1999, June 11). Retrieved from New York Times: http://www.nytimes.com/1999/06/11/business/minnesota-sues-us-bank-on-privacy-data.html
4. Joseph Karl Grant, (2010, March 26), "What the Financial Services Industry Puts Together Let No Person Put Asunder: How the Gramm-Leach-Bliley Act Contributed to the 2008-2009 American Capital Markets Crisis." Albany Law Review, 371-420.

## New Lending Policies: Why Some Banks Will Not Lend

### Citation(s):

1. Michael S. Derby, "Ending Interest on Reserves Won't Help," WSJ Blogs, July 21, 2010. http://blogs.wsj.com/economics/2010/07/21/ending-interest-on-reserves-wont-help-economy-much/
2. U.S. Small Business Administration (SBA) Office of Advocacy's 2010 edition of "The Small Business Economy: A Report to the President" (Jan 2011) http://www.sba.gov/sites/default/files/files/sb_econ2009.pdf
3. "For want of a loan: America's best job creators are being hit by a credit crunch," The Economist, December 10, 2009. http://www.economist.com/node/15065782
4. "The Bank of North Dakota: A Model for Massachusetts and Other States?" Federal Reserve Bank of Boston http://www.bos.frb.org/economic/neppc/researchreports/2011/neppcrr1102.pdf

### Selected Resources:

Afonso, Gara Alfonso, Anna Kovner, and Antoinette Schoar, "What happened to US interbank lending in the financial crisis?" www.VoxEU.org, April 26, 2010.

Brown, Ellen, "Why Banks Aren't Lending: The Silent Liquidity Squeeze," www.webofdebt.com, July 15, 2011. http://www.webofdebt.com/articles/why_banks.php

Zywicki, Todd J., "Why Aren't Banks Lending?" Washington Times, Opinion page, June 8, 2010. http://www.washingtontimes.com/news/2010/jun/8/why-arent-banks-lending/

Mason, John M., contributor, "Why Banks Aren't Lending" Seekingalpha.com, September 23, 2011. http://seekingalpha.com/article/295630-why-banks-aren-t-lending

## A Golden Parachute

### Citation(s):

1. Gary Strauss, "CEOs' exit packages blow past $100 million," USA Today (November 2011). http://www.usatoday.com/MONEY/usaedition/2011-11-08-100M-chairmen_ST_U.htm
2. Ibid

### Selected Resources:

Albano, M., Alcock, M., Emberger, K., LaPorte, L., & Bonnett, E. (2011). "The SEC's Final 'Say': SEC Adopts Final Say-on-Pay and Shareholder Advisory Vote Regulations," Corporate Governance Advisor, 19(2), 20-33.

Bagley, C. (2005). "How Corporate Parachutes Unfurled," Business Week. [Available] Online: http://www.businessweek.com/magazine

Cochran, P. L., Wood, R. A., & Jones, T. B. (1985). THE COMPOSITION OF BOARDS OF DIRECTORS AND INCIDENCE OF GOLDEN PARACHUTES. Academy Of Management Journal, [Available] Online: https://ehis.ebscohost.com

Evans, J. D., and Hefner, F. (2009). "Business Ethics and the Decision to Adopt Golden Parachute Contracts: Empirical Evidence of Concern for All Stakeholders." Journal Of Business Ethics.

SEC Issues Final Rules Regarding Say-On-Pay and Golden Parachute Requirements Under the Dodd-Frank Financial Reform Act. (2011). Venulex Legal Summaries, 1-9.

Task, A., "Another Corporate Outrage: Golden Parachutes for Failed CEOs," The Daily Ticker (2011). [Available] Online: http://finance.yahoo.com/blogs/daily-ticker

Hodgson, Paul and Greg Ruel, "Twenty-One US CEOs with Golden Parachutes of More Than $100 Million," GMI Ratings http://origin.library.constantcontact.com/download/get/file/1102561686275-69/GMI_GoldenParachutes_012012.pdf

## Corporate Handouts and Welfare

### Citation(s):


1. Chris Edwards and Tad DeHaven. (2003). Cato Handbook for Congress. Washington, D.C.: Cato Institute.
2. Global Forum on Competition - Competition, State Aids and Subsidies. (February 2010) Paris, France (Conference Location): Federal Trade Commission (Report submitted for Conference Inclusion).
3. Corn Subsidies in United States in 2010. (2010). Retrieved from Environmental Working Group: http://farm.ewg.org/top_recips.php?fips=00000&progcode=corn&yr=2010&regionname=theUnitedStates
4. "Do We Need Big Government?" (2011, December 14). Retrieved from Cato Institute: http://www.cato.org/pub_display.php?pub_id=13935
5. Chris Edwards and Tad DeHaven. (2003). Cato Handbook for Congress. Washington, D.C.: Cato Institute.
6. "Epoch Times: Warren Buffett Off the Mark," (2011, September 9). Retrieved from Citizens for Tax Justice: http://ctj.org/ctjinthenews/2011/09/epoch_times_warren_buffett_off_the_mark.php
7. David Cay Johnson, "State and local corporate welfare are mind-boggling. Where's the reporting?" (2011, January, 8) Retrieved from Nieman Watchdog: http://www.niemanwatchdog.org/index.cfm?fuseaction=ask_this.view&askthisid=488
8. "Solyndra Highlights Long History of Energy Subsidies". (2012, January 15). Retrieved from NPR - National Public Radio: http://www.npr.org/2011/11/16/142364037/solyndra-highlights-long-history-of-energy-subsidies
9. "Policy Basics: Where Do Our Federal Tax Dollars Go?" (2011, April 15). Retrieved from Center on Budget and Policy Priorities: http://www.cbpp.org/cms/index.cfm?fa=view&id=1258
10. "Policy Basics: Where Do Our State Tax Dollars Go?" (2011, April 12). Retrieved from Center on Budget and Policy Priorities: http://www.cbpp.org/cms/index.cfm?fa=view&id=2783
11. "Campaign to cut waste: Vice President Biden announces U.S. will halt production of excess dollar coins and Department of Justice recovered a record $5.6 billion in fraud in 2011," (2011, December 13). Retrieved from U.S. Department of Health & Human Services and U.S. Department of Justice: http://www.hhs.gov/news/press/2011pres/12/20111213a.html

## Outsourcing and Other Offshore Business

### Citation(s):

"The Offshore Outsourcing of Information Technology Jobs in New York State," September 2010. http://www.labor.ny.gov/stats/PDFs/Offshore_Outsourcing_ITJobs_NYS.pdf

### Selected Resources:

Elliot, Larry and Patrick Wintour, "Tax evasion crackdown will raise £62bn for G20 nations, says OECD." The Guardian (November 2011). http://www.guardian.co.uk/business/2011/nov/03/global-tax-evasion-crackdown-will-raise-billions-says-oecd

OECD: Tax Haven Criteria http://www.oecd.org/document/23/0,3343,en_2649_33745_30575447_1_1_1_1,00.html

REPATRIATING OFFSHORE FUNDS www.levin.senate.gov/download/repatriating-offshore-funds

Werdigier, Julia. "Tax Evaders Face Greater Scrutiny as National Debts Pile Up," New York Times. (November 2011). http://www.nytimes.com/2011/11/03/business/global/tax-evaders-face-greater-scrutiny-as-national-debts-pile-up.html

## Special Interests and Lobbyists

### Citation(s):

1. OpenSecrets.org Details What Special Interest Groups Spent Most on Third-Quarter Lobbying. (2011, October 31). Retrieved from Open Secrets.org: http://www.opensecrets.org/lobby/top.php?showYear=2011&indexType=i
2. Burdett Loomis, "From the Framing to the Fifties: Lobbying in Constitutional and Historical Contexts," Extensions - a Journal of the Carl Albert Congressional Research and Studies Center (2006, Fall).
3. Ibid
4. Ibid
5. The Federal Election Campaign Laws: A Short History. (1985). Retrieved from Federal Election Commission: http://www.fec.gov/info/appfour.htm

6. Lobbying Database. (2012). Retrieved from OpenSecrets.org –Center for Responsive Politics: http://www.opensecrets.org/lobby/index.php
7. Top Lobbying Firms, (2012) Retrieved from OpenSecrets.org – Center for Responsive Politics: http://www.opensecrets.org/lobby/top.php?showYear=2011&indexType=l
8. Richard S. Dunham and Stewart Powell, "Critics blame energy lobby for lax safety rules," (Washington Bureau: 2010, May 8). Retrieved from Houston chron.com: http://www.chron.com/business/energy/article/Critics-blame-energy-lobby-for-lax-safety-rules-1597469.phpecial Interests and Lobbyists

## SECTION 3: Brave New World

### Global Financial Crisis Update

#### Citation(s):

Juan Forero, "In Role Reversal, Latin America May Help IMF," Washington Post, World section, December 2011. http://www.washingtonpost.com/world/in-role-reversal-imf-comes-hat-in-hand-to-latin-america/2011/12/03/gIQAjPbYPO_story.html

#### Selected Resources:

The Wall Street Journal online

Forbes online

The Charlotte Observer online

Reuters

United Nations website

### The Eurozone Experiment

#### Selected Resources:

www.bloomberg.com

www.efsf.europa.eu

www.businessweek.com

www.theeconomist.com

www.dasspiegal.de

www.schoolvoorjournalistiek.com

www.ft.com

www.europa.come Eurozone Experiment

## The Global Economic Shift

### Citation(s):

1. "A Game of Catch Up: The shift in economic power from West to East," Economist (Dec. 17, 2011). http://www.economist.com/node/21528979
2. "The Big Tilt: The rise of the East and what it means for business," Economist Intelligence Unit Limited 2010. http://graphics.eiu.com/upload/eb/the_big_tilt.pdf
3. Barry Eichengreen, "Why the Dollar's Reign is Near an End." http://online.wsj.com/article/SB10001424052748703313304576132170181013248.html

### Selected Resources:

Economist.com

Wall Street Journal

New York Times

## China: The Rise of an Empire

### Citation(s):

1. "The world's biggest defense budgets," The Economist (March 2011) http://www.economist.com/blogs/dailychart/2011/03/defence_budgets
2. http://www.globalfirepower.com/

3. "Report: China to raise defense budget in 2011," CNN Wire staff (March 2011) http://articles.cnn.com/2011-03-04/world/china.defense.budget_1_defense-budget-china-plans-military-spending?_s=PM:WORLD
4. "An Analysis of China's 2011 Defense Budget and Total Military Spending — The Great Unknown," Dennis J. Blasko (March 2011). http://www.jamestown.org/single/?no_cache=1&tx_ttnews%5Btt_news%5D=37631
5. "Chinese Curbs on Raw-Material Exports Break Rules, WTO Says," Jennifer M. Freedman, Bloomberg (July 2011). http://www.bloomberg.com/news/2011-07-05/chinese-curbs-on-raw-material-exports-break-rules-wto-says-1-.html
6. "China's Economy: Two twists in the dragon's tail," The Economist (Jan 2012). http://www.economist.com/node/21543176
7. "China's Fall, Not Its Rise, Is the Real Global Threat," (October 2011). http://www.businessweek.com/news/2011-10-03/china-s-fall-not-its-rise-is-the-real-global-threat-view.html#fadetoblack
8. "Why China is an energy consumption hog," Steve Hargreaves, (November 2010). http://money.cnn.com/2010/11/26/news/international/china_energy_efficiency/index.htm
9. "Q&A: Why China has become the Middle East's favorite customer," Sarah A. Topol, (July 2010). http://www.csmonitor.com/World/Asia-Pacific/2010/0713/Q-A-Why-China-has-become-the-Middle-East-s-favorite-customer
10. "How China has created a new slave empire in Africa," Peter Hitchens (September 2008). http://www.dailymail.co.uk/news/article-1063198/PETER-HITCHENS-How-China-created-new-slave-empire-Africa.html
11. "Expanding China-Africa Oil Ties" Christopher Alessi, Associate Staff Writer, and Stephanie Hanson Council on Foreign Relations (Feb 2012). http://www.cfr.org/china/expanding-china-africa-oil-ties/p9557?cid=rss-energy_environment-expanding_china_africa_oil_tie-020812
12. "Fueling the dragon: China's race into the oil market" http://www.iags.org/china.htm
13. China's Economy Predicted to Overtake the U.S. Economy within Two Years (November 2010). http://www.instituteforenergyresearch.org/2010/11/17/china%E2%80%99s-economy-predicted-to-overtake-the-u-s-economy-within-two-years/

14. "Expanding China-Africa Oil Ties" Christopher Alessi, Associate Staff Writer, and Stephanie Hanson Council on Foreign Relations (Feb 2012). http://www.cfr.org/china/expanding-china-africa-oil-ties/p9557?cid=rss-energy_environment-expanding_china_africa_oil_tie-020812
15. "Chinese Oil Giant Buys Into Canadian Oil Sands," Vivian Wai-yin Kwok, Forbes (September 2009). http://www.forbes.com/2009/09/01/petrochina-oil-sand-markets-commodities-canada.html
16. "Venezuela, China Sign Oil Deals" Darcy Crowe (December 2009). http://online.wsj.com/article/SB126152693744102097.html

**Selected Resources:**

CIA.gov

The Economist

Bloomberg

CNN

Wall Street Journal

chinadaily.com.cn

## SECTION 4: State of Affairs

### The Gig Economy: Age of the Independent Worker

**Citation(s):**

1. Tina Brown, "The Gig Economy." (2009, January 12). Retrieved from The Daily Beast: http://www.thedailybeast.com/articles/2009/01/12/the-gig-economy.html
2. Sara Horowitz, "The Freelance Surge is the Industrial Revolution of Our Time." (2011, September 1).Retrieved from The Atlantic: http://www.theatlantic.com/business/archive/2011/09/the-freelance-surge-is-the-industrial-revolution-of-our-time/244229/
3. Ibid
4. Sara Horowitz, "A Jobs Plan for the Post-Cubicle Economy." (2011, September 5).Retrieved from The Atlantic: http://www.theatlantic.

com/business/archive/2011/09/a-jobs-plan-for-the-post-cubicle-economy/244549/

5. Eve Tahmincioglu, "Need a job? Contract work could be new normal." (2010, May 6)Retrieved from Careers on msnbc.com: http://www.msnbc.msn.com/id/36826679/ns/business-careers/t/need-job-contract-work-could-be-new-normal/#.T2k9exG3OSo

### Technological Innovations in Commerce

## Citation(s):

1. "E-commerce," The Economist, October 8, 2009, http://www.economist.com/node/14298940
2. Ibid
3. Ibid
4. "Borders Forced to Liquidate, Close All Stores," Wall Street Journal, (July 19, 2011), http://online.wsj.com/article/SB10001424052702303661904576454353768550280.html
5. Kee-Hung Lai and Cheng, T. C. E. Just-in-Time Logistics, p. 2, http://www.iped-uk.com/Just-in-Time_Logistics_Intro.pdf
6. "The click and the dead," The Economist, (July 1, 2010), http://www.economist.com/node/16478931
7. "Internet Retailer Survey: International E-Commerce," Internet Retailer, (March 31, 2010), http://www.internetretailer.com/2010/03/31/internet-retailer-survey-international-e-commerce
8. Ibid
9. "Internet Sales Tax Fairness," New Rules Project, (May 23, 2011), http://www.newrules.org/retail/rules/internet-sales-tax-fairness
10. Ibid
11. Annette Nellen, "Federal Internet Tax Freedom Act: The Myths and Realities," (February 1999), http://www.cob.sjsu.edu/nellen_a/ITFA.html
12. Ibid, "Internet Sales Tax Fairness"
13. "What is NFC?" NFC Forum, http://www.nfc-forum.org/aboutnfc
14. "Bits and Bob," The Economist, (June 13, 2011), http://www.economist.com/blogs/babbage/2011/06/virtual-currency
15. Ibid

# SECTION 5: Solutions for a Better Tomorrow

## Government Financial Tools and Effect on Behavior

### Citation(s):


1. New laws toughen rules on abortions, immigrants, voters. (2011, December 31). Retrieved from MSNBC.com: http://www.msnbc.msn.com/id/45819570/ns/us_news-life/t/new-laws-toughen-rules-abortions-immigrants-voters/#.TxbwMm-3OSo
2. Ibid
3. The World Bank 1999. (Washington, D.C.). Curbing the Epidemic: Governments and the Economics of Tobacco Control. Washington, D.C.: The Bank.
4. ICAP Reports 18. Alcohol Taxation. (May 2006) Washington, D.C.: International Center for Alcohol Policies.
5. Congressional Budget Office, Effects of Gasoline Prices on Driving Behavior and Vehicle Markets, (Washington, D.C.: CBO. January 2008).
6. CBO. (n.d.). Changes in Health Habits and Medical Practices. Retrieved from Congressional Budget Office: http://www.cbo.gov/ftpdocs/99xx/doc9924/Chapter7.11.1.shtml
7. Ibid
8. Bank of America Settles Claims Stemming From Mortgage Crisis. (2011, June 29). Retrieved from The New York Times: http://www.nytimes.com/2011/06/30/business/30mortgage.html?pagewanted=all
9. Ibid
10. U.S. Smoking Rate Still Coming Down. (2008, July 24). Retrieved from Gallup: http://www.gallup.com/poll/109048/us-smoking-rate-still-coming-down.aspx
11. CDC. (2011, October). Drinking and Driving. Retrieved from Centers for Disease Control and Prevention: http://www.cdc.gov/vitalsigns/DrinkingAndDriving/index.html
12. Steven Dowshen, (2007, January). Most Infant Car Seats Fail Consumer Reports Crash Test. Retrieved from Children's Hospital Colorado: http://www.childrenscolorado.org/wellness/info/news/54744.aspx

13. Melissa C. Lott, "The US Now Uses More Corn for Fuel Than for Feed." (2011, October 7). Retrieved from Scientific American: http://blogs.scientificamerican.com/plugged-in/2011/10/07/the-u-s-now-uses-more-corn-for-fuel-than-for-feed/Government Financial Tools and Effect on Behavior

## Alternatives to Layoffs: Managing People in a Tough Economy

### Citation(s):

1. http://www.pbs.org/newshour/bb/business/jan-june12/germany_02-08.html

### Selected Resources:

Davidowitz, H., The Daily Ticker, (2011). [Available] Online: http://finance.yahoo.com/blogs/daily-ticker.

De Meuse, K. P., Vanderheiden, P. A., & Bergmann, T. J. "Announced Layoffs: Their Effect on Corporate Financial Performance." Human Resource Management, (1994) 33(4), 509-530.

Heathfield, S., "7 Tips for Compassionate Layoffs," Human Resources. [Available] Online: http://humanresources.about.com/od/layoffs-downsizing-strategies.

Olson, R. "Downsizing Is Rough.' Public Management (00333611), (2004) 86(11), 10.

Schnurr, L. "Planned Layoffs Surge in January," Reuters (2012). [Available] Online: http://www.reuters.com/article/2012/02/03/us-usa-economy-jobs.

## Large Corporations vs. Small Businesses

### Citation(s):

1. "Small Business is Good for Local Economies; Big Business is Not, Researchers Say," BusinessNewsDaily Staff (Aug 2011). http://www.businessnewsdaily.com/1298-small-business-good-for-economy.html
2. Goldman, David, "Most firms pay no income taxes – Congress," CNNMoney.com (Aug 2008). http://money.cnn.com/2008/08/12/news/economy/corporate_taxes/

3. "Mutual Benefits, Shared Growth: Small and Large Companies Working Together," (September 2010). http://businessroundtable.org/studies-and-reports/mutual-benefits-shared-growth-small-and-large-companies-working-togeth?
4. Ibid.
5. Arnold Anderson, "Disadvantages of Small Business," http://www.ehow.com/print/list_6552079_disadvantages-small-business.html
6. Big-Box Economic Impact Studies (www.HometownAdvantage.org) http://web.mit.edu/course/4/4.293/!Phoenix/Research/Tenant%20Research/bigboxstudies.pdf
7. Nin-Hai Tseng, "A bright spot for small businesses: Job creation," Fortune (November 2011). http://finance.fortune.cnn.com/2011/11/01/small-business-hiring/
8. http://money.cnn.com/2008/08/12/news/economy/corporate_taxes/
9. David Callahan, "Loophole Land: Time to Reform Corporate Taxes," (April 2011). http://www.ourfiscalsecurity.org/taxes-matter/2011/4/12/loophole-land-time-to-reform-corporate-taxes.html
10. David Goldman, "Most firms pay no income taxes – Congress," CNNMoney.com (Aug 2008). http://money.cnn.com/2008/08/12/news/economy/corporate_taxes/
11. "Mutual Benefits, Shared Growth: Small and Large Companies Working Together," (September 2010). http://businessroundtable.org/studies-and-reports/mutual-benefits-shared-growth-small-and-large-companies-working-togeth?
12. Ibid.

**Selected Resources:**

Fortune Magazine

Big-Box Economic Impact Studies

CNN Money

Business Roundtable

## Government Partnerships

### Citation(s):

1. www.SBA.gov
2. "What is the role of government to encourage small business innovation?" philmckinney (Jan 2010). http://philmckinney.com/archives/2010/01/role-of-government-to-encourage-small-business-innovation.html
3. "Firms' Access to Finance: Entry, Growth, and Productivity" http://siteresources.worldbank.org/INTFINFORALL/Resources/4099583-1194373512632/FFA_ch02.pdf
4. "Ohio could benefit from business incubator legislation" U.S. Sen. Sherrod Brown (March 2011) http://www.timesreporter.com/opinion/x1315031081/Ohio-could-benefit-from-business-incubator-legislation
5. Ibid.
6. Emily Maltby and Angus Loten, "Tale of Two Loan Programs," (October 2011). http://online.wsj.com/article/SB10001424052970204138204576603100469929700.html
7. http://money.cnn.com/news/storysupplement/economy/bailouttracker/
8. "Factbox: How the TALF loan program worked," (September 2011) http://www.reuters.com/article/2011/09/15/US-eurozone-talf-idUSTRE78E64Y20110915
9. "Sources of Corporate Finance" http://www.ehow.com/list_6538333_sources-corporate-finance.html
10. http://siteresources.worldbank.org/INTFINFORALL/Resources/4099583-1194373512632/FFA_ch02.pdf
11. "Startup Boot Camps Seek Army of Entrepreneurs" John Tozzi (March 2011) http://www.businessweek.com/smallbiz/content/mar2011/sb20110329_239744.htm
12. http://www.nyc.gov/html/om/html/2010b/pr453-10.html
13. "Lawmaker Seeks to Incubate Incubators" Angus Loten (April 2011) http://blogs.wsj.com/in-charge/2011/04/07/lawmaker-seeks-to-incubate-incubators/
14. "A bright spot for small businesses: Job creation," Nin-Hai Tseng, Fortune (November 2011). http://finance.fortune.cnn.com/2011/11/01/small-business-hiring/

15. Lynnley Browning, "Study Tallies Corporations Not Paying Income Tax," (Aug 2008) http://www.nytimes.com/2008/08/13/business/13tax.html
16. "Reducing your tax legally with the use of an offshore company" https://webspace.utexas.edu/dtt56/Offshore-Company.html
17. Jillian Berman, "Thirty Of America's Most Profitable Companies Paid 'Less Than Zero' In Income Taxes In Last 3 Years" (November 2011) http://www.huffingtonpost.com/2011/11/03/major-corporations-tax-subsidies_n_1073548.html
18. Big-Box Economic Impact Studies (www.HometownAdvantage.org)
19. Phil McKinney, "What is the role of government to encourage small business innovation?" (Jan 2010) http://philmckinney.com/archives/2010/01/role-of-government-to-encourage-small-business-innovation.html
20. http://www.human-rights-online.org/human-rights/Article-56-Oursourcing-Corporations-and-Consumers.htm
21. "The Benefits of Outsourcing for Small Businesses," http://www.allbusiness.com/human-resources/workforce-management-hiring/1084-1.html

**Selected Resources:**

Small Business Administration

Fortune Magazine

Loophole Land: Time to Reform Corporate Taxes

Big-Box Economic Impact Studies

Times Reporter

Wall Street Journal

Money.CNN.com

Business Week

Huffington Post

Reuters

www.SBA.gov

## America Competing in the Global Economy

### Citation(s):


1. http://www.dol.gov/oasam/programs/history/herman/reports/futurework/trends/trendsVII.htm
2. "Why Google Invests in Clean Energy," Marc Gunther (Feb 2012). http://www.greenbiz.com/blog/2012/01/01/why-google-invests-clean-energy
3. Ibid
4. "Viewpoint: Businesses Must Stimulate U.S. Manufacturing By Buying American-made Products," (October 2010). http://www.industryweek.com/PrintArticle.aspx?ArticleID=23054
5. http://www.bea.gov/newsreleases/international/trade/tradnewsrelease.htm
6. "Viewpoint: Businesses Must Stimulate U.S. Manufacturing By Buying American-made Products," (October 2010). http://www.industryweek.com/PrintArticle.aspx?ArticleID=23054
7. Peter Valdes-Dapena, "American cars are back at last," (January 2011). http://money.cnn.com/2011/01/06/autos/american_car_quality/index.htm
8. Fuller, Brian, "Quality crisis in electronics industry-survey," (November 2011). http://www.eetimes.com/electronics-blogs/pop-blog/4230725/Quality-crisis-in-electronics-industry
9. Ibid
10. "Viewpoint: Businesses Must Stimulate U.S. Manufacturing By Buying American-made Products," (October 2010). http://www.industryweek.com/PrintArticle.aspx?ArticleID=23054
11. Brian Fuller, "Quality crisis in electronics industry-survey," (November 2011). http://www.eetimes.com/electronics-blogs/pop-blog/4230725/Quality-crisis-in-electronics-industry
12. http://www.dol.gov/oasam/programs/history/herman/reports/futurework/trends/trendsVII.htm
13. Ibid
14. Ibid
15. Ibid

16. David DiSalvo, "The Fall of Kodak: A Tale of Disruptive Technology and Bad Business," (October 2011). http://www.forbes.com/sites/daviddisalvo/2011/10/02/what-i-saw-as-kodak-crumbled/
17. http://findarticles.com/p/articles/mi_mCNK/is-2008_March_25/ai_n25020498/
18. http://futureforall.org/whatscoming.htm
19. http://amcleanenergy.com/about-solar/government-incentives
20. http://www.afdc.energy.gov/afdc/laws/fed_summary
21. Ibid
22. "Why Google Invests in Clean Energy," Marc Gunther (Feb 2012). http://www.greenbiz.com/blog/2012/01/01/why-google-invests-clean-energy
23. Ibid
24. http://knowlede.emory.edu/article.cfm?articleid=975
25. http://www.investopedia.com/terms/c/corporate-culture.asp
26. "Corporate Culture: The Only Truly Sustainable Competitive Advantage," George Bradt, (Feb 2012). http://www.forbes.com/sites/geogebradt/2012/02/08/corporate-culture-the-only-true-sustainable-competitive-advantage/
27. "The Smartest Guys in the Room," directed by Alex Gibney. New York, NY: Jigsaw Productions, 2005. DVD.
28. "How Is Financial Leverage Related to Bankruptcy?" Jay Way, http://www.ehow.com/print/about_7528586_financial-leverage-related-bankruptcy.html
29. "Are U.S. Companies Doomed to Keep Planning for the Short Term?" (July 2006). http://knowledge.emory.edu/article.cfm?articleid=975
30. Ibid
31. Ibid
32. Ibid
33. "Alternatives to Layoff" http://www.ehow.com/print/info_8208600_alternatives-layoff.html
34. http://www.whitehouse.gov/21stcenturygov/actions/21st-century-regulatory-system
35. http://www.forbes.com/lists/2011/6/best-countries-11_United-States_CHI004.html

**Selected Resources:**

The United States Department of Labor

Forbes

Time

Futureforall.org

"The Smartest Guys in the Room" – Enron

Made in United States
Troutdale, OR
11/03/2026

56852534R00149